'An essential read for the many police staff, officers and leaders who care about applying evidence based practice in protecting victims from domestic abuse and securing justice for them.'

Louisa Rolfe, *Metropolitan Police, National Police Chief Council lead for DA*

'*Policing Domestic Violence* offers practical, policing-based strategies for how to better support victims–survivors of domestic violence abuse, facilitate robust risk assessments, and ensure that all perpetrators are held accountable for committing violence against women and children. The book also considers and summarises the implications of police failure to protect actual and potential victims–survivors, using case studies to offer ways forward for rebuilding trust across all aspect of policing these crimes. Written in a clear and accessible way, this book addresses the importance of police work in revealing some of the ways in which multi-agency and multidisciplinary cooperation work in practice. It also illuminates the possible unintended consequences of particular interventions.'

Aisha K. Gill, *Professor of Criminology, Social Sciences, University of Roehampton*

'I can only recommend this great book to every young police officer (and maybe a couple of old hands too), as it manages to unpick this extremely complex topic of Domestic Abuse in a very accessible and practical and holistic way. I am convinced that it will make a great contribution to society as it will help us to learn to deal with this difficult topic.'

Tom Kirchmaier, *Director of the Policing and Crime research group, London School Economics*

'From recognition to response, domestic abuse presents profound challenges for policing. It is an old problem that constantly requires new thinking as we grapple with lockdowns, a housing deficit, and digital forms of violence and control. The authors are uniquely placed to provide the guide that is needed for 21st century policing.'

Nigel South, *Emeritus Professor of Sociology, University of Essex*

'Providing an effective and informed response to domestic abuse is of enormous importance. This comprehensive and timely text draws together research on the nature, dynamics and consequences of domestic abuse alongside policy, legislation and developments in policing practice. Vividly written, it is essential reading for frontline police professionals, as well as academics and students concerned with how best to identify, respond to and prevent domestic abuse in the pandemic era. This is a timely and unique book, in that it blends the voices and expertise of academics and police practitioners to advance practice and understanding relating to the policing of domestic abuse. Although the domestic abuse crisis predates the pandemic, the past couple of years are testament to how important it is that we retain a sharp focus on tackling and responding to domestic abuse in all of its forms – so it is fantastic to see this collaboration come to fruition, and produce such a useful and practical resource.'

Michele Burman, *Professor of Criminology, University of Glasgow*

'This is a courageous and inspiring book addressing everyday challenges in policing domestic abuse, from definitions and measurement to assessing risk, intersectionality in victimisation to effective treatment options. Its blend of academic research and theory, legal developments and practical applications make it a must read for operational police officers, academics and those in allied agencies.'

Loraine Gelsthorpe, *Director, Institute of Criminology, University of Cambridge*

'This is a timely and unique book, in that it blends the voices and expertise of academics and police practitioners to advance practice and understanding relating to the policing of domestic abuse. Although the domestic abuse crisis predates the pandemic, the past couple of years are testament to how important it is that we retain a sharp focus on tackling and responding to domestic abuse in all of its forms – so it is fantastic to see this collaboration come to fruition, and produce such a useful and practical resource.'

Kelly Johnson, *Assistant Professor in Criminology, Department of Sociology, Centre for Research into Violence and Abuse*

Policing Domestic Abuse

This book is dedicated to improving the practice of the policing of domestic abuse. Its objective is to help inform those working in policing about the dynamics of how domestic abuse occurs, how best to respond to and investigate it, and in the longer term how to prevent it.

Divided into thematic areas, this book uses recent research findings to update some of the theoretical analysis and to highlight the areas of good practice: 'what works and why'. An effective investigation and the prosecution of offenders are considered, as well as an evaluation of the success of current treatment options. Policing domestic abuse can only be dealt with through an effective partnership response. The responsibilities of each agency and the statutory processes in place when policy is not adhered to are outlined.

Core content includes:

- A critique of definitions and theoretical approaches to domestic abuse, including the coverage of the myths surrounding domestic abuse and their impact on policing.
- An exploration on the challenges of collecting data on domestic abuse, looking at police data and the role of health and victim support services.
- A critical review of different forms of abuse, different perpetrators and victims, and risk assessment tools used by the police.
- A critical examination of the law relating to domestic abuse; how police resources are deployed to respond to and manage it; and best practice in investigation, gathering evidence, and prosecution.
- Key perspectives on preventing domestic abuse, protecting victims, and reducing harm.

Written with the student and budding practitioner in mind, this book is filled with case studies, current research, reports, and media examples, as well as a variety of reflective questions and a glossary of key terms, to help shed light on the challenges of policing domestic violence and the links between academic research and best practice.

Katy Barrow-Grint is a Chief Superintendent in Thames Valley Police with over 20 years of police experience. She has an academic interest in Domestic Abuse, completing her Masters at Warwick Business School, and has written on domestic abuse attrition rates in the Criminal Justice System.

Dr Jacqueline Sebire is an Assistant Chief Constable with Bedfordshire Police. She has 30 years of police service specialising as a detective in homicide and safeguarding and public protection. She has a PhD in Psychology from the University of Leicester researching the risk factors associated with domestic abuse homicide.

Jackie Turton is an Emeritus Professor in the Department of Sociology at Essex University. She joined the university after a career in the health service and has taught sociology and criminology since 1996. Family violence is a key focus of her research work.

Dr Ruth Weir is a Senior Research Fellow in the Violence and Society Centre at City University. She specialises in using quantitative methods and Geographic Information Systems (GIS) to analyse gender-based violence and abuse. Prior to working in academia Ruth held several research and policy positions in local government and the Home Office.

Routledge Advances in Police Practice and Knowledge

Series Editors

Dr Tom Cockcroft, Leeds Beckett University, UK, and Dr Martin Wright, Canterbury Centre for Policing Research, UK

Routledge Advances in Police Practice and Knowledge is a new series of books which brings together established academics and authors in the field of police studies to provide themed textbooks that will support students engaging with professional police studies within higher education. The focus of the series is to provide academically rigorous accounts of research and knowledge and to contextualise them in the practical and applied context of policework. In doing so, the books that make up the series will provide an invaluable resource to students studying policing through a variety of academic and vocational routes.

The Editors, Dr Tom Cockcroft and Dr Martin Wright, dedicate this series to the memory of Professor PAJ (Tank) Waddington who believed policing to be an honourable profession, and whose career's work embodied the values that inform the direction of the series.

Policing Structures
Colin Rogers

Improving Intelligence Analysis in Policing
Stuart Kirby and Scott Keay

Criminology for the Police
Craig Paterson and Ed Pollock

Policing Domestic Abuse
Risk, Policy and Practice
Katy Barrow-Grint, Jacqueline Sebire, Jackie Turton, and Ruth Weir

Policing Domestic Abuse

Risk, Policy, and Practice

Katy Barrow-Grint,
Jacqueline Sebire,
Jackie Turton, and Ruth Weir

Routledge
Taylor & Francis Group
LONDON AND NEW YORK

Cover image: Baac3nes, Creative #:1357296414, Royalty-free

First published 2023
by Routledge
4 Park Square, Milton Park, Abingdon, Oxon OX14 4RN

and by Routledge
605 Third Avenue, New York, NY 10158

Routledge is an imprint of the Taylor & Francis Group, an informa business

British Library Cataloguing-in-Publication Data
A catalogue record for this book is available from the British Library

ISBN: 978-0-367-68414-3 (hbk)
ISBN: 978-0-367-68415-0 (pbk)
ISBN: 978-1-003-13741-2 (ebk)

DOI: 10.4324/9781003137412

Typeset in Times New Roman
by codeMantra

This book is dedicated to all the police officers, staff and partners engaged in policing domestic abuse.

Contents

Figures

Tables

Boxes

Abbreviations

ACE	Adverse Childhood Experiences
ACPO	Association of Chief Police Officers (dissolved in 2015 and re-established as the National Police Chiefs Council NPCC)
APP	Authorised Professional Practice
BCS	British Crime Survey (changed in 2012 to CSEW Crime Survey for England and Wales and Scotland had its own survey SCJS Scottish Crime and Justice Survey)
CAADA	Co ordinated Action Against Domestic Abuse renamed Safe Lives (SafeLives.org.uk)
CAFCASS	Children and Family Court Advisory and Support Service
CARA	Cautioning and Relationship Abuse
CBT	Cognitive Behaviour Therapy
CCHI	Cambridge Crime Harm Index
CCR	Coordinated Community Response
CED	Connected Energy Device
CID	Criminal Investigation Department
CJS	Criminal Justice System
COP	College of Policing
CPS	Crown Prosecution Service
CSP	Community Safety Partnership
CSEW	Crime Survey for England and Wales
CCS	Crime Severity Scores
CTS	Conflict Tactic Scale
CYPIDVA	Child and Young People IDVA role
DAHA	Domestic Abuse Housing Alliance
DAPN	Domestic Abuse Notices (in April 2021 replaced by Domestic Abuse Protection Notices)
DAPO	Domestic Abuse Protection Orders (in April 2021 replaced by Domestic Abuse Protection Orders)
DART	Domestic Abuse Reference Tool
DASH	Domestic Abuse Stalking Honour based violence risk assessment tool

DHR	Domestic Homicide Review
DPP	Director of Public Prosecutions
DVDS	Domestic Violence Disclosure Scheme
DVPN	Domestic Violence Protection Notices (in April 2021 replaced by Domestic Abuse Protection Notices)
DVPO	Domestic Violence Protection Orders (in April 2021 replaced by Domestic Abuse Protection Orders)
DVPP	Domestic Violence Perpetrator Programme
DOH	Department of Health
EIF	Early Intervention Foundation
FCO	Foreign and Commonwealth Office
FGM	Female Genital Mutilation
FM	Forced Marriage
FMPO	Forced Marriage Protection Order
FMU	Forced Marriage Unit
HBV/A	Honour Based Violence or Abuse
HMIC	Her Majesty's Inspectorate of Constabulary (changed in 2017 to HMICFRS Her Majesty's Inspectorate of Constabulary and Fire and Rescue Services)
HMICFRS	Her Majesty's Inspectorate of Constabulary and Fire and Rescue Services
HO	Home Office
IDVA	Independent Domestic Violence Advisers
IMR	Independent Management Review
IOPC	Independent Office for Police Conduct
IPV	Intimate Partner Violence
LCJB	Local Criminal Justice Board
LSOA	Lower Super Output Area
MASH	Multi-Agency Safeguarding Hub
MAPPA	Multi-Agency Public Protection Arrangements
MARAC	Multi-Agency Risk Assessment Conference
MATAC	Multi-Agency Tasking and Coordination
MHI	Mental Health Investigation
MOJ	Ministry of Justice
MPS	Metropolitan Police Service
NHS	National Health System
NICE	National Institute for Health and Care Excellence
NCVS	National Crime Victimisation Survey
NLDVS	North London Domestic Violence Survey
NPCC	National Police Chiefs Council
NRPFP	No Recourse to Public Funding Requirement
ONS	Office for National Statistics
PACE	Police and Criminal Evidence Act 1984
PEEL	Police Effectiveness, Efficiency and Legitimacy

PKF	Police Knowledge Fund
PNC	Police National Computer
PPSLP	Public Protection and Safeguarding Leaders Programme
PTSD	Post Traumatic Stress Disorder
RCN	Royal College of Nursing
RFGV	Recency, Frequency, Gravity and Victims tool
SAR	Safeguarding Adult Review
SCJS	Scottish Crime and Justice Survey
SDVC	Specialist Domestic Violence Courts
SPO	Stalking Protection Order
UN	United Nations
VAW	Violence Against Women
VAWG	Violence Against Women and Girls
WHO	World Health Organization
YDVA	Youth Domestic Abuse Advisor
YOS	Youth offending Service

Foreword

A personal account of domestic abuse

Making the decision to call the police to report domestic abuse was one of the hardest but best decisions I have made in my life. I remember the mix of emotions I felt as I dialled 101 and the sense of relief I felt when the call-handler started speaking to me. It's not an exaggeration to say that the positive approach by the officers who responded to that call and took on the investigation gave me the courage to take the steps to change my life, for the better.

When the responding officers came into my house, I saw them switch on their body worn video cameras, spot the broken crockery on the floor and start to film. From the start their words and actions reassured me that I had done the right thing to call police and that they were there to help me. They made an early arrest which led to a charge. They went through a risk assessment and discussed a safety plan with me. They were patient, sensitive and thorough with their questions. They gave me details of charities and agencies for follow-up support. They provided me with their contact details and kept me updated.

I find it hard to explain why I didn't take action sooner. I was a police officer myself in the Metropolitan Police, and I was familiar with domestic abuse from a policing perspective. I knew things were wrong at home, but I didn't acknowledge the impact of what was going on. I didn't recognise it in my own case until it was pointed out to me by the Police Constable (PC) sitting opposite me at our kitchen table. He said that based on what I was telling him, there was a pattern of behaviour here rather than just the assault I had phoned 101 to report. He told me that the pattern of behaviour I'd described was unacceptable. The PC was right, and I will always be grateful to him for recognising the situation and helping me to take the steps to deal with it.

You also have the responsibility to help victims in the way that the PC helped me. Domestic abuse is complex – every case is different, and every victim will have different needs. But the impact that your response will have on the victims you deal with should not be underestimated. You can make such a positive, life-changing impact.

Of course, preventing and responding to domestic abuse is not only the responsibility of the police, a whole system partnership approach is essential. This book will tell you more about that approach to give you a wider understanding of this subject. This will help you when you are thinking about the best options for the victims you are dealing with.

Since I disclosed my own experiences of being in a controlling and abusive relationship, I have been contacted by many people who have asked for advice, either for themselves, or because they are worried about friends, family members, neighbours, or colleagues. Domestic abuse is everyone's business, and it doesn't discriminate. As one of my colleagues said to me, if it can happen to the Borough Commander, it can happen to anyone. There are both victims and perpetrators of domestic abuse in the police service. Employers – including the police service – have a responsibility to spot the signs and support their employees who are impacted by it. I'm pleased that this book contains useful guidance on this.

For people trapped in an abusive relationship, the obstacles to leaving can seem insurmountable. Police officers have to be the bringer of hope because in fact those obstacles are not insurmountable, but the path out of the relationship is seldom easy. The victims you are dealing with may not have acknowledged the power and control in their relationships. The perpetrators may be difficult for you to deal with. The threats of post-separation abuse and control need to be recognised.

It takes confidence and skill to deal well with domestic abuse calls as a police officer. This textbook will help equip you so that you can provide the best possible service in this area of policing. Thank you for reading it, for providing that excellent service and for prioritising the safety of the victim who has called you for help. Through your actions you are going to change lives and save lives.

Sally Benatar

This personal recollection was courageously provided as an opening for this book by Sally Benatar, a retired Chief Superintendent from the Metropolitan Police Service.

Chapter 1

Introduction

The purpose of this book

Sally Benatar's story is introduced at the very beginning of this book to highlight that domestic abuse can be experienced by anyone. More importantly, it shows how the police respond when a victim makes the first step of acknowledging domestic abuse and then asking for help can make a positive difference to their lives. But where the service they receive is less than professional it can destroy any subsequent trust and confidence in the police service and may result in victims not reaching out for help again.

Many officers joining the police service have expectations of spending days chasing after 'bad guys' in high-speed pursuits with blue lights flashing and sirens wailing (Herrington and Sebire, 2021). However, this is not the reality. A considerable amount of day-to-day front-line policing involves responding to domestic incidents within families, and relationships often involving the worst people can do to those they claim to love and care for. What have historically been perceived as private, or family matters are now a priority for policing given the devastating effect domestic abuse has on individuals and society (Walby, 2004).

Policing domestic abuse is not easy. Dealing with people who have been controlled and coerced throughout their relationships, traumatised, beaten, and injured and the children and others who witnessed such abuse is a significant responsibility. The actions taken by police can be life changing through supporting victims to leave violent and abusive relationships and bringing perpetrators to justice through diligent evidence capture and prosecution. However, where the policing response has not been timely or risk assessments are inappropriate, lives have been lost.

This book has been written to assist those working within policing and those researching domestic abuse in understanding the theory and practical application of this most challenging area of policing. It does not replace any force policies or the College of Policing's approved professional practice. Whilst primarily aimed at policing and legislation in England and Wales, the principles outlined are widely applicable in policing domestic

DOI: 10.4324/9781003137412-1

abuse internationally. It provides guidance in how to support victims, complete risk assessments and manage perpetrators with examples, signposting additional resources and suggesting critical thinking points in order to assist those who police domestic abuse and improve their practice. This book identifies key developments in terms of new legislation such as the Domestic Abuse Bill 2020, which works in abuse prevention and of course the impact of the COVID-19 pandemic.

Whilst the police have a significant role to play, it is essential that this is done in partnership. This book explains the statutory role of agencies in providing support to families suffering from abuse. Only a whole system response where agencies and the community work together can bring about sustained change to address this 'wicked problem'.

Dealing with traumatic incidents can lead to stress and anxiety. Managing self-resilience and well-being of yourself and colleagues is essential. We examine the impact of trauma and share current best practice and available resources to assist in managing well-being.

There will be perpetrators of domestic abuse who are also police officers and staff. Such behaviour impacts on police legitimacy and public confidence, and we consider the misconduct process and the code of ethics when the standards police are held to are broken.

Being a police officer or staff member is a privilege but comes with responsibility. Protecting the vulnerable and abused is our highest priority. We hope this book will assist you in the execution of that duty.

Structure of the book

There are many ways this text could be constructed; however, the chapters below allow students the opportunity to examine specific areas of interest as required.

Chapter 2 offers an overview of domestic abuse from the historical to how it emerged from a private to public concern. It relates the legacy of the myths and misunderstandings that arise when dealing with both victims and perpetrators. The extent of domestic abuse is measured in a variety of ways; Chapter 3 considers how data is collected as well as the advantages and disadvantages of using quantitative data. One of the difficulties of supporting victims is the ability to assess risk, and the theories of risk are explored in Chapter 4 alongside the various methods of identifying risk factors. No risk assessment tools are infallible but current tools, their application, and best practice are reviewed, including the multi-agency processes for managing risk.

No book on domestic abuse is complete without offering an understanding of the ways in which the law, both civil and criminal, responds. This is the essence of Chapter 5, which reviews the legal and policy strategies for responding to domestic violence. There are numerous factors to examine from 'golden hour' investigative principles to the limitations of police resources and ultimately the impact that policy has on front-line decision-making.

The victims (Chapter 6) and perpetrators (Chapter 7) require careful risk and behaviour appraisal. Chapter 6 highlights the need to understand victims as individuals. They are not all 'the same' and some must contend with numerous social inequalities, which effect their response to domestic abuse and to those who offer support. Police and other professionals need to account for difference taking a more intersectional approach to their decision-making. The discussion of perpetrators in Chapter 7 unravels not only some of the theories of perpetration but also how police manage these offenders faced with limits to resources, whilst striving to prioritise risk in terms of levels of dangerous. This chapter also reviews some of the treatment options available for perpetrators.

Throughout this text there are references to the efficacy of working together with other agencies. Chapter 8 details some of the ways in which multi-agency and multi-disciplinary cooperation works in practice. Domestic violence is a complex problem that often requires more than a criminal justice response; many victims never reach the police statistics and are involved with other statutory and support agencies. Regardless of best intentions sometimes things go wrong, and all agencies should be prepared to meet the challenge to change. This is when both practice and policy need careful review through processes such as Domestic Violence Homicide Reviews.

Those who work in the police and related services are just a representative selection of society. Therefore, it is not surprising that domestic abuse occurs within the policing community. Chapter 9 explores the problems of domestic violence within the police and cites high-profile examples to reinforce the difficulties of disclosure for victims as well as risk-assessing suspected perpetrators. How do the police deal with victims and offenders within their own community?

Chapter 10 brings the book to a conclusion, although there is no definitive end as domestic abuse cases and victims' deaths continue. However, it is useful to reflect on the past and to consider new directions. For instance, the recent COVID-19 pandemic has brought to the fore the extra dangers victims face in a national lockdown or where service provision, particularly face-to-face, is either unavailable or restricted. Further the full effect of recent changes in the law, the appointment of the Domestic Abuse Commissioner and the Violence Against Women and Girls agenda more generally are yet to be revealed. These changes raise hopes that domestic abuse and violence against women and girls more generally will remain a priority for government and policing.

References

Herrington, V., Sebire, J, 2021. *Policing the future – The future of policing.* Policing Insights.

Walby, S., 2004. *The cost of domestic violence.* Women and Equality Unit.

Chapter 2

What is domestic abuse?

KEY POINTS

- Domestic abuse only emerged as a public concern in the 20th century.
- Recognising and defining the problem is complex as domestic abuse is not 'one' crime.
- Understanding perpetrators and victims helps dispel myths and supports risk management.

Introduction

This chapter covers three key areas. First, how did the apparently private act of domestic abuse come to public notice and emerge as one of the highest priorities on the policing agenda? Taking an historical approach, we will uncover the process from private to public concern. Second, this chapter will review the difficulties and challenges of recognising and defining domestic abuse and highlight some of the myths and assumptions that can inhibit detection. Third, this leads us to consider how researchers and academics have described and explained domestic abuse and reflect on some of the contemporary debates.

History

As we have discussed, domestic abuse is not new; there has always been violence and abusive behaviour within family households. What has changed is the social response to this behaviour. It has moved from acts that were deemed acceptable, and in fact normalised, to being recognised as inappropriate, anti-social and in some cases criminal. Analysing some of the historical backdrop to domestic abuse offers some clarity-concerning issues and dilemmas that arise when thinking about cases today. It is impossible to detail all the actions that have led us to our current system of support and policing of domestic abuse. However, what this section attempts to do is to highlight some important key events and consider their significance

DOI: 10.4324/9781003137412-2

enabling us to make links with successes as well as some challenges and failures of policing, legislation, and victim support.

Until the early 1970s domestic abuse was very much a private, family problem, and as the literature suggests there was little appetite for challenging or changing that situation.

> The husband [. . .], by the old law, might give his wife moderate correction. For, as he is to answer for her misbehaviour, the law thought it reasonable to intrust him with this power of restraining her, by domestic chastisement, in the same moderation a man is allowed to correct his apprentices or children, for whom the master or parent is also liable in some cases to answer.
>
> (Sir William Blackstone, 1763: Quoted in (Hecker, 1911), p. 125)

The family unit was perceived as an ideal and idealised social building block offering the opportunity to husbands to control their wives and their children with little if any restraint from outside forces (Buzawa and Buzawa, 1996). Men hitting their wives, with 'moderation', was not seen as criminally or morally wrong as women were 'possessions' of their husbands (Dobash and Dobash, 1979), and as a result, wives had little or no recourse to law if assaulted (Edwards, 1989), although this did not mean that it was completely tolerated. According to Clark (1992) "(b)y the 1780s and 90s at least one woman a week appeared before the Middlesex justices to prosecute her husband. . . for assault" (1992, p. 192). But as marriage was seen as a social and sexual contract, action was limited,

> . . . this contract justified the denial of individual rights to women on the grounds they would be protected by their husbands, a fiction which worked in the interests of maintaining and reinforcing patriarchy.
>
> (Abrams, 1999, p. 120)

The male domination of Western societies within politics, the workplace, and the family largely excluded women from any power or voice, leaving them vulnerable. Patriarchy described the inequality and power relationship between women and men and was to become the bedrock for understanding and analysing the problem of domestic abuse.

As early as the 19th century Frances Power Cobbe was a key voice of reform against the prevalence of domestic violence. According to Smith (1989),

> . . . Cobbe (1878) systematically collected evidence of that abuse and presented it in her pamphlet Wife torture in England. Although she delineated four main incitements to violence – alcohol, prostitution, heteropathy (that is the converse of sympathy and comprises both anger

> and cruelty) and squalid living conditions – she saw the cause of such violence as the inequality of the sexes.
>
> (1989, p. 4)

The legacy of male rights over wives was slow to dispel continuing well into the 20th century (Box 2.1). Consequently, the themes of inequality and patriarchy were adopted by feminists in the 1970s and 1980s as foundations of their research, analysis, and campaign work.

BOX 2.1 ATTITUDES TO 'WIVES'

Smith (1989) records some fairly recent court reports that reflected the social attitudes to women as wives. He states that ". . . judges have . . . defended the right of a husband to correct his wife:

- in 1946 (although the judgement was reversed by the Court of Appeal).
- in 1959 when the judge stated that it would not have been cruel to punish a wife as 'one punishes a naughty child'.
- and again in 1976 when a Scottish judge expressed the view that 'reasonable chastisement should be the duty of every husband if his wife misbehaves', precisely qualifying that 'it is a well-known fact that you can strike your wife's bottom if you wish, but you must not strike her on the face'.
- It should not be thought that these were peculiarities of English (and Scottish) law. Jolin (1983). . . claims that as recently as 1976 a Pennsylvania town ordinance sanctioned a husband's violence against his wife provided he did not act in such a manner after 10 o'clock in the evening or on Sundays" (Smith, 1989, p.4).

Apart from the concerns of inequality and patriarchy, wife-beating and family violence generally was perceived as a class issue. The middle classes tended to be exempt from the scrutiny of early social reformers who took the view that men who assaulted their wives were amongst the disorderly working class or immigrant poor (Dobash and Dobash, 1992). This anecdotal notion has taken some time to temper as (Wilson, 1983) highlighted within the 20th-century discussions of working-class 'problem families', 'bad' mothers and 'nagging' wives. The lack of support for exiting these violent marriages resulted in domestic abuse remaining hidden invoking shame and self-reprisal for any victims who spoke out. Shame and fear of dishonouring the family were and have remained concerns, particularly for some minority ethnic groups (Femi-Ajao et al.,

2020; Gill, 2004). In such cases victims have been a fearful of disclosing any abuse, a problem exacerbated by the interrelated social disadvantages of racism, classism, and sexism. Furthermore, on-going relationship difficulties between the police, other statutory organisations and some minority groups have discouraged victims from reaching out for support, making policing of domestic abuse more complicated. As this short historical backdrop indicates, we have inherited a complex series of unresolved legacies for those currently working with cases of domestic abuse around the problems of power, inequality, and victimhood, as well as ethnicity, race, and class.

Feminist campaign for change

From the 1950s therapeutic discourses were very prevalent in the USA and, while less influential, they also had some impact in the United Kingdom (Saraga, 1996). The therapeutic model changes the dynamics of understanding domestic abuse moving the discourse away from a multi-layered problem with social, cultural, and political dimensions introduced above into a medical syndrome suggesting women in some way provoked or deserved the violence meted against them (Dobash and Dobash, 1992). As Saraga observed in this way the victims ". . . were seen as either responsible for provoking the violence or even seeking it out, and frequently as being in need of treatment themselves" (1996, p. 207) all of which deflected the ". . . attention from the inequalities of marriage itself" (Clark, 1992, p. 187) and indeed deflected attention away from the perpetrators. It was a popular model within the USA throughout the 1970s and early 1980s during which time therapeutic discourses battled with the radical feminist campaigns against patriarchy and the growing work of the socialist and liberal feminists for equal rights for women in the home and at work (Naffine, 1990).

It was the second wave of feminism in the 1970s that set the challenge for change with two core missions. The first was campaigning to raise the profile of domestic abuse both as a public concern and as violent behaviour that should be open to public scrutiny. After all, violent acts on the street were treated as crimes but the same acts, where identified, behind closed doors tended to be ignored, down-graded, or 'no-crimed'. The feminists also recognised the needs of domestic abuse victims and developed a series of support networks alongside the awareness-raising.

The second core mission for the feminists was to develop an empirically sound contemporary knowledge about the problem of domestic abuse. So, alongside the campaigning and victim support, there was a plethora of research to both encourage a public understanding of the problem and to offer challenges to the legal system and policy makers to take family violence seriously. The early feminist researchers took a qualitative, active research approach listening to the testimonies of female survivors, and that research revealed a number of immediate concerns:

- Domestic violence (as domestic abuse was then known) was not just one type of action or act. In fact, occasionally the fear of the violence was the biggest concern for victims.
- The extent of domestic abuse was much broader than revealed through police records or even national statistics such as the British Crime Survey (now the Crime Survey for England and Wales – CSEW) – many victims were not admitting their abuse to anyone.
- There was a consistent failure of all statutory services to protect victims of domestic abuse.
- Finally, as Edwards (1989) found the police were less likely to intervene in any domestic disturbance, particularly within poorer inner-city areas or among black or Asian communities (Gill, 2004).

The feminist campaigning had a lasting effect on the perception of domestic crime. During the first 10 years the movement forced the issues of domestic abuse onto the public agenda, opened and staffed refuges for supporting victims as well as developing a strong campaigning group for funding, and supporting new policies and laws to protect women and children.

It was the work of feminists in the 1970s that led to the very first select committee on the Rights of Women in the House of Commons in 1975, and during the same decade the research evidence gathered led to a number of civil acts including the Domestic Violence and Matrimonial Proceedings Act (1976) and the Domestic Violence and Magistrates Court Act (1978). All of these changes pointed to the increasing awareness of domestic abuse as a major problem (Groves and Thomas, 2014) – although they failed to make any amendments to the criminal justice system. Despite all the work, political and judicial projects were slow to move forward leaving the police to consider the problem as one for social services and counselling therapists rather than the law. In fact, at this time police were actively encouraged "... to give advice, to keep the peace and most of all prevent injury" (Select Committee, 1975; quoted in Dobash and Dobash, 1992, p. 150). Day's (2018) work also revealed an example that highlighted the problems of policing domestic abuse in the 1970s and 1980s in a statement by the Association of Chief Police Officers,

> ... whilst such problems [domestic violence] take up considerable police time during say, 12 months, in the majority of cases the role of the police is a negative one. We are, after all, dealing with persons 'bound in marriage', and it is important for a host of reasons, to maintain the unity of the spouses.
>
> (House of Commons Select Committee on Violence in Marriage, 1975, p. 336)

A number of contemporary research studies into police responses confirmed the extent of this approach to domestic abuse (Faragher, 1985; Grace, 1995; Pagelow, 1981; Wright, 1995), and this was perhaps just a reflection of general social attitudes to the problem.

Police response to domestic abuse

The early police response to domestic abuse often erred on the side of caution reflecting the contemporary social attitudes by avoiding interfering with the family wherever possible (Bourlet, 1990; Burton, 2016). The legacy of this approach lingered well into the late 20th century causing the police to develop a "... certain ideological caution" (Bourlet, 1990, p. 15). Even when the need for more appropriate training to enable front-line officers to cope with domestic abuse situations was recognised in the early 1970s and 1980s, this apparent move forward was hampered by the caveats within early police guidance. These suggested that any criminal offense in cases of domestic abuse was unusual; therefore, the main role of the police at the scene was to 'restore the peace' (Home Office, 1986). As Burton rightly points out,

> ...domestic violence was not viewed as a crime but as a civil or private matter, it is, perhaps, not surprising that the police did not perceive arrest and prosecution to be appropriate responses.
>
> (2016, p. 38)

Police reaction to domestic cases was further compounded by the low priority generally attached to domestic abuse. Bourlet (1990) highlighted that the HMIC report in 1989 did not once mention domestic abuse as a policing problem, leaving it as an issue of 'discretion' for front-line officers and at Chief Constable level in terms of resources and creating gaps in both the protection of victims and any form of risk assessment.

Thus, we can identify the core barriers for working with domestic offences during the late 20th century:

- The problems with taking domestic abuse seriously beyond that of a 'breach of the peace' remained as did the expected role of encouraging reconciliation to preserve the family unit.
- Partly as a result, domestic offences continued to be seen as not 'proper' police work – not 'real' police work (Dobash and Dobash, 1979; Groves and Thomas, 2014) and often delegated to junior police, usually female officers; these offences were perceived as 'women's' work.
- In some cases, a lack of victim sympathy proved a stumbling block. As such this was exacerbated by the patriarchal police culture combined with attitudes of 'undeserving victims', especially concerning the withdrawal of complaints (Edwards, 1989). The failure to understand this victim behaviour has been an on-going difficulty (Bourlet, 1990; Duggan, 2018).

Significant changes began from the 1990s onwards with the Home Office (HO) guidance encouraging police forces to take domestic abuse more seriously, by arresting perpetrators using contemporary criminal law, thus provoking a more in-depth investigation of the offences. The HO also recommended the development of specialist police units to ensure the development of a pool of experienced officers, although not all forces adopted this advice. However, during the 2000s there was considerable progress within the management of domestic abuse:

- In recognition of the need for specialist skills in dealing with domestic abuse some Specialist Domestic Violence Courts (SDVCs) were established in 2006. This move offered the opportunity to facilitate multi-disciplinary/multi-agency approaches by supporting victims through the court process. Unfortunately cuts in public spending have led to the demise of this initiative in many areas along with other schemes such as Independent Domestic Violence Advisers (IDVA).
- A new risk assessment tool was approved in 2009 – the Domestic Abuse, Stalking, Harassment and Honour-based Violence Assessment Tool (DASH) which is currently under review; despite its drawbacks it has acted as an aid memoir for assessment at the scene as well as a data source for recognising repeat offences and for research.
- The Crime and Security Act (2010) introduced victim protection orders.
- The HO consultation document 'Call to End Violence Against Women and Girls', first published by the Home Office in 2010, emphasised prevention and victim support and most importantly the role of the police in working with other agencies in local partnerships.
- The Domestic Violence Disclosure Scheme or Clare's Law was implemented in 2014 following the enquiry into the killing of Clare Wood by her partner. This enables police to disclose to potential victims, relevant past violent offences relating to new or current partners.

All these changes emphasised the prevention, the support for victims, and the importance of working with other agencies. But we know by the number of serious domestic abuse events – including deaths – that difficulties have remained including:

- Grading the importance of calls to police for assistance (HMIC, 2014);
- Inadequate training for front-line officers (Jenner, 2021) which is also emphasised by the victims' experiences (Grace, 1995);
- The slow movement of policy into practice on the frontline (HMIC, 2014) often hampered by cutbacks and reductions in resources.

Domestic abuse still poses a dilemma after 50 years of campaigning, research, and activism by feminists, supporters of women's rights and others, as well as the changes within policy, legislation, and policing. We know that the statistics offer us only the tip of the iceberg and that domestic crime is far less likely to be reported even when victims have been violently attacked. Anxieties about the removal of children, economic concerns and fear of the offender silence victims. The social stigma relating to domestic abuse leads to shame and blame (Flood and Pease, 2009) often leaving victims unsupported within their communities. Furthermore, if charity fiscal donation is an indication of support for women in abusive relationships, Booth (2008) suggested in his article that donations to donkey sanctuaries are far greater than to charities supporting domestic abuse victims. Some victims seek support from refuges and other victim focussed on agencies, but the CSEW indicates that even now only 21% report to the police (Flatley, 2016). The current situation creates difficulties for policing, resourcing, and research as there is no easy way to collate information accurately, but more importantly this lack of knowledge works against any agenda focussed on protecting victims, assessing risk, prevention, and treatment of offenders.

Recognising domestic abuse

This section will consider who are the victims and perpetrators of domestic abuse and the events, behaviours, and harms that definitions have attempted to encompass. Domestic abuse is not a simple action, and unlike some other crimes it is very rarely a singular act (RCN, 2020). Although early feminist research revealed the multiple dimensions of abusive behaviour (see Kelly, 1988) these are sometimes difficult to articulate in policies and legislation. Often the act of abuse itself requires the narrative around the context and history to enable an understanding of the risk and harm faced by the victim.

Defining domestic abuse

We have only recently begun to use the term 'domestic abuse' within legal definitions. 'Domestic violence' was the standard terminology in the United Kingdom for violence within households, but it is useful to understand why criticism from some academics and policy makers led to change and how sometimes language can limit our recognition and understanding of events.

One of the key problems with the word 'domestic' is that it conjures up an image of marital status (Edwards, 1989). But these acts are much broader and more complex. The intention is to encompass all intimate relationships whether co-habitees or not and contractual or not (Walklate, 2001). As we know from the research abuse may occur prior to co-habitation or after relationships have ended. Further Weir (2020) suggests, "(i)t also might be experienced between family members who do not live together, such as an older parent and their adult child". Furthermore ". . . the violence may not occur exclusively in the home but may take place in the public sphere" (p, 23).

The word 'violence' – while still popular with many of the feminist researchers, for example, Myhill and Kelly (2021), Walby and Towers (2018), and other support groups – has also come under criticism. It emphasises the physical side of abuse sometimes neglecting the huge range of other abusive behaviours (Box 2.2) that victims suffer including emotional and economic abuse as well as coercive control (Kelly and Westmarland, 2014; Myhill and Hohl, 2016; Stark, 2006; Women's Aid, 2016). While some difficulties around the use of 'domestic' remain, the adoption of domestic abuse as the over-arching term does cover non-violent abuse and offers an opportunity to include both criminal and non-criminal behaviours (Richards et al., 2008).

BOX 2.2 SOME MYTHS AND ASSUMPTIONS ABOUT DOMESTIC ABUSE

- Alcohol and drugs make men violent.
  - Many perpetrators are violent when sober and partners who drink are often not abusers. Blaming drink or drugs is a way of denying responsibility.
- Domestic violence only happens in poor families.
  - Domestic abuse occurs in all parts of society. Anyone can be a victim. Perpetrators can be lawyers and judges as well as unemployed.
- If it was that bad, she would leave.
  - Leaving is not a simple decision. The victim may be concerned about the well-being of any children in the family, have no access to finance or may feel shamed and silenced. Lack of self-esteem can also act as a barrier to both disclosure and escape from an abusive household.
- Stress or loss of temper causes violent behaviour.
  - Neither of these emotions are caused by themselves. Stress and bad temper can be present in many relationships that are not abusive. This excuse infers a lack of control, but most perpetrators are very much in control.
- Domestic violence is a private not a public matter.
  - The fact that it happens 'behind closed doors' does not excuse violence. Speaking out, protecting victims, and challenging perpetrators support change.

For more information: www.refuge.org.uk

The HO has been using the term 'domestic abuse' since 2013, and the resulting definition is used by the police forces and most other statutory and voluntary organisations in the United Kingdom.

> Any incident or pattern of incidents of controlling, coercive or threatening behaviour, violence, or abuse between those aged 16 or over who are or have been intimate partners or family members regardless of gender or sexuality. This can encompass but is not limited to the following types of abuse: Psychological, physical, sexual, financial and emotional.
> (Home Office, 2013)

While this definition encompasses all types of abuse including coercive control, it is important to note that currently domestic abuse itself is not a single criminal offence, but most forms of domestic abuse are crimes, such as harassment, assault, and coercive control. Even so, according to the ONS (2018) only 50% of offences have led to criminal investigation. However, this could be all set to change with the new Domestic Abuse Bill (UK Parliament, 2021).

Unpacking the crime

Box 2.3 details various types of abuse that can occur within intimate relationships. On many occasions, victims are subject to one or more of these and any demarcation may be blurred. It is the complex and diverse nature of domestic abuse that creates dilemmas for professionals working with victims, and some of these issues and concerns have been addressed in the literature.

BOX 2.3 TYPES OF DOMESTIC ABUSE

Physical abuse: Probably amongst the more obvious signs of domestic abuse such abuse is not just hitting but also punching, pinching, shoving, and throwing objects sometimes claiming that this behaviour is 'just a joke' (National DA Helpline, 2019). The results of physical abuse are often visual and often how society comes to view a victim, which can lead to other abuse being overlooked.

Sexual abuse: As with all sexual crime acts like this are sometimes difficult to process and within domestic relationships even more complicated to prove. Some perpetrators may coerce or manipulate victims to comply with unwanted sexual acts. Rape in marriage was only made illegal in 1991 – prior to this it was not possible to rape a spouse – and is particularly underreported. Victims of marital rape are loath to disclose for the fear of not being recognised as a 'real' rape victim (Flood & Pease, 2009).

Emotional abuse: All victims of domestic abuse suffer at least some emotional abuse such as threats and belittling, and perpetrators are very adept at passing the blame for any abusive behaviour onto their victims. Sometimes this form of abuse occurs early within the relationship and works with coercive control to manipulate the victim to believe it is all her fault.

Economic abuse: Nearly one third of respondents in a recent survey by Women's Aid suggested that their access to money was controlled by their partner. Being a way of controlling the victim within a relationship the lack of finance also acts as a barrier to leaving the perpetrator. Some victims are encouraged to stop work to make them more financially dependent and more isolated.

Online/digital abuse: Many victims find that the experience of online abuse follows the pattern they experienced offline from partners and ex-partners. There have been a number of incidents where perpetrators have loaded location software onto victims' phones to maintain their harassment and control.

Coercive control: According to the ONS (2020) 17,616 offences of coercive control were recorded by the police in year ending, March 2019. "Coercive control creates invisible chains and a sense of fear that pervades all elements of a victim's life. It works to limit their human rights by depriving them of their liberty and reducing their ability for action" (Women's Aid, 2019).

https://www.womensaid.org.uk/information-support/what-is-domestic-abuse/coercive-control/

Most of the household violence that reaches media headlines involves either a homicide or significant physical injury; but this is just the very tip of the iceberg. In her early work, Kelly (1988) developed the concept of a continuum to describe the extent of the behaviours the women in her study found abusive. By using the idea, she was able to incorporate both the everyday and the less common abusive behaviours experienced. This was not a line of continuum measuring the seriousness of any event because the reaction to abuse for any particular victim varies. Kelly was interested in considering prevalence and recognised,

> . . . that there are forms of sexual violence which most women experience in their lives and which they are more likely to experience on multiple occasions. While these common forms are more likely to be defined by men as acceptable behaviour (for example, see sexual harassment as 'a harmless bit of fun'), they are connected to the forms of violence which are currently defined as crimes within the law.
>
> (Kelly 1988, p. 76)

Understanding the different forms of violence and the range of abuse much of which does not fall into any neat analytical categories is important if we are to protect and support victims.

Walby et al.'s (2017) research has extended some of these ideas by highlighting the variety of dimensions to be considered and recorded to ensure victim safety. Domestic abuse defies the concept of a crime as one perpetrator, one victim, and one event (Walby et al., 2017). At the very least, each case of domestic violence necessitates a close look at the act, the victim perspective, and the perpetrator to consider the amount of harm done, the intention of the perpetrator, the duration of the abuse and consequences of the action as well as some history of the frequency of the behaviour. All these dimensions play a part in unravelling the risk of any abusive situation and builds the picture of the behaviour. Acts of domestic abuse never occur once.

Walby et al. (2017) and other researchers (Day, 2018; Nixon and Humphreys, 2010) have used other intersecting dynamics within their research, for instance, the power differentials within the family unit, between victims and the judicial system and within society more generally. How do these effect the behaviour and response of perpetrators and victims? Other social factors such as ethnicity, class, gender, and age all influence both the actions and the reactions of victims, the power of perpetrators, and the responses of professionals, and each one can have an impact, not always positive, on the outcome of a domestic abuse event.

Who are the perpetrators?

Discussions about who are the perpetrators of violence in the heterosexual domestic sphere have drawn attention to two different commentaries: symmetrical, where both partners are perceived to be involved as perpetrators and victims of violence, and asymmetrical, where one partner, usually the male, is the perpetrator and the other partner, usually the female, is the victim. We do know that men can be victims of violence and abuse in heterosexual relationships; therefore, women can be perpetrators (Gadd et al., 2002; Huntley et al., 2019; Renzetti, C., 2009). But understanding the extent of any gender balance is important for policy and practice. Currently the weight of resources and investigation assumes, in the main, female victims and male perpetrators – at least in heterosexual relationships. If that balance was proved to be wrong then the approach to understanding domestic abuse, assessing risk, and resourcing for victims and the perpetrator programmes would need rethinking. This section considers what we know.

There have been two core strands considering domestic abuse: Family Violence Research and Violence Against Women. The Family Violence Research focus has suggested that intimate violence stems from symmetrically violent households and that assaults by women (as well as those committed by men) present a serious problem (Straus, 1993). This premise has led Straus to suggest "... assaults by wives are one of the main causes of wife beating" (1993, p. 80). Therefore, male violence in the household must in some ways be dependent on women's behaviour or at the very least there is symmetry in terms of violence. There have been a number of critiques of these findings (Dobash and Dobash, 2004; Walby et al., 2017; Walklate, 2001), which centre on the methodology used by Straus. First, the core sample groups were very small from very specific cohorts – mostly therapeutic practice – and results generalised. Straus et al. (1980) revised their methods to extend the data and developed a new scale for measuring the extent of domestic abuse within household surveys – the Conflict Tactics Scale (CTS). But the CTS scale generated further concerns. According to Dobash and Dobash (2004), it was more likely to find gender symmetry between partners using this scale. For instance, there was little or no differentiation between frequency of acts and types of violence, and neither defensive nor retaliatory actions were recorded. Therefore, there is no allowance for context, motivation (Renzetti, C., 2009), or the harm caused nor the intent of the perpetrator (Walby et al., 2017). Furthermore, assuming the equal distribution of power within the family unit denies the risk posed by domestic abuse and blames the victim both for provoking abuse and for not leaving. Staying in a violent relationship appears irrational, so onlookers might assume that the situation cannot be 'so bad' (Walklate, 2001).

The second approach to understanding perpetrators of domestic crime considers domestic abuse, rape, and sexual assault as Violence Against Women (Walklate 2001). According to Dobash and Dobash (2004) evidence, both quantitative and qualitative, from across the globe suggests that women suffer more victimisation and more violence over a lifetime than men, many suffer chronic levels of abuse, and the harm inflicted is more serious, as is the fear of harm. Their review of the research literature found that "... women's violence differs from that perpetrated by men in terms of nature, frequency, intention, intensity, physical injury and emotional harm" (Dobash and Dobash, 2004, p. 343).

There have been other reviews of gender symmetry (Johnson, 2006, 1995; Johnson and Ferraro, 2000) that divided heterosexual partner violence into four different types: intimate terrorism, violent resistance, situational couple violence, and mutual violent control. The important issue for Johnson is the need to understand the variety of controlling behaviours and who has the control within a relationship (Johnson 2006). Situational couple violence, where violence occurs but neither partner displays controlling behaviour, and mutual violent control – only found in five couples in Johnson's data set, where both parties are violent and controlling, which are situations that could be considered gender symmetric. However, the more concerning behaviours were intimate terrorism and violent resistance. He refers to intimate terrorism as "... relationships in which only one of the spouses is violent and controlling. The other spouse is either nonviolent or has used violence but is not controlling" (2006, p. 1009). In heterosexual relationships the perpetrator in this group is nearly always the male. Violent resistance are cases where ". . . the focal spouse is violent but not controlling, and his or her partner is violent and controlling . . . and it is almost entirely a woman's type of violence" (Johnson 2006, p. 1010). Further findings suggest that victims of intimate terrorism suffer more violent and frequent attacks, experience more harm, and are more likely to seek help and support (Leone et al., 2004).

Females can sometimes be violent perpetrators although research data suggests that women are more commonly victims of violent behaviour in domestic abuse situations (Gadd et al., 2002; Johnson, 2006; Saunders, 2002; Walby et al., 2017; Walby and Allen, 2004). Reviews of the literature indicate that most "*serious* intimate violence is asymmetrical, with men usually violent to women" (Dobash and Dobash 2004, p. 343) and that intimate violence is a gendered crime (Renzetti, 2009). While maintaining gender as a key variable there are other important issues to be unravelled including the intent behind and context of the crime. But there is little room to doubt that the back-story to violent acts differ for men and women.

> Traditionally, while male violence has been condoned, as acknowledged, for example, in the common law right to beat one's wife. . . women's violence against men has been viewed as a rebellion against authority.
>
> (Hooper, 1996, p. 177)

Understanding victims

The first step to understanding victims is to appreciate there is no typical domestic abuse victim. While routine and regular encounters may give rise to certain stereotypical notions about victims by supporting common myths and assumptions – these are just the tip of the iceberg. Domestic abuse occurs in all parts of society as the example of former Chief Superintendent Sally Benatar demonstrates (see Chapter 8).

Nevertheless, there are victim behaviours that are sometimes difficult to understand. For instance, 'why does she stay?' is a question often voiced and sometimes difficult to answer, but Stark's (2006) analysis of coercive control offers some insights. Coercive control isolates victims from family and friends and offers some insight into the victim's dilemma. It builds on existing sexual inequalities and therefore is less visible, and more importantly, it is an often overlooked aspect of domestic abuse (Swan and Snow, 2003).

Stark (2009) uses his work to distinguish between violent and controlling abuse to reveal one reason that domestic abuse is so complicated lies in the fact that physical abuse is not always present. Coercive control is insidious and works through the ". . . enforcement of gender stereotypes" (Stark 2009,

p. 1511) to 'trap' victims by intimidation, isolation, and lack of access to either economic or social resources. Where violence is part of the controlling behaviour using the victim's fear of repeated violent attacks one of the many tactics used by abusers. Whatever tactics used by the perpetrators, Stark suggests that such behaviours ". . . erodes confidence" and forces victims to ". . . adapt their behaviour to avoid abuse" (Sharp-Jeffs et al., 2018, p. 165). The subtle nature of coercive control is so normalised within these relationship that many victims fail to recognise the behaviour as abusive. Silvestri and Crowther-Dowey (2008) highlighted links between understanding torture and the enactment of coercive control, whereby passive methods can be used to destroy the sense of self.

> Like torture . . . domestic violence has its own interrogation-type questions, accusations, insults and orders: 'Where were you today?' 'Who were you with?' 'Why is the house dirty?' are all fairly typical forms of interrogation that those in abusive relationships face. The goal of such interrogation is not to elicit the truth necessarily, but to instil a sense of dread, humiliation and submission in the victim.
>
> (2008, p. 99)

Such power in a relationship may offer both explanations of victim behaviour and lead to some effective interventions where "incident-specific definition(s) have failed" (Stark 2006, p. 1021). Experiencing coercive control ". . . would explain why 'abuse' continues even when couples separate, why 'minor' violence can have such significant consequences, why battered women are entrapped and develop a unique problem profile" (ibid), maybe leading to withdrawal of complaints and difficulty in leaving the partnership.

So, in answering the question of why women stay in controlling dangerous and violent situations Walklate suggests such a response is far from irrational.

> Home is a risky and highly dangerous place for women. Women in violent relationships . . . know this. They devise many and diverse strategies of coping with and surviving the violence. From this viewpoint, staying in such a relationship is symbolic of women's rationality and their local expert knowledge of the risks and dangers associated with any other options available to them. It is particularly associated with their knowledge of the men in their lives.
>
> (Walklate 2001, p. 116)

Any attempt to escape from a violent relationship can escalate the abuse and increase victim vulnerability (Duggan, 2018) with few if any guaranteed safeguards.

Who are the victims?

We have suggested above women are disproportionately victims of serious domestic abuse. However, there are other issues and concerns to be considered in order to appreciate the different dimensions of domestic abuse. While gender is the inter-connecting thread, other social locations are all pieces of the jigsaw that we need to understand the crime and support victims.

This section moves away from the vision of victim as white and female to other victims of domestic abuse. Anyone can be a victim of domestic abuse and the message we should be promoting is that emotional control and violence by anyone in the family unit, or any intimate relationship, is not acceptable (Dixon and Graham-Kevan, 2011).

Men as victims

As discussed above women do experience more, and certainly more severe domestic abuse, than men (Gadd et al., 2002). But some men are victims of partners and ex-partners too, both in heterosexual and in homosexual relationships (see Box 2.4). Recent research (Huntley et al., 2019) suggests that male victims failed to report domestic abuse expressing many of the anxieties and concerns revealed in studies of female victims – such as shame, a lack of self-confidence and worries about the welfare of their children. Some of the barriers to help-seeking were different. There were fears about disclosing abuse not just in terms of being believed but of being falsely accused as the perpetrator, and uncertainties voiced especially in connection with both their own ". . .personal sense of and societal interpretations of masculinity" (2019, p. 10). Sometimes male victims fail to recognise their partners' behaviour as abusive and remain in a state of unspoken shame often connected to a feeling of fear and inability to protect themselves (Dutton and Nicholls, 2005). The fears raised by male victims in Huntley et.al. (2019) reinforces a move away from a continuum of male violence (Kelly, 1988) towards the recognition and examination of the differences between men as championed by Connell (1995). Such an analysis could offer a better understanding of why some men become victims of intimate abuse as well as why some men are perpetrators.

BOX 2.4 MALE VICTIM OF DOMESTIC ABUSE – THE BBC TELLS HIS STORY

"A male domestic abuse survivor said he was "10 days away from death" before he was helped by police and medics.

Alex Skeel, 22, from Stewartby, Bedfordshire has urged other victims in abusive relationships to speak out. His former partner, Jordan

Worth, 22, subjected him to multiple physical injuries, denied him food and isolated him from his family, a court was told.

Pleading guilty to grievous bodily harm and coercive controlling behaviour, she was jailed for seven-and-a-half years. The prosecution is the United Kingdom's first conviction for coercive control involving a female offender, Bedfordshire Police said. Luton Crown Court was told Worth and Mr Skeel met at college in 2012 when they were both 16. From an early stage she had control over him, telling him what he should wear and attacking him physically.

During the last nine months of their relationship, Worth subjected her partner to multiple physical injuries, often requiring hospital treatment.

The abuse came to an end one evening last June when a neighbour called the police after hearing shouts from the couple's home. Ambulance staff noted injuries to his hand and burns to his arms and legs which had been self-treated with cling film. The court was told Worth had thrown boiling water over him and that he had second and third-degree burns.

Mr Skeel said he had not been allowed to get treatment for his wounds. "The hospital told me I was 10 days away from death", Alex Skeel said.

Worth broke all his mobile phones so he could not contact friends or family. He said on one occasion she told him her mother had received a message to say his grandfather had died.

"Half-way through me crying she said, 'Do you want to go downstairs and talk to my Mum about this?' So, you think, it is real", Mr Skeel said. But after watching him sob for two hours, Worth then revealed the death had not happened before berating him for caring about his family.

On another occasion he woke up after Worth had beaten him on the head with a beer bottle before chasing him and hitting him on the hands and face with a hammer.

Det Ch Insp Jerry Waite said: "Coercive control is subtle. The victim may not immediately recognise the behaviour as abuse...and (it) can lead to violence. . . You're far more of a person if you speak out. You're only going to get better if you talk about it", he said.

Worth was also made the subject of a restraining order, which prevents her from contacting Mr Skeel for an indefinite period".

https://www.bbc.co.uk/news/uk-england-beds-bucks-herts-43799850

Victims in the LGBT+ communities

The Council of Europe (2022) suggests that LGBT+ is an overarching term that stands for lesbian, gay, bisexual, and transgender/transexual people. This includes all those who feel their sexuality is not heterosexual hence the + symbol.

The domestic abuse research within these communities is limited but we do know that it is a sizeable problem (Donovan et al., 2006) and about 25% experience abuse from partners or ex-partners (End the fear, 2021). This figure is comparable with the victimisation rate amongst heterosexual women. Therefore, "MARACs and domestic abuse services should expect to see more than 2.5% of referrals for LGBT+ people" (SaveLives, 2018).

There are many similarities between heterosexual and LGBT+ victims including the types of abuse suffered and victim hesitation in recognising and reporting domestic abuse. However, there are some particular issues for LGBT+ victims:

- One form of control used by the perpetrator is to threaten to 'out' the victim to family, friends, and others.
- Victim denial of the abusive behaviour is common, especially in cases where physical abuse is not a factor (Donovan et al., 2006). Where the abusive behaviour is recognised, some victims assume that their sexual orientation or gender identity is a factor (End the Fear, 2021).
- It is hard for these victims to seek help. There is considerable silence around domestic abuse within LGBT+ communities leading to further disbelief and misinformation (End the Fear, 2021). Furthermore, public agencies have not always responded appropriately or sympathetically to disclosures from LGBT+ victims in the past (Donnovan et al., 2006).

LGBT+ domestic violence victims often have complex needs as they delay seeking help. Furthermore, the dangers they face are likely to be high risk (SafeLives, 2018). Currently statutory and non-statutory organisations are missing opportunities and failing to recognise not just the victims but also the perpetrators. Given these factors it is important for both central and local governments to develop pathways for specialist funding for LGBT+ service provision and ensure appropriate guidance to reflect inclusion in strategic and local policy-making (SafeLives, 2018).

Ethnicity

While domestic abuse can be identified in all ethnic groups (Mooney, 2000) it is important to realise victims are not a homogenous group and to recognise the interplay between race and gender (Gill, 2004). According to

Gill "South Asian women are often doubly victimised: first by the violence perpetrated against them by their partner, and then by (a) society" (2004, p. 466) that fails to protect them. Some victims abide in multigenerational households and as a result may experience multigenerational violence and control. Despite their abusive situations they can be slow to disclose as they are fearful of causing the family shame and dishonour.

The crimes of Forced Marriage (FM) and Female Genital Mutilation (FGM) tend to be specific to some minority groups, although not exclusively so. FM is not the same as an 'arranged marriage' where families may help you choose a suitable partner and marriage only occurs with the consent of both parties. People of all ages, cultures, and religions can be forced or pressurised into marriage (FCO, 2013), which is a crime in England, Scotland, and Wales under the Anti-Social Behaviour Crime and Policy Act 2014. It is also possible to apply for a Forced Marriage Protection Order (FMPO) through the family courts. FGM involves the mutilation of female genitalia, is sometimes performed on very young children and is a criminal offence – Female Genital Mutilation Act 2003. Like FM this may be performed under the guise of tradition, though neither are supported by any religious doctrine (GOV.UK, 2021).

Unlike FM and FGM, Honour-Based Violence or Abuse (HBV/A) is not a specific statutory offence. HBV/A is complex and involves patriarchal controls, usually over a young girl/woman. Rather than just a partner this abuse can involve the wider family and community (Gill, 2009). The abuse may start as a response to a young woman's refusal to marry or her attempt to escape from a violent relationship (see Box 2.5).

HBV/A is prosecuted according to the laws that regulate the specific offence committed. HBV/A can be distinguished from domestic abuse and other forms of violence because it is often committed with some degree of approval and/or collusion from family and/or community members in response to perceived immoral/shameful behaviour on the part of the victim (Gill et al., 2018, p. 579).

BOX 2.5 HONOUR KILLING

A 17-year-old Shafilea disappeared from her home in Warrington, Cheshire, on 11 September 2003; she was reported missing by her teacher a week later. After several police appeals to find her, workmen found her decomposed remains in the River Kent in Cumbria February 2004 and she was identified by her dental records and jewellery.

Her parents, Iftikhar, 52, and Farzana Ahmed, 49, had denied murder but the jury at Chester Crown Court returned guilty verdicts against them both. The couple suffocated Shafilea with a plastic bag after she had suffered years of abuse. Mr Justice Roderick Evans said they would both serve a minimum of 25 years. The judge told them: "Your concern about being shamed in your community was greater than the love of your child".

After the trial, Det Supt Geraint Jones described the killing as a "vile and disgraceful act against someone they should have been very proud of". He added: "For me this is not an 'honour killing', it's a clear case of murder". The prosecution claimed she was murdered by her parents because they believed she brought shame on the family.

Source: www.bbc.co.uk/news/uk-england-19068490

On the 6th Day of Memory for the Victims of Honour Killings, charities say more education is needed to tackle so-called 'honour'-based violence.

The charity Karma Nirvana (www.karmanirvana.org.uk) is one of the main organisations that helps victims of honour-based abuse. As well as running a national helpline to support victims in immediate danger, they offer training to professionals and regularly work with police forces, the NHS, social services, local government, and teachers.

The HO estimates that between 5,000 and 8,000 people are at risk of being forced into marriage every year in the United Kingdom. But last year, Karma Nirvana's helpline received just over 12,000 contacts from the United Kingdom alone, and the charity believes this is a huge underestimate of the actual scale of honour-based abuse.

Source: https://www.standard.co.uk/front/honour-abuse-killings-day-of-memory-a4198036.html

There are other multi-dimensional problems effecting the lives of some victims that create difficulties for reporting abuse, particularly in cases where women are controlled by the perpetrator and extended family or community. When professionals do become involved finding safe locations and ensuring the availability of interpreters where needed can raise further risk for these victims. Women from recent migrant populations and asylum seekers may have particular fears and concerns in the current 'hostile' UK environment as ". . .UK immigrations laws frequently bind migrant women to their perpetrators, who may be their sponsor in obtaining legal status" (Day 2018, p. 40). Migrant victims without secure status have very little access to support under the No Recourse to Public Funding Requirement (NRPFR) and therefore are not eligible for any basic domestic abuse services including safe accommodation or emergency finance (Voolma, 2018). All of these extra dilemmas add to the complexities of mitigating risk in cases of domestic abuse, and as a recent report from Sisters for Change (2019) suggested multiple social locations generate multiple concerns.

Black, Asian, minority ethnic and migrant women experience higher rates of domestic homicide and are three times more likely to commit suicide than other women in the United Kingdom, and 50% of these victims of violence experience abuse from multiple perpetrators. In addition, 40% of these women live in poverty and are more likely than other women to be living in a deprived area, have experienced of the State care system, and suffer from discrimination and racism (Sisters for Change report, 2019, p. 2)

Elder abuse

Older people in domestic abuse situations share many of the same problems about seeking help as other cohorts. But long periods of abuse can also lead to a severe loss of self-confidence and isolation (Zink et al. 2003). Given that these victims are less able to access resources to support a more timely exit from their relationship they develop strategies of coping that allowed them to maintain and invest in a tolerable lifestyle, which in some cases becomes a "... philosophy of life and survival" (Zink et al., 2006, p. 648). Alongside these coping strategies, which for some have been a lifetime's investment, many older victims are economically dependent and feel less able to develop new social networks.

While none of the issues raised are unique to older people, there are some particular differences highlighted in the literature.

- There is evidence of a slight gender shift in terms of victims suggesting a slightly higher number of male victims, two to every five females (Clarke et al., 2016) within intimate partner violence.
- The perpetrators of coercive control and violence among older victims are more varied, commonly involving close relatives, including sons and grandsons, and carers (Clarke et al., 2016) as well as intimate partners.
- Research into elders and domestic abuse is in its infancy compared to other domestic abuse situations. More consideration of the differences in terms of the event and who are the perpetrators and victims (see Walby et al., 2017) is required to enable the most appropriate and supportive interventions.

According to Age UK, victims of domestic abuse amongst the older population have been neglected by professionals and policy makers. Yet it is hardly an insignificant problem. In their report, No Age Limit (2020) they note that the Crime Survey for England and Wales 2018/19 recorded about 180,000 older women between 64 and 75 years and 98,000 older men between 64 and 75 years as victims of domestic abuse in England and Wales (Henderson et al. 2020). Furthermore, as it stands, the new Domestic Abuse Bill also fails to offer older people appropriate protection. The Age UK report suggests that older people are systematically overlooked in favour of younger victims – who may well have more access to support – and that there is not enough data to be able to assess the problem appropriately. This is partly because the CSEW does not collect data on adults over the age of 74, resulting in ageist and stereotypical assumption concerning older people. The provision of services is affected as a result (Clarke et al., 2016).

The recent HMICFRS (2019) report has highlighted many of the same concerns. The report included a review of cases where victims were over 60 years of age and found inconsistency of treatment across the forces. In particular, older people were not considered a 'special' group and therefore vulnerability and safeguarding needs went unrecognised in many cases. While more research data would help support calls for increase in resourcing and victim support, raising awareness of the possibility of intimate violence in the older population amongst all front-line professionals should be a priority.

Young people and domestic abuse

As with elder abuse the research literature data gathered about young people and domestic abuse is limited. A recent report by SafeLives (2017) defined three concerns relating specifically to young people and intimate abuse (see Box 2.6). The first highlights the problems for children who are witnesses to domestic abuse within their family. Research suggests that this group of children are more prone to develop abusive or self-harming behaviours, and as such it is mandatory, under the Children Act 1989, for all professionals involved with cases of domestic abuse to alert social services if children are in the household. Children witnessing domestic violence within the household are at the very least subject to emotional abuse endangering their mental health as well as their understanding of future intimate relationships (Holt et al., 2008). Children observing violent abuse and coercive control between their parents can result in a normalisation of violent behaviour which in turn effects their future relationships (ibid).

BOX 2.6 SAFE YOUNG LIVES

A report published in 2017 by SafeLives offers some insights into the concerns about children and young people as witnesses and victims of domestic abuse. Key findings include:

- The data gathered shows that children and young people experience domestic abuse and that the most severe forms of abuse ". . .may be highest for the youngest age group".

- An NSPCC study indicates that 25% of girls and 18% of boys amongst 13–17 year olds involved in the research had experienced ". . .physical violence from an intimate partner". And 31% of the girls as well as 18% of boys disclosed ". . .some form of sexual abuse within their relationships".
- The SafeLives data has shown that 1:4 13–17 year olds who do seek help through the young people's domestic abuse service ". . .demonstrate harmful behaviour". And 61% of this group directed harmful behaviour towards their mothers.

Amongst the most concerning findings include:

- "49% of boys and 33% of girls aged 13–14 thought that hitting a partner would be 'okay' in at least one of twelve scenarios they were presented with".
- "SafeLives Children's Insights data shows that less than half (45%) of young people in an abusive intimate relationship were known to social services".
- "Young people were more than twice as likely to self-harm compared to older victims (30% compared to 14%)".
- And overall 1:5 children are exposed to domestic abuse in the household.

Source: SafeLives (2017) Safe young lives: young people and domestic violence, www.safelives.org.uk

The second concern raised by SafeLives involves children and young people who are perpetrators within households – harming or using controlling behaviour over other members of the family. There has been very little data collected on this group within the United Kingdom, which has led to limited specialist support services in this area for young people and made more complicated by the difficulty in finding a suitably sensitive and nuanced response to the violent behaviour within any policing, child protection, or domestic abuse policy frameworks (Miles and Condry, 2016).

The third group discussed comprise victims of abusive relationships – mainly girls (95%) who are more likely to have older boyfriends. Very little is understood about teenage experience of partner violence in the United Kingdom, except that it exists in a range of forms from rape to emotional abuse (Barter, 2009) and from coercive control to the micro-management of daily life (Stark, 2009). The SafeLives (2017) report draws out some key areas that require some careful consideration. For instance, children under 16 are unable to access specialist domestic abuse services. Although this changed for 16- and 17-year olds in 2013, SafeLives research findings indicate that on average abusive relationships begin one to one and a half years prior to the 16-cut-off age, at 14 or 15. This leaves victims under the age of 16 reliant on ". . . limited specialist Young People Domestic Abuse Services (YPDA) and although social services should pick up these young people, only 45% are known to the authorities". A final troubling point was uncovered within the qualitative data of the SafeLives report (2017) about the use of technology by perpetrators for controlling and stalking victims which found that while,

> . . . technology could play a positive role in a victim's abilities to stay safe from domestic abuse, concluded that perpetrators currently remain one step ahead of both victims and professionals in re-purposing technology to their advantage.
>
> (SafeLives, 2017, p. 21)

Digital technology has been highlighted as a key issue for concern and should be included alongside other forms of 'in person' abuse as part of any risk assessment (Harris and Woodlock, 2019).

Class

The research and surveys agree with the early campaigners that physical abuse and class are statistically related. In effect physical abuse is more prevalent among the working class (Bograd, 1999; Fang and Corso, 2008; Mooney, 2000; Flatley, 2016; Renzetti, 2009). According to Mooney (2000), the North London Domestic Abuse Survey (NLDAS) results also supported this discrepancy of physical abuse and class.

However, qualitative research undertaken after the NLDAS survey uncovered two key issues:

- Professional women were more aware of other types of abuse.
- Within most of the relationships there was a period when the perpetrator exercised power and control over the victim.

Mooney (2000) suggests that professional women may well have the resources, and fewer domestic commitments such as children, to leave relationships before they become physically abusive. However, there are exceptions as some victims feel unable to seek help sometimes not recognising the perpetrators' behaviour as abuse or feeling loath to report abuse for fear of losing face. Economics and the ability to maintain financial independence play important roles in escaping abusive relationships. They can offer the gateway to access safe and secure housing, which alongside a regular viable income is a major factor in enabling women to escape the insidious coercive control that limits the space for victims to act (Sharp-Jeffs et al., 2018). Those without economic or social capital have a practical barrier to leaving an abusive relationship. Current employment trends, especially in a post-COVID world, are complex for those with low or no qualifications or experience especially if young children are involved. Recent cuts to the Women's Refuge networks, the complex access to government benefits and universal credits, and the lack of social housing all create further limitations on the 'space for action' that women experience (Kelly, 2003).

Understanding domestic abuse

The purpose of this section is to consider some of the key research findings that enable us to better understand domestic abuse as a problem. As we have seen in the discussion above, the second-wave feminists, particularly the radical feminists, were instrumental in challenging the problems of private crime and progressing theoretical explanations of domestic abuse. Not only did they recognise that abuse in the home was a major social problem, but also recognised that violence is gendered, which they laid at the door of a masculinised and patriarchal social order. They also suggested that the maintenance of this social order was controlled by the 'threat' of violence towards women.

> Radical feminists see all forms of male violence against women including the threat and fear of violence, as functioning as a social control mechanism forcing women to modify their behaviour. . . male violence serves to keep women in their place.
>
> (Mooney 2000, p. 90)

There is no doubt that this analysis developed by the feminists forged a pathway to support for domestic abuse and rape victims through activism and research. However, the dominance of the radical perspective, and indeed some of the early feminist discourse more generally, has given rise to criticism. One of the key problems was its focus on a universal notion of 'woman' to the exclusion of other discriminatory factors such as race, ethnicity, class, and sexuality. This was a major omission that was followed up and questioned by the black feminists such as hooks (1981) and led to a move towards a more inclusive, intersectional approach.

The use of intersectionality as an analytic tool has been an important development (Patil, 2013). We know some of the early work does look at a variety of inequalities and how they interlink (Kelly, 1988) but the core intersectionality theory was developed by Crenshaw (1989). This approach identifies the ways in which gender is affected by other social locations such as race, ethnicity, class, age, disability, and sexuality. All inequalities are interdependent so victims may suffer multiple injustices which compound the problems of any domestic abuse (Strid et al., 2013) especially with regard to disclosure. The important issue for research, policy, and practice is threefold:

- To ensure that these disadvantages are recognised by naming them.
- To consider how recognition of these inequalities is played out in practice.
- To ensure the inclusion of voices of vulnerable victims who have been marginalised.

Using an intersectional approach works towards developing good quality policy and practice that should enable all women and men to access the services they need. It also ensures any intervention or support is effective in order to overcome the multitude of injustices that compound the problems of domestic abuse (Strid et al., 2013). It has proved to be a useful tool for understanding domestic abuse and allows us to develop policies that are inclusionary. For instance, an appreciation of the range of inequalities offers us an awareness of the limited choices available to some victims and emphasises the importance of activating multi-agency support to reduce risk.

So, understanding the inequalities faced by a victim can be significant in any domestic abuse incident but some domestic crime, like coercive control, is insidious and difficult to identify even though it can be a core element of domestic abuse. Coercive control needs to be an important focus as it encapsulates ". . .what living with domestic violence means for women and children" (Myhill and Kelly, 2021, p. 3). The main purpose of Stark's (2007) work is to show how domestic violence limits the free will of women by micro-managing their everyday lives. This goes beyond the physical assault to the ". . . microregulation of everyday behaviours associated with stereotypic female roles" (Stark 2007, p. 13). While understanding that both men and women may use coercive control, it is sexual inequality that allows men to be more successful according to Myhill and Kelly (2021). However, despite legislation coercive control is difficult to police as the abusive behaviour experienced by survivors may not align with the current legal framework (Myhill & Kelly, 2021).

We have come a long way since the 1970s, and as a result domestic abuse is now very much a public and political concern. What seems clear from the research is that, perhaps more than other crimes, domestic abuse must be considered in context. Walby and her colleagues (2017) identified that domestic abuse needs careful consideration in order to put the crime into perspective. Domestic abuse is not a single event, and the tendency to remove the behaviour from the whole context misunderstands the crime and complicates the assessment of risk in terms of both victims and perpetrators (Dasgupta, 2002).

Conclusion

Feminist campaigning and research have highlighted the scale of domestic abuse raising it as an issue of public and political importance as well as challenging the response of the criminal justice system. Part of the problem has been that domestic abuse is not 'one' crime, there is no single law relating to domestic abuse, and therefore, any definition needs to encompass various perspectives. What this chapter has shown is that it is important to look at the past to understand the present. There is a historical legacy of myths and assumptions about domestic abuse that linger today which sometimes influence current practice. Furthermore, the careful analysis of current research and theories of the causes, alongside a better understanding of the victims and the perpetrators of domestic violence, offers policy and practice ways to recognise abuse, support victims, and lower the risk of harm.

Reflective questions

- How did private acts of domestic abuse emerge as a public concern?
- How do myths and assumptions about domestic abuse effect a police response?
- Why does domestic abuse occur? How is it defined?
- What insights does research offer policy and practice?

Useful websites

Professor Evan Stark – explaining the use of coercive control by perpetrators of domestic abuse and its effect on children in the family https://www.youtube.com/watch?v=kvHbVzTzpX0&ab_channel=WelshWomen%27sAid

Unequal regard, unequal protection: A report on the responses to violence against BME women in England, 2017 https://www.sistersforchange.org.uk/2017/11/20/unequal-regard-unequal-protection/

Professor Aisha Gill – research on honour-based violence and forced marriage has improved victim protection and prosecution of perpetrators https://esrc.ukri.org/news-events-and-publications/impact-case-studies/countering-honour-crimes-and-forced-marriage/

Help guide for men who are suffering domestic abuse https://www.helpguide.org/articles/abuse/help-for-men-who-are-being-abused.htm

UN Women.org An explanation of intersectionality and why it matters https://www.unwomen.org/en/news/stories/2020/6/explainer-intersectional-feminism-what-it-means-and-why-it-matters

References

Abrams, L., 1999. Crime against marriage? Wife-beating, divorce and the law in nineteenth century Hamburg, in: Arnot, M., Usborne, C. (Eds.), *Gender and Crime in Modern Europe*. UCL Press & Taylor Group, pp. 118–136.

Barter, C., 2009. In the name of love: Partner abuse and violence in teenage relationships. *British Journal of Social Work* 39, 211–233.

Bograd, M., 1999. Strengthening domestic violence theories: Intersections of race, class, sexual orientation, and gender. *Journal of Marital and Family Therapy* 25, 275–289.

Booth, R., 2008. Britons give more to donkey sanctuary than abuse charities. *The Guardian*.

Bourlet, A., 1990. Police intervention in marital violence. Open University Press Milton Keynes.

Burton, M., 2016. A fresh approach to policing domestic violence, in: Hilder, S., Bettinson, V. (Eds.), *Domestic Violence: Interdisciplinary Perspectives on Protection, Prevention and Intervention*. Palgrave Macmillan UK, pp. 37–57.

Buzawa, E.S., Buzawa, C.G., 1996. *Domestic violence: The criminal justice response*. Sage.

Clark, A., 1992. *Humanity or justice? Wifebeating and the law in the eighteenth and nineteenth centuries*. Routledge.

Clarke, A., Williams, J., Wydall, S., 2016. Access to justice for victims/survivors of elder abuse: A qualitative study. *Social Policy and Society* 15, 207–220.

Cobbe, F.P., 1878. Wife-torture in England. *Contemporary Review*.

Connell, R.W., 1995. *Masculinities*. Polity Press.

Council of Europe, 2022. LGBT+, https://www.coe.int/en/web/gender-matters/lgbt- (accessed 7.10.22).

Crenshaw, K., 1989. *Demarginalizing the intersection of race and sex: A Black feminist critique of antidiscrimination doctrine, feminist theory, and antiracist politics*. University of Chicago Legal Forum.

Dasgupta, S.D., 2002. A framework for understanding women's use of nonlethal violence in intimate heterosexual relationships. *Violence Against Women* 8, 1364–1389.

Day, A.S., 2018. *Partnership and power: Domestic violence, the women's sector, and the criminal justice system*. University of Essex.

Dixon, L., Graham-Kevan, N., 2011. Understanding the nature and etiology of intimate partner violence and implications for practice and policy. *Clinical Psychology Review* 31, 1145–1155.

Dobash, R.E., Dobash, R.P, 1979. *Violence against wives: A case against the patriarchy*. Free Press New York.

Dobash, R.E., Dobash, R.P., 1992. *Women, violence and social change*. Routledge.

Dobash, R.P., Dobash, R.E., 2004. Women's violence to men in intimate relationships: Working on a puzzle. *British Journal of Criminology* 44, 324–349.

Donovan, C., Hester, M., Holmes, J., McCarry, M., 2006. *Comparing domestic abuse in same sex relationships*. University of Bristol.

Duggan, M., 2018. 'Idealising' domestic violence victims, in: Duggan, M (Ed.), *Revisiting the 'Ideal Victim': Developments in Critical Victimology*, pp. 159–174.

Dutton, D.G., Nicholls, T.L., 2005. The gender paradigm in domestic violence research and theory: Part 1—The conflict of theory and data. *Aggression and Violent Behavior* 10, 680–714.

Edwards, S.S., 1989. *Policing 'domestic' violence: Women, the law and the state.* SAGE.

End the Fear, 2021. Same sex domestic violence. Greater Manchester Against Domestic Abuse. EndtheFear.co.uk/same-sex-domestic-violence (accessed December 2021).

Fang, X., Corso, P.S., 2008. Gender differences in the connections between violence experienced as a child and perpetration of intimate partner violence in young adulthood. *Journal of Family Violence* 23, 303–313.

Faragher, T., 1985. The police response to violence against women in the home, in: Pahl, J. (Ed.), *Private Violence and Public Policy.* Routledge, pp. 16–48.

FCO, 2013. *Forced marriage.* Foreign and Commonwealth Office.

Femi-Ajao, O., Kendal, S., Lovell, K., 2020. A qualitative systematic review of published work on disclosure and help-seeking for domestic violence and abuse among women from ethnic minority populations in the UK. *Ethnicity & Health* 25, 732–746.

Flatley, J., 2016. *Intimate personal violence and partner abuse.* Office for National Statistics.

Flood, M., Pease, B., 2009. Factors influencing attitudes to violence against women. *Trauma, Violence, & Abuse* 10, 125–142.

Gadd, D., Farrall, S., Dallimore, D., Lombard, N., 2002. *Domestic abuse against men in Scotland.* Scottish Executive Central Research Unit.

Gill, A., 2009. Honor killings and the quest for justice in black and minority ethnic communities in the United Kingdom. *Criminal Justice Policy Review* 20, 475–494.

Gill, A., 2004. Voicing the silent fear: South Asian women's experiences of domestic violence. *The Howard Journal of Criminal Justice* 43, 465–483.

Gill, A.K., Cox, P., Weir, R., 2018. Shaping priority services for UK victims of honour-based violence/abuse, forced marriage, and female genital mutilation. *The Howard Journal of Crime and Justice* 57, 576–595.

GOV.UK, 2021. Female genital mutilation. https://www.gov.uk/government/collections/female-genital-mutilation (accessed 11.13.21).

Grace, S., 1995. *Policing domestic violence in the 1990s.* HM Stationery Office.

Groves, N., Thomas, T., 2014. *Domestic violence and criminal justice.* Routledge.

Harris, B.A., Woodlock, D., 2019. Digital coercive control: Insights from two landmark domestic violence studies. *The British Journal of Criminology* 59, 530–550.

Hecker, E.A., 1911. *A short history of women's rights.* The Knickerbocker Press.

Henderson, R., McCarron, E., Trew, A., 2020. *No age limit: The blind spot of older victims and survivors in the domestic violence bill.* Age UK.

HMIC, 2014. *Everyone's business: improving the police response to domestic abuse.* Her Majesty's Inspectorate of Constabulary.

HMICFRS, 2019. The poor relation: The police and Crown Prosecution Service's response to crimes against older people. *Her Majesty's Inspectorate of Constabulary and Fire and Rescue Services.*

Holt, S., Buckley, H., Whelan, S., 2008. The impact of exposure to domestic violence on children and young people: A review of the literature. *Child Abuse & Neglect* 32, 797–810.

Home Office, 2013. *New government domestic violence and abuse definition* (Home Office Circular No. 0032).

Home Office, 1986. *Police initial training notes.* HMSO.

Hooks, B., 1981. *Ain't I a woman Black women and feminism.* London: Pluto Press.

Hooper, M., 1996. When domestic violence diversion is no longer an option: What to do with the female offender. *Berkeley Women's Law Journal* 11, 168–181.

House of Commons Select Committee on Violence in Marriage, 1975. *Violence in marriage report and papers.* HMSO.

Huntley, A.L., Potter, L., Williamson, E., Malpass, A., Szilassy, E., Feder, G., 2019. Help-seeking by male victims of domestic violence and abuse (DVA): A systematic review and qualitative evidence synthesis. *BMJ Open* 9, e021960.

Jenner, A., 2021. *What police do? What victims need? A qualitative analysis of the police response to domestic violence (in Essex).* University of Essex.

Johnson, M.P., 2006. Conflict and control: Gender symmetry and asymmetry in domestic violence. *Violence Against Women* 12, 1003–1018.

Johnson, M.P., 1995. Patriarchal terrorism and common couple violence: Two forms of violence against women. *Journal of Marriage and the Family* 57, 283–294.

Johnson, M.P., Ferraro, K.J., 2000. Research on domestic violence in the 1990s: Making distinctions. *Journal of Marriage and Family* 62, 948–963.

Kelly, L., 2003. The wrong debate: Reflections on why force is not the key issue with respect to trafficking in women for sexual exploitation. *Feminist Review* 73, 139–144.

Kelly, L., 1988. *Surviving sexual violence.* John Wiley & Sons.

Kelly, L., Westmarland, N., 2014. *Time for a rethink—Why the current government definition of domestic violence is a problem.* Trouble & Strife, p. 14.

Leone, J.M., Johnson, M.P., Cohan, C.L., Lloyd, S.E., 2004. Consequences of male partner violence for low-income minority women. *Journal of Marriage and Family* 66, 472–490.

Miles, C., Condry, R., 2016. Adolescent to parent violence: The police response to parents reporting violence from their children. *Policing and Society* 26, 804–823.

Mooney, J., 2000. *Gender, violence and the social order.* Springer.

Myhill, A., Hohl, K., 2016. The "golden thread" coercive control and risk assessment for domestic violence. *Journal of Interpersonal Violence* 34, 4477–4497.

Myhill, A., Kelly, L., 2021. Counting with understanding? What is at stake in debates on researching domestic violence. *Criminology & Criminal Justice* 21, 280–296.

Naffine, N., 1990. *Law and the sexes: Explorations in feminist jurisprudence.* Allen & Unwin Sydney.

National DA Helpline, 2019. *What is abuse?* https://www.nationaldahelpline.org.uk/en/What-is-abuse (accessed 4.21.19).

Nixon, J., Humphreys, C., 2010. Marshalling the evidence: Using intersectionality in the domestic violence frame. *Social Politics* 17, 137–158.

ONS, 2020. Domestic abuse prevalence and trends, England and Wales – Office for National Statistics. https://www.ons.gov.uk/peoplepopulationandcommunity/crimeandjustice/articles/domesticabuseprevalenceandtrendsenglandandwales/yearendingmarch2020#crime-survey-for-england-and-wales (accessed 9.7.21).

ONS, 2018. Domestic abuse in England and Wales – Office for National Statistics. https://www.ons.gov.uk/peoplepopulationandcommunity/crimeandjustice/bulletins/domesticabuseinenglandandwales/yearendingmarch2016#are-there-differences-between-local-areas (accessed 2.17.19).

ONS, 2016. Intimate personal violence and partner abuse. Office for National Statistics. https://www.ons.gov.uk/peoplepopulationandcommunity/crimeandjustice/compendium/focusonviolentcrimeandsexualoffences/yearendingmarch2015/chapter4intimatepersonalviolenceandpartnerabuse (accessed 7.4.22).
Pagelow, M., 1981. *Woman Battering: victims and their experiences.* Sage.
Patil, V., 2013. From patriarchy to intersectionality: A transnational feminist assessment of how far we've really come. *Signs: Journal of Women in Culture and Society* 38, 847–867.
RCN, 2020. *Domestic abuse.* The Royal College of Nursing.
Renzetti, C., 2009. Social class, race, and intimate partner violence. *Racism Review*, http://www.racismreview.com/blog/2009/03/14/social-class-race-and-intimate-partner-violence/ (accessed 7.4.22).
Richards, L., Letchford, S., Stratton, S., 2008. *Policing domestic violence: Blackstone's practical policing.* Oxford University Press.
SafeLives, 2018. *Free to Be Safe: LGBT+ people experiencing domestic abuse*, https://safelives.org.uk/knowledge-hub/spotlights/spotlight-6-lgbt-people-and-domestic-abuse (accessed 7.10.22).
SafeLives, 2017. *Spotlight #3: Young people and domestic abuse|SafeLives.* https://safelives.org.uk/knowledge-hub/spotlights/spotlight-3-young-people-and-domestic-abuse (accessed 11.2.21).
Saraga, E., 1996. Dangerous places: The family as a site of crime, in: Muncie, J., Mclaughlin, E. (Eds.). *The problem of crime 2.* US Department of Justice. https://www.ojp.gov/ncjrs/virtual-library/abstracts/problem-crime-0
Saunders, D.G., 2002. Are physical assaults by wives and girlfriends a major social problem? A review of the literature. *Violence Against Women* 8, 1424–1448.
Sharp-Jeffs, N., Kelly, L., Klein, R., 2018. Long journeys toward freedom: The relationship between coercive control and space for action—Measurement and emerging evidence. *Violence Against Women* 24, 163–185.
Silvestri, M., Crowther-Dowey, C., 2008. Gender and crime. SAGE.
Sisters for Change, 2019. Unequal regard, unequal protection: spotlight on Manchester report. https://www.sistersforchange.org.uk/ (accessed 11.3.21).
Smith, L.J.F., 1989. *Domestic Violence: an overview of the literature, Home Office Study no 107.* HMSO.
Stark, E., 2009. Rethinking coercive control. *Violence Against Women* 15, 1509–1525.
Stark, E., 2007. *Coercive Control: How Men Entrap Women in Personal Life.* New York, NY: Oxford University Press.
Stark, E., 2006. Commentary on Johnson's "Conflict and control: Gender symmetry and asymmetry in domestic violence." *Violence Against Women* 12, 1019–1025.
Straus, M., Gelles, R., Steinmetz, S.K., 1980. *Behind closed doors: A survey of family violence in America.* Routledge.
Straus, M.A., 1993. Physical assaults by wives: A major social problem, in: Gelles, R.J., Loseke, D.R. (Eds.), *Current Controversies on Family violence*, California, Sage Publications, pp. 67–87.
Strid, S., Walby, S., Armstrong, J., 2013. Intersectionality and multiple inequalities: Visibility in British policy on violence against women. *Social Politics: International Studies in Gender, State & Society* 20, 558–581.

Swan, S.C., Snow, D.L., 2003. Behavioral and psychological differences among abused women who use violence in intimate relationships. *Violence Against Women* 9, 75–109.

UK Parliament, 2021. *Domestic Abuse Act 2021 – Parliamentary Bills – UK Parliament* [WWW Document]. URL https://bills.parliament.uk/bills/2709 (accessed 12.1.21).

Voolma, H., 2018. "I must be silent because of residency": Barriers to escaping domestic violence in the context of insecure immigration status in England and Sweden. *Violence Against Women* 24, 1830–1850.

Walby, S., Allen, J., 2004. *Domestic violence, sexual assault and stalking: Findings from the British Crime Survey.* Home Office.

Walby, S., Towers, J., 2018. Untangling the concept of coercive control: Theorizing domestic violent crime. *Criminology & Criminal Justice* 18, 7–28.

Walby, S., Towers, J., Balderston, S., Corradi, C., Francis, B.J., Heiskanen, M., Helweg-Larsen, K., Mergaert, L., Olive, P., Palmer, C.E., 2017. The concept and measurement of violence against women and men. *Policy Press.*

Walklate, S., 2001. *Gender, crime and criminal justice.* Willan.

Weir, R., 2020. *Individuals, families and neighbourhoods: Predictors of domestic abuse in Essex.* University of Essex.

Wilson, E., 1983. *What is to be done about violence against women?* Penguin Books.

Women's Aid, 2019. Women's aid, the IOPC and the NPCC launch make yourself heard campaign this national stalking awareness week. *Womens Aid.* https://www.womensaid.org.uk/womens-aid-the-iopc-and-the-npcc-launch-make-yourself-heard-campaign-this-national-stalking-awareness-week/ (accessed 11.28.21).

Women's Aid, 2016. Annual survey 2016. *Womens Aid.* https://www.womensaid.org.uk/research-and-publications/annual-survey-2016/ (accessed 3.14.19).

Wright, S., 1995. The role of the police in combating domestic violence, in: Walklate, S. (Ed.), *Gender and Crime.* University of Wales Press, 9, 936267.

Zink, T., Jacobson Jr, C.J., Pabst, S., Regan, S., Fisher, B.S., 2006. A lifetime of intimate partner violence: Coping strategies of older women. *Journal of Interpersonal Violence* 21, 634–651.

Zink, T., Regan, S., Jacobson Jr, C.J., Pabst, S., 2003. Cohort, period, and aging effects: A qualitative study of older women's reasons for remaining in abusive relationships. *Violence Against Women* 9, 1429–1441.

Chapter 3

Measuring the extent of domestic abuse

KEY ISSUES

- How is data on levels of domestic abuse captured across the CJS.
- What are the advantages and disadvantages of survey data?
- What do we know from police data and what is missing?

What do other agencies outside of the CJS collect on domestic abuse?Introduction

The two main sources of domestic abuse data are the Crime Survey in England and Wales (CSEW) and police-recorded crime data. However, domestic abuse is one of the most underreported crimes and the CSEW estimates that only about 20% of victims report their abuse to the police (Flatley, 2016). This therefore leaves a significant gap in our understanding of who the victims are, the nature of their abuse, who is perpetrating the abuse, when and where the abuse is taking place, and whether they are repeat victims. To try and ensure that everybody has access to support and relevant services it is therefore very important to understand the challenges in collecting data on domestic abuse. This chapter explores these issues by unpacking the uses and limitations of data; the way in which data is captured and interlinked across the CJS and other agencies; and the gaps that still exist in our knowledge.

Uses and limitations of data

Data on domestic abuse is used by a wide range of individuals and organisations for several different purposes. Elected representatives and national and local government agencies use the data to develop and monitor policies, to develop awareness campaigns, to allocate resources, and to commission services. Third-sector organisations rely on data to design and run their services and to bid for funding to maintain future provision. Police forces and the partner agencies that they work with use the information at both an

DOI: 10.4324/9781003137412-3

operational and strategic level. The specific activities include responding to incidents; assessing risk; gathering evidence and further data; developing good practice; allocating and prioritising short- and long-term resources; and setting and monitoring strategic priorities.

The data is also used by journalists to report on patterns of domestic abuse prevalence or to add context to a news report or a campaign. Academic researchers use the data to carry out in-depth studies of domestic abuse victimisation or perpetration and to evaluate the success of interventions. They also use data to teach their students about domestic abuse and students in turn use the data in their projects and theses.

Individuals and organisations also use data to take a collaborative approach to reducing domestic abuse through membership of Community Safety Partnerships (CSPs) and Local Criminal Justice Boards (LCJBs). They also pool data from several organisations to manage high-risk victims through Multi-Agency Risk Assessment Conferences (MARACs) and Multi-Agency Public Protection Arrangements (MAPPAs) (see Chapter 5 for more details).

It is therefore extremely important that the limitations of the data that these individuals and organisations are relying on are understood. To begin with it is important to recognise how data is captured and connected across the Criminal Justice System (CJS).

How is data captured and interlinked across the CJS

Figure 3.1 highlights just how complicated it is to capture data on domestic abuse within the CJS and beyond. It demonstrates that at every stage of the criminal justice process the number of victims in the system reduces. This process of losing people is known as **attrition**. Another limitation is that statistics are produced by several different agencies using different timescales and reference periods. So, the data does not follow individual cases at each stage of the CJS, which means direct comparisons cannot be made.

The actual level of abuse will never be known, but survey data has been used to predict the scale of the problem. In 2019/2020 the CSEW estimated that there were 2.3 million victims in England and Wales. We know, however, that this is already an underestimate as the methodology used in the survey only captures victims aged between 16 and 74.

The initial decision by the victim on whether to report or disclose abuse is fundamental to their recognition in the system in terms of support and justice. If a victim does report (or somebody else reports on their behalf), where they report is also important. There are a range of agencies to which victims might report and some might report to more than one. In 2019/2020 for those who reported to the police, there were just under 1.3 million incidents recorded by police forces in England and Wales. It should be noted

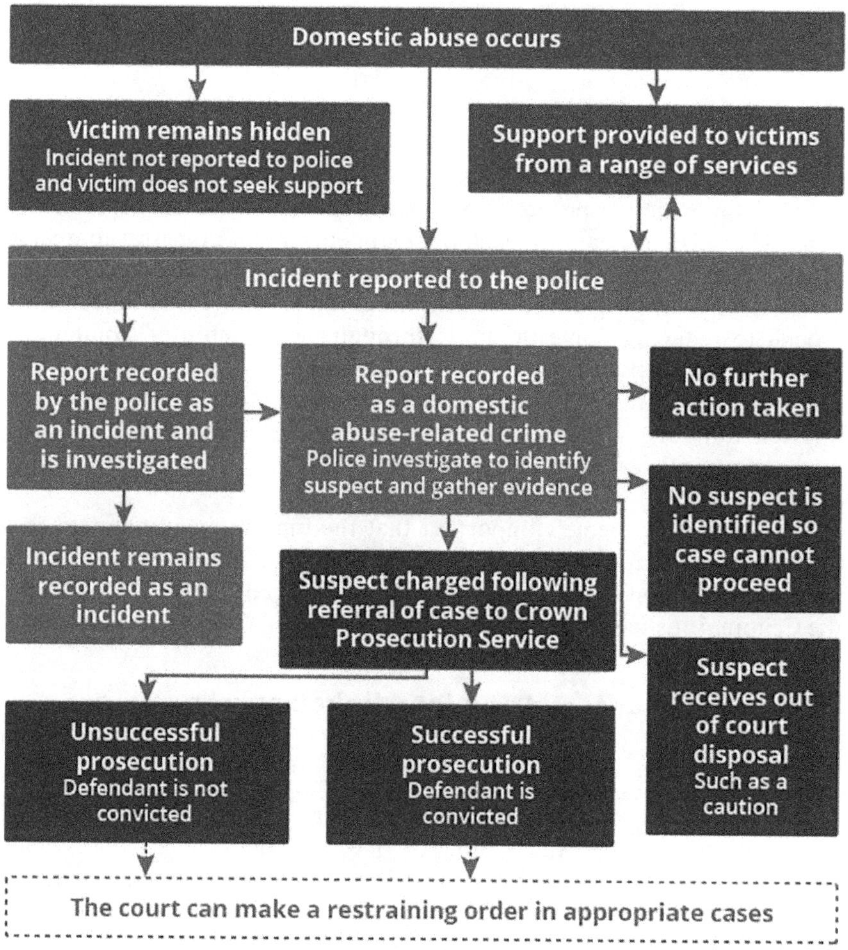

Figure 3.1 How data are captured and interlinked across the CJS.

that some of these incidents will be repeat victims, so the number is not comparable to the CSEW estimate.

After a domestic abuse incident is recorded some cases will be converted to a crime, whereas others will remain recorded as an incident. Police forces have been working hard over recent years to increase the number of incidents that become crimes, and as a result the percentage recorded as a crime has increased. In 2019/2020 the crime conversion rate in England and Wales was 59%, which was a 2% increase in the previous year (ONS, 2020).

Domestic abuse prosecutions account for about 14% of all CPS prosecutions in England and Wales (ONS, 2020). How far a domestic abuse-related crime will progress in the CJS is quite variable and, in a similar way to sexual offences, the level of attrition within the CJS is one of the reasons thought to be behind the low levels of reporting (Flood and Pease, 2009), with victims not believing that the CJS will provide redress.

Once a domestic abuse-related crime is reported an initial investigation will be conducted where the police collect relevant evidence and identify a suspect. Some cases may have taken place in another police force area and will therefore be transferred to the relevant forces, who will then conduct the investigation. For the case to continue further the suspect needs to be referred to the Crown Prosecution Service (CPS) and be charged. Not all cases will make it this far, with some cases resulting in no further action. Reasons for no further action include not having enough evidence for the police to take the case forward; an offender having died; the crime report being cancelled, where further investigation did not find a crime that took place; where an out of court disposal is given, such as a caution; or where the police cannot identify a suspect (ONS, 2020).

Crime surveys

Surveys have made an important contribution to our understanding of a range of crimes and have been particularly helpful in understanding those crimes, such as domestic abuse, which are underreported to the police. This section explores the range of surveys from the international to local levels and the understanding that has been drawn from them over time. It unearths the strengths and limitations of using surveys as an alternative to data collected by the police and other agencies.

Range of surveys

National and international surveys

At the international and national level there are two main models for collecting survey data on domestic abuse. The first is through generic crime surveys and the second through more specialised violence against women surveys. The former are generally linked to crime codes, meaning that they are more aligned with data collected in the CJS, whereas the latter collect more information on the act of violence that has been committed and are usually based on a modified form of the Conflict Tactics Scale (CTS) (Walby et al., 2017).

The CTS was developed by Straus (1979) as part of the New Hampshire's Family Violence Research Programme to measure the rate of violent acts between married couples (Walsh, 2018). It was formed on the basis of two nationwide surveys in the United States (Natarajan, 2017). The revised Conflict Tactics Scale (known as CTS2) was introduced in 2000 and used 39 questions. Respondents were asked paired questions to report the number of times in the last 12 months that they have been victims and the number of times they had perpetrated various behaviours to resolve conflicts with their intimate partners. There are a number of questions on five different behaviour types: Physical Assault, Injury, Psychological Aggression, Sexual Coercion, and Negotiation. However, methodologically the CTS and CTS2 have been heavily criticised for only capturing actions and not harm and intention, and therefore creating the impression that the violence shows gender symmetry (Walby et al., 2017).

The most wide-reaching survey in the United Kingdom is the Crime Survey in England and Wales, formerly known as the British Crime Survey (BCS). There is also the Scottish Crime and Justice Survey. In terms of coverage, the CSEW invites around 35,000 households to participate in a self-reported survey and it has a response rate of around 70% (ONS, 2020) covering all 43 police forces in England and Wales. The questions on domestic abuse in the CSEW have evolved over time. They began in 1982 in the BCS, with face-to-face questions in the main interview. However, low levels of disclosure, owing to the face-to-face nature, led to the development of a separate model on Intimate Personal Violence, where questions, based on a modified version of the CTS, are asked on a computer, rather than verbally. Box 3.1 shows the partner/ex-partner questions that are included in the survey. There are also similar styled questions about abuse between other family members (including siblings and parents and adult children). There are still also some domestic abuse questions in the main face-to-face survey as well. The Intimate Personal Violence module, which was introduced in 2001, did increase the number of respondents disclosing abuse tenfold (Flatley, 2016); however, methodologically it has received criticism, which will be discussed further below.

BOX 3.1 CRIME SURVEY IN ENGLAND AND WALES SELF-COMPLETION MODULE: DOMESTIC ABUSE, STALKING VICTIMISATION AND STALKING MODULE. DOMESTIC ABUSE QUESTIONS FOR PARTNER/EX-PARTNER

1 Since you were 16 has a partner or ex-partner ever done any of the things listed below?

By partner we mean a boyfriend, girlfriend, husband, wife, or civil partner.

Prevented you from having your fair share of the household money
Stopped you from seeing friends and relatives
Repeatedly belittled you to the extent that you felt worthless

2 And has a partner or ex-partner done any of these things to you in the last 12 months?

Prevented you from having your fair share of the household money
Stopped you from seeing friends and relatives
Repeatedly belittled you to the extent that you felt worthless

3 In the last 12 months, has a partner or ex-partner ever repeatedly or continuously done any of the things listed below?
Please select all that apply.

1 Unfairly controlled how much money you could have or how you spent it
2 Isolated you from your friends and family
3 Monitored your letters, phone calls, emails, texts, or social media
4 Enforced rules or activities which humiliated you
5 Controlled how household work or childcare is done
6 Kept track of where you went or how you spent your time
7 Bullied or intimidated you, for example, by punching walls or destroying property
8 Forced you to engage in sex or certain sexual acts against your will
9 Threatened to harm children in the household
10 None of these
11 Don't know/can't remember
12 Don't wish to answer

4 Thinking about these actions you experienced in the last 12 months, to what extent did you suffer any of the following as a result? [Response options for each impact = Very much/quite a lot/a little/not at all/don't know/can't remember/don't wish to answer/does not apply]

A Fear that violence would be used against you
B Feeling unable to leave the relationship/household due to fear of coming to harm
C Constantly living in fear which affected your day-to-day activities
D Significant changes in routine, behaviour, or appearance to try to avoid the abuse
E Forced to give up work, education, or volunteering due to fear of coming to harm
F Fear that you would lose contact with your children

5 Since you were 16 has a partner or ex-partner ever frightened or threatened you in any way? For example, they may have threatened to hurt you, to kill you, to use a weapon on you, or to hurt someone close to you [such as your children]?

1 Yes
2 No
3 Don't know/can't remember

6 And has a partner or ex-partner frightened or threatened you in any way in the last 12 months? For example, they may have threatened to hurt you, to kill you, to use a weapon on you, or to hurt someone close to you [such as your children]?

1 Yes
2 No
3 Don't know/can't remember
4 Don't wish to answer

7 Since you were 16 has a partner or ex-partner ever used force on you? For example, they may have pushed you; slapped you; hit, punched, or kicked you; choked you; or used a weapon against you.

1 Yes
2 No
3 Don't know/can't remember
4 Don't wish to answer

8 Have you ever been injured (even if only slightly) as a result of the force used on you? By injured we mean things such as bruises, black eyes, cuts or scratches, or broken bones.

1 Yes
2 No
3 Don't know/can't remember
4 Don't wish to answer

9 Has a partner or ex-partner used force on you in the last 12 months? For example, they may have pushed you; slapped you; hit, punched, or kicked you; choked you, or used a weapon against you.

1 Yes
2 No
3 Don't know/can't remember
4 Don't wish to answer

10 And have you been injured (even if only slightly) in the last 12 months as a result of the force used on you? By injured we mean things such as bruises, black eyes, cuts or scratches, or broken bones.

1 Yes
2 No
3 Don't know/can't remember
4 Don't wish to answer

In addition to victim surveys administered by the Office for National Statistics (ONS) there is also an annual survey of refuge services and community-based services conducted by Women's Aid. There are two separate surveys for England and Wales (see Box 3.2).

BOX 3.2 WOMEN'S AID ANNUAL SURVEY

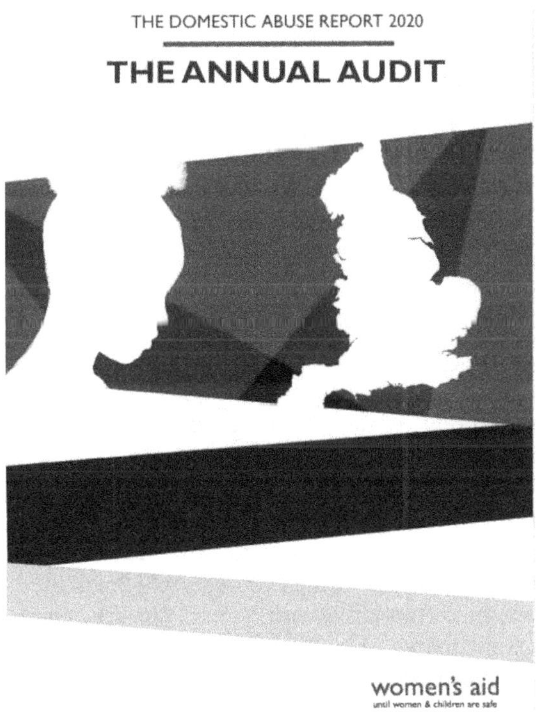

Women's Aid, a national domestic abuse charity, runs an annual survey. The survey collects information from Women's Aid local services and the thousands of women and children that they support. The survey records the number of referrals to refuges, the number that Women's Aid were able to support (and the number they were unable to support), and the biggest challenges faced by the services.

There is a live dashboard on the Women's Aid website where you can explore service provision across England. The chart below shows the estimated number of referrals accepted and the estimated number of children accommodated each year by all refuge services on Routes to Support in England.

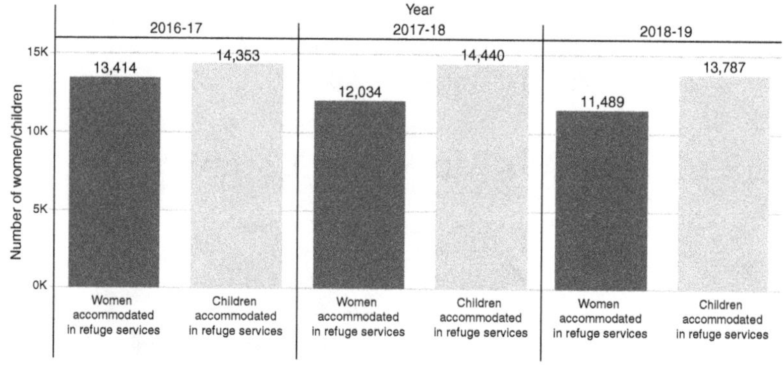

Source: https://www.womensaid.org.uk/domestic-abuse-provision-annual-survey/#link_tab-1579018361843-4-9

Results over time

Using survey data means that a sample of the population are asked questions and estimates about the whole population are made from this data. This means that unlike police data, which records the number of incidents that have taken place, the survey data estimates the proportion of the population that has been victimised either in the last year or in their lifetime. Figure 3.2 illustrates that over time there has been a reduction in the prevalence of domestic abuse experienced. In the year ending March 2005 8.9% of those surveyed had experienced abuse in the last year, which equated to an estimate of 2.3 million victims, compared with 5.5% in the year ending March 2020, where there were estimated to be 2.1 million victims (ONS, 2020).

The most significant reduction was seen in the year ending March 2009, after which the changes over time have not seen considerable variation. When broken down into partner abuse and family abuse there have been reductions in both over time (ONS, 2020). Of course, it is difficult to tell whether this is the result of a downward trend in domestic abuse or whether people were more hesitant to disclose their abuse to a survey.

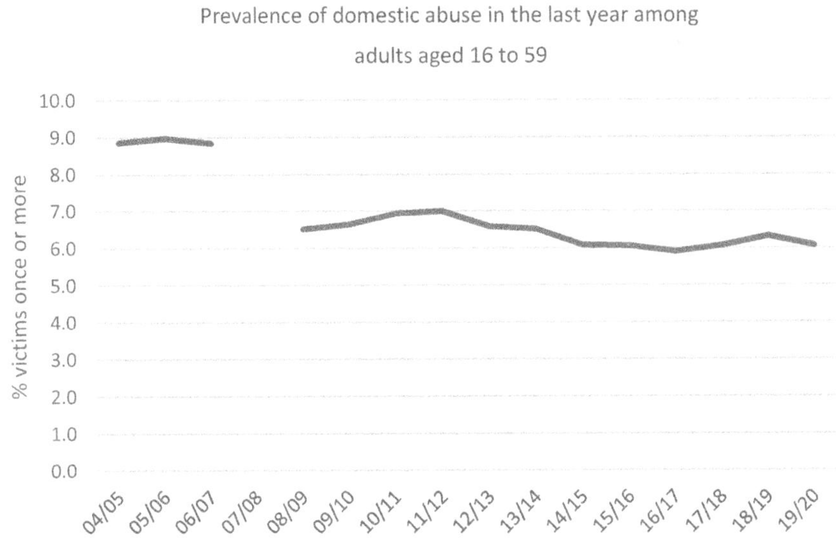

Figure 3.2 Prevalence of domestic abuse in the last year amongst adults aged 16–59.

Accessing the CSEW data

The CSEW data is published in a series of annual reports and data tables on the ONS website. There is a separate report for the domestic abuse data which analyses both the CSEW and police-reported crime data which is collected by the Home Office. The report has the headline results and analysis of the demographics of victims.

Academics or other researchers seeking to conduct more in-depth analysis of the Intimate Personal Violence module in the CSEW data can apply for secure access status to the UK Data Archive as an accredited researcher. Researchers need at least an undergraduate degree and be able to demonstrate at least three years of quantitative research experience. They also need to successfully complete a Safe Researchers training course. If access is granted, then the CSEW data can be downloaded at the national level or at a lower level of geography (down to Lower Super Output Area level, which has a population of approximately 1,500 people).

Strengths and weaknesses of crime surveys

The main benefit of survey data is that it helps capture the prevalence of domestic abuse and whether people are reporting it to the police, other agencies, friends, and family or not at all. Whilst crime surveys are thought to give a more accurate estimate of the extent of domestic abuse than recorded crime data, they are still believed to underestimate the number of victims. There are, however, several problems with crime surveys identified in the academic literature.

One of the key debates that has stemmed from the use of victims' surveys to explore the nature and extent of domestic abuse has been around gender. Feminists argue that domestic abuse is an asymmetrical crime, with men largely perpetrating the abuse and women being the victims, whereas victimologists argue that the crime shows symmetry, with men and women being both victims and perpetrators (Gelles and Straw, 1979; Straus, 1979; Straus et al., 1980).

Repeat victimisation is higher for women, and they are more likely to be killed or seriously injured (ONS, 2018; Walby and Allen, 2004; Walby and Towers, 2017). Removing repeat victimisation and severity from analysis reduces gender asymmetry. This has been an issue identified in the CSEW where repeat victimisation was being capped at five incidences (Farrell and Pease, 2007; Walby et al., 2014). Research found that removing the cap increased the number of violent offences by 60%, when compared to the published results where the cap had been implemented (Walby et al., 2014). More recently the concerns raised by Walby et al. (2014) have been addressed and the cap has finally been replaced, with data from 2019 onwards using a crime-specific imputation method, based on the 98th percentile, to set a cap for each crime type, rather than using the arbitrary limit of five incidents (ONS, 2019).

Women have also been found to have higher levels of fear of domestic abuse and are more likely to experience coercive control (Dobash and Dobash, 2004; Hester, 2013; Myhill, 2017, 2015). Analysis of the National Crime Victimisation Survey (NCVS) in the United States found women are more likely to need protection than men and are less likely to regard the issue as private or to view it as a trivial issue. The main inhibitor to women reporting their abuse was the fear of reprisal from the perpetrator (Felson and Pare, 2007).

As discussed further in Chapter 6, there is limited data in the CSEW on domestic abuse in LGBT relationships. This is because the sample size of the survey means that the data on sexuality has not been analysed from the IPV computer-based module, which typically only has about 3,000 disclosures of domestic abuse across all respondents. The sub-sample of those in LGBT relationships is therefore found to be too small to be able to carry out any statically robust analysis. There has been some more general analyses of LGBT victims for other crimes, which has been achieved by aggregating several years of CSEW data, but this has not yet been carried out for domestic abuse. As explored in Chapter 6 there have been specialist surveys on domestic abuse in LGBT relationships conducted by charities such as Stonewall (Stonewall, 2018).

Another problem was that interviews using the IPV computer-based module were only conducted with people between the ages of 16 and 59, which lead to a lack of representation for both youngest and oldest victims (Groves and Thomas, 2014). Since 2017 the methodology has been changed to include those between 16 and 74 but still excludes anyone over the age of 75. Following two independent reviews of the BCS in 2006 the BCS was extended to children aged 10–16, but only as experimental statistics, and the question on domestic abuse was removed after piloting as it became clear that it was difficult for some children to differentiate between parental discipline and abuse. Issues were also found around truthfulness and disclosure when the parents were in the same room (Groves and Thomas, 2014). Separate surveys, such as the United Kingdom Study of Abuse and Neglect of Older People (O'Keeffe et al., 2007), have been used to gain information about older people's experiences of abuse, but with a different methodology and approach the results are not comparable.

Coverage issues have also been a problem for both the CSEW and BCS. The questions are only asked to people in their own homes, so this excludes hard to reach victims, who may be living in alternative accommodation, such as refuges, hotels, travellers' sites, prisons, or for those living with friends or homeless (Mooney, 2000; Walby and Allen, 2004).

Another issue across all surveys has been the accuracy of responses given in self-completion interview techniques. Gadd et al. (2003) conducted some additional research following the Scottish Crime Survey in 2000. They managed to re-contact and interview some of the men who had disclosed abuse in the original survey. Two-thirds confirmed the accuracy of their record, but 28% refuted the record and claimed not to have been forced or threatened by a partner, and the remainder neither confirmed nor denied their record. The reasons given for the inaccurate reports varied but included that the men had been assaulted by a stranger in a public place, had been attacked by their girlfriend's other partner, had been involved in verbal altercations with a friend or other incidents that had happened at home, but would not be classified as domestic abuse, such as being frightened by trick or treaters (Gadd et al., 2003).

Another problem identified with self-completion questionnaires is that the victim may not self-identify their experiences as domestic abuse or as a crime (Walby and Myhill, 2001). They may not recognise everyday coercive control as abuse, or there may be elements of self-blaming, which mean it is unlikely that they will report the abuse. They are also less likely to report the abuse if the perpetrator is at home (Groves and Thomas, 2014).

Local crime surveys

An alternative to national and international surveys has been local crime surveys. Harne and Radford (2008) suggest in-depth local surveys, such as the Islington Crime Surveys and the North London Domestic Violence Survey (NLDVS), offer a better estimate of the true extent of the crime, but these surveys are very expensive to complete, so they have not been carried out in many areas. The NLDVS was conducted in 1993, and it had a sample size of 1000 and individuals were randomly selected. The survey used mixed methods, and its focus was on women's experiences of violence from husbands or boyfriends (including ex-husbands and ex-boyfriends). The interviews were face to face, but the interviewers ensured that nobody else was at home and if they were, they gave callback cards. In the first stage, men and women were interviewed. The second stage was women only and involved filling in a self-completion questionnaire, which was returned in a stamp-addressed envelope. The third stage consisted of in-depth interviews with women who had disclosed domestic violence. Mooney (2000) compared the results of the main 1996 BCS, the 1996 BCS self-completion module, and the NLDVS to compare the percentage incidence of domestic violence against women in a 12-month period. The results found that the self-completion module only showed a third of the incidences that the NLDVS recorded. Mooney (2000) suggested this was due to the methods employed in the BCS, which did not ensure anonymity. Other surveys also experienced low response rates to the domestic abuse question. The 1993 Aberystwyth Crime Survey found a 14% 'no response' rate (with respondents neither confirming nor denying abuse) in the 16–34 age group. The survey was, however, conducted in front of family members, which would explain the interviewees' reticence in answering the question (Koffman, 1996).

Despite their limitations, national and local surveys have been very useful in developing more of an understanding of the true extent of domestic abuse. They have also given more insights into some of the reasons why victims do not report their abuse to the police or in some cases, anybody. Reasons why people do not report will be explored later in this chapter.

Police data

The domestic abuse data collected by the police is the richest source of data on victims, perpetrators, and the nature of abuse recorded by any agency. The problem is that only around 20% of victims are thought to report their abuse to the police, which leaves a substantial gap in our knowledge of both victims and perpetrators. This section explores what is collected before examining why victims may not report their abuse to police.

Data collection and national trends

As discussed above, the ONS publish an annual domestic abuse report and Excel tables with data from both the CSEW and police-recorded crime data. Unlike the CSEW, the collection of domestic abuse data at the national level

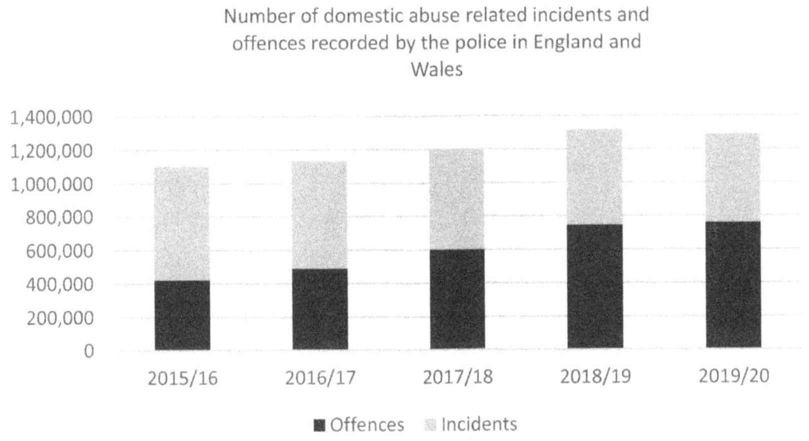

Figure 3.3 Number of domestic abuse-related incidents and offences recorded by the police in England and Wales, April 2016–March 2020 (ONS, 2020: Note the 2019/2020 figure is missing Greater Manchester Police data).

has only been conducted by the Home Office since 2016. Prior to that police forces would send in their returns, but the incident level data was not submitted to a central repository. This means that comparable data is only available from 2016 onwards. Figure 3.3 highlights that since the data has been collected there has been an annual reduction in the number of domestic abuse-related incidents recorded by the police, but an increase in the number of offences. Individual forces will have more historic data. Forces have undergone a series of crime data integrity inspections since an initial nationwide inspection in 2014, which has changed recording significantly (HMICFRS, 2021).

In the year ending March 2019 14% of all crime, which equated to 746,219 crimes, were recorded by the police as domestic abuse related in England and Wales. Figure 3.4 shows that the largest proportion of those offences that were recorded as domestic abuse related were violence against the person (44%), followed by sexual offences (18%) and criminal damage and arson (12%).

In the same time frame a further 570,581 domestic abuse-related incidents were recorded (these incidents were not recorded as a crime) and 17,616 coercive control offences were recorded (ONS, 2020).

Between April 2016 and March 2019 there were 357 domestic homicides, of which 77% of the victims were female. Where the victim was female 96% of the suspects were male. However, where the victim was male just under half (47%) of the suspects were female.

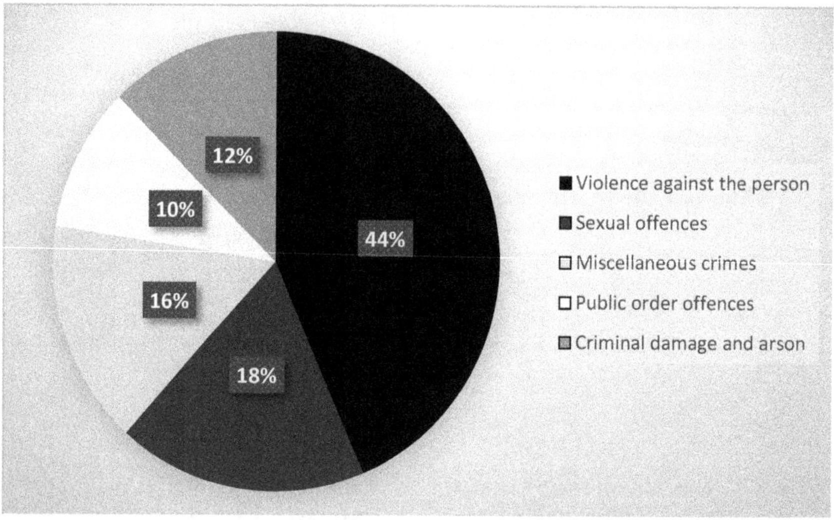

Figure 3.4 Proportion of offences recorded by the police in England and Wales which were flagged as domestic abuse-related year ending March 2019.

Police-recorded domestic abuse data is the richest source of information on victimisation, perpetration, and the nature of the incident. Each force records details on where and when the incident took place, whether the incident was alcohol or drug related, whether a child was present, and whether it was a repeat incident. They also collect demographic information on the age, gender, ethnicity, and address of both the victim and perpetrator. Linked to every incident are the responses from the 27 questions asked to victims in the DASH risk assessment and the free text fields associated with each question (see Chapter 6). We can therefore learn a lot from those who do report their abuse to the police, but for many reporting to the police is not their preferred option.

Why don't people report

The CSEW found that whilst 81% of victims told someone about their abuse, only 21% of victims reported their abuse to the police, with women more likely (26%) than men (10%) to report. As will be discussed in the next section, there are a number of other agencies where victims might disclose and the CSEW found 19% had reported to health services and 29% to other professional or organisational support such as counsellors or therapist, Victim Support, helplines, or specialist support services. But 73% of victims would confide in someone they knew personally, such as family, friends, a neighbour or work colleague (Flatley, 2016). However, when these support mechanisms prove inadequate or are unavailable then victims are more likely to report to official agencies (Pahl, 2016).

The time elapsing before domestic abuse is reported is also an issue. On average it takes a high-risk victim 2.3 years and medium-risk victim three years before they get help. Before getting help 68% of high-risk victims have attempted to leave the relationship on average two to three times (Safelives, 2015).

There are both personal reasons and societal causes which mean that victims do not tell anyone about their abuse. Reporting to the police is more likely if the incentives outweigh the costs of reporting (Felson et al., 2002). One of the key incentives to report is protection, particularly when children are involved. Reporting is also more likely if the assault is serious and there is a weapon involved or an injury is sustained. Another key reason is the desire for retribution or justice (Felson et al, 2007). On the other hand, the costs may be greater if the victim fears retaliation or consequences if they report. Or the perpetrator may offer remorseful apologies, promising that the abuse will never happen again (Harne and Radford, 2008; Mooney, 2000). In other situations, the perpetrator may convince the victim that they brought the abuse on themselves or some victims self-silence, by placing their partners' needs above their own (Margolis, 1998) or are just too embarrassed to report (Felson et al., 2002). Victims also find it difficult to leave if they are economically dependent on the perpetrator. Others just want the violence to stop but would not wish their partner to be labelled as a criminal (Harne and Radford, 2008).

Despite domestic abuse awareness campaigns and attempts to bring the offence into the public sphere, societal causes for not reporting still exist, including imbalanced power relations between men and women, the idea of family privacy, and victim-blaming attitudes (Gracia, 2004). Some 37% of CSEW respondents did not report their abuse because they regarded it as a private or family matter rather than an issue for the police. Perceptions of others' attitudes lead to fear that family and friends will blame them for bringing it on themselves or that the CJS will not intervene (Felson et al., 2002; Flood and Pease, 2009; Kingsnorth and Macintosh, 2004; Lievore, 2003). An example of this is marital rape, a type of abuse that is particularly underreported. One reason for the lack of disclosure has been attributed to the crime not fitting the stereotype of rape, with it being neither committed by a stranger nor an outsider, with victims not feeling they will be believed or seen as a real rape victim (Flood and Pease, 2009). It is not only the public that have shown negative attitudes to marital rape. When rape was first included in the Sexual Offences Act in 1976, legislators were particularly hesitant to include marital rape and excluded if from the legislation for a further 18 years (Groves and Thomas, 2014).

Walklate (2004) identified that a lot of victim-blaming attitudes stem from the thought that if a situation is so bad then the victim would leave and staying in a violent relationship is symbolic of women's irrationality. The feminist movement on the other hand has asked the question, why does she stay? Gracia (2004) questions whether it is unreported ignorance or social silence and acknowledges that, if it is the latter, then action is needed. Those with traditional gender role attitudes have been found to be less likely to report, and were more likely to blame themselves and therefore less likely to report it to the police or other authorities (Harris et al., 2005; see also Chapter 6).

The incentives and costs of reporting were also found to vary depending on the gender of the victim and the type of relationship (Felson et al., 2002). Grady (2002) suggests that men abused in the home are less likely to report their abuse. This may be because men and women are socialised to express themselves differently. Men may be less able than women to reveal the emotional impact that domestic abuse has on their lives (Goodey, 2005). However, analysis of data from the BCS and CSEW found that the severity and volume of abuse experienced by women is greater, as is the impact it has on their lives (Walby and Allen, 2004), which could result in more women reporting their abuse than men.

Historically, society had constructed women with children as the 'ideal victims' of domestic violence (Christie, 1986). However, there are certain groups of women that fall outside the definition of the ideal victim and are therefore even less likely to report their abuse, particularly to the police. These groups include non-EU migrant women who have no right to support from state funds (Gill and Sharma, 2007), those involved in criminality, including prostitution (Douglas, 2008; Dutton, 1993), and the travelling community (Burman et al., 2004; Harne and Radford, 2008)

Attitudes towards the police have been found to influence reporting, with 25% of CSEW respondents believing that the police could not help them. Others feared more violence from involving the police, or they did not think the police would be sympathetic, whilst others feared or disliked the police (Flatley, 2016). A report by Her Majesty's Inspectorate of Constabulary (HMIC) (now Her Majesty's Inspectorate of Constabulary and Fire & Rescue Services (HMICFRS)) found gross failings in the way that the police deal with domestic abuse. The findings included attitudes towards the victim that led to them being disbelieved, accused of violence themselves, and even 'chatted up' by the police officer. Domestic abuse was often treated as a second-class crime, with police officers having the attitude that it was only a 'domestic' (HMIC, 2014).

The media has played an important role in bringing the previously private issue into public debates and discussions. Several soap operas, including EastEnders and Radio 4s, The Archers, have run stories where characters have experienced abuse (BBC, 2017, 2016). The Archers storyline coincided with a 20% increase in reporting to the National Domestic Abuse Helpline, which was particularly significant given the middle class, who are the main listener group for Radio 4 and are thought to be even less likely to report their abuse. The stories reinforced the message that domestic abuse can happen to anyone regardless of their age, class, sexuality, ethnicity, or gender. Celebrities, such as Nigella Lawson, have also spoken out in the hope that a high-profile case such as hers will encourage others to escape their abuse. The disclosure had the desired effect, with a spike in reporting to domestic abuse helplines following the publication of a photograph of Nigella's husband with his hands around her throat in a restaurant (Scott, 2013).

What this section has highlighted is that the reporting and disclosure of abuse is complicated by a range of personal, societal, and organisational factors. A further complication is that victims will also present to other agencies. In the absence of multi-agency data collection, this therefore adds to the difficulty in gaining a full understanding of the problem. The next section explores the other agencies where victims may present and report and what we already know from the data that they collect.

Other agencies

As discussed above, victims of domestic abuse do not always seek a criminal justice response to their abuse. The introduction of three civil acts – Domestic Violence and Matrimonial Proceedings Act 1976; Housing Act 1977; and Domestic Violence and Magistrates Court Act 1978 – raised the profile of domestic abuse amongst other professionals and practitioners (Groves and Thomas, 2014; Sanders-McDonagh and Neville, 2017; Ward and Bird, 2005).

As a result, there are a number of agencies that offer support to victims, some with statutory responsibilities and others without. Whilst having a range of agencies offers victims a number of options as to where they can seek support, the downside of this is that some victims become lost in the system (Groves and Thomas, 2014). This has become particularly evident in some of the Domestic Homicide Reviews (DHRs), which found that victims were known to a number of agencies, but that the agencies had not spoken to each other. This lack of communication between agencies resulted in vital information not being shared and important links not being made, which in some cases could have potentially prevented the untimely death of the victim (Home Office, 2013).

The range of support agencies also creates an issue for those commissioning domestic abuse services and for those trying to estimate the full extent of victimisation. The purpose of data collection varies across agencies, and as a result the quality and type of data collected differs considerably. Some agencies have a statutory responsibility to respond to domestic abuse, whereas other are operating in a charitable capacity. Fundamentally, the information is not always shared between agencies, unless victims are under multi-agency arrangements, such as MARACs (see Chapter 8 for further details). It can therefore be difficult to identify and support victims and know the number of agencies that an individual might be engaged with or if they are known to any at all.

To further understand this complexity a brief overview of each of the main agencies that may come across victims of domestic abuse is given below. For each agency there is a discussion of the legislation, guidance, or principles that the organisation works to and how this may affect what is known about the victims that might access their services.

Family courts

Cases of domestic abuse are not only disclosed in the criminal courts but also come to light in the family courts. The Family Procedure Rules 2010 cover all proceedings relating to children, and its Practice Direction 12J (PD12J) tells those involved in judicial proceedings how to interpret court rules regarding child arrangements and contact orders where there is domestic abuse (Ministry of Justice, 2017). The Family Justice System has come under scrutiny recently, following recommendations from the All Party Parliamentary Group on Domestic Violence and a Women's Aid report, 'Nineteen Child Homicides' (Womens' Aid, 2016). The recommendations called for amendments to PD12J, after the group and report found inadequate compliance with the Practical Direction. Justice Cobb was asked to review PD12J, and a number of amendments were made in October 2017. This included reminding courts that this is a mandatory requirement and instructing courts to immediately stop the cross-examination of victims by their alleged perpetrator (Family Law, 2017).

Research conducted by Women's Aid and the Children and Family Court Advisory and Support Service (CAFCASS) found that 62% of child custody cases feature allegations of domestic abuse (CAFCASS, 2017). Disclosures to other agencies for those with cases in the family courts appear to be higher than those reporting to the CSEW. A recent survey conducted for Women's Aid found that the abuse of 82% of those women who had been a victim of domestic abuse and had had a child contact case held in the family court in the last 5 years was known to the police. Sixty-six percent of respondents also said that their abuse had been disclosed to health and domestic abuse services, 58% to social services, 50% to education services, 37% to Victim Support services, and 31% to housing (Birchall and Choudhry, 2018). This suggests that when domestic abuse is mentioned in court a number of agencies will already be aware of the abuse. It should be noted, however, that this is a very small-scale survey (76 respondents), compared to the national data collected by the CSEW.

A limitation to data about domestic abuse in family court proceedings is in gaining access, with the current sources limited to small studies or surveys. There is not currently a central database that researchers or practitioners can easily access.

Housing

Domestic abuse is one of the key causes of homelessness, particularly for women (Menard, 2001; St Mungos, 2014). In 2018 domestic abuse contributed to homelessness for at least one in ten people who required local authority support (Department for Communities and Local Government, 2018), but like police-reported domestic abuse the true scale of the issue is unknown (Safelives, 2018). Housing providers have had a key role to play in providing shelter to victims, and they have become a key partner to the MARAC (see Chapter 8). As discussed earlier in the chapter, the forming of the House of Commons Select Committee in 1975 led to three civil law acts. One of these acts was the Housing (homeless persons) Act 1977, which gave the housing departments of district and borough councils the statutory responsibility to house those fleeing domestic abuse regardless of where they came from within the United Kingdom. This legislation was updated to become the Housing Act 1996 and Homelessness Act 2002. The Acts require somebody to be treated as homeless if they are seen to be at risk of violence or abuse in their home (Shelter, 2018).

A link has been identified between the reports of anti-social behaviour and domestic abuse, with 40% of tenants who have suffered domestic abuse having had complaints made against them for anti-social behaviour (Jackson, 2013). With other research finding that people experience abuse for an average of 3 years before engaging with support services (Safelives, 2015), housing providers have found that they are ideally placed to identify domestic abuse and act as a first point of contact. Key to pushing this work forward has been the Domestic Abuse Housing Alliance (DAHA), which was set up as a partnership between three agencies (Gentoo, Peabody, and Standing Together) aimed at improving the housing sectors response to domestic abuse (DAHA, 2018). Box 3.3 gives an example of the ways in which housing providers are collecting information on domestic abuse through their anti-social behaviour data.

BOX 3.3 HOUSING PROVIDER ASB DATA

Data on domestic abuse is often recorded in anti-social behaviour data that is collected by housing providers. However, the way that it is collected may vary between providers. Analysis of Colchester Borough Homes' ASB data found that domestic abuse was the fifth most reported category of ASB. Unlike police-reported ASB which tends to centre on the town centre night-time economy, ASB reported to Colchester Borough Homes was focussed on residential areas. Deprivation was found to be the strongest predictor of ASB even when controlling for the level of housing stock in the area, was controlled for.

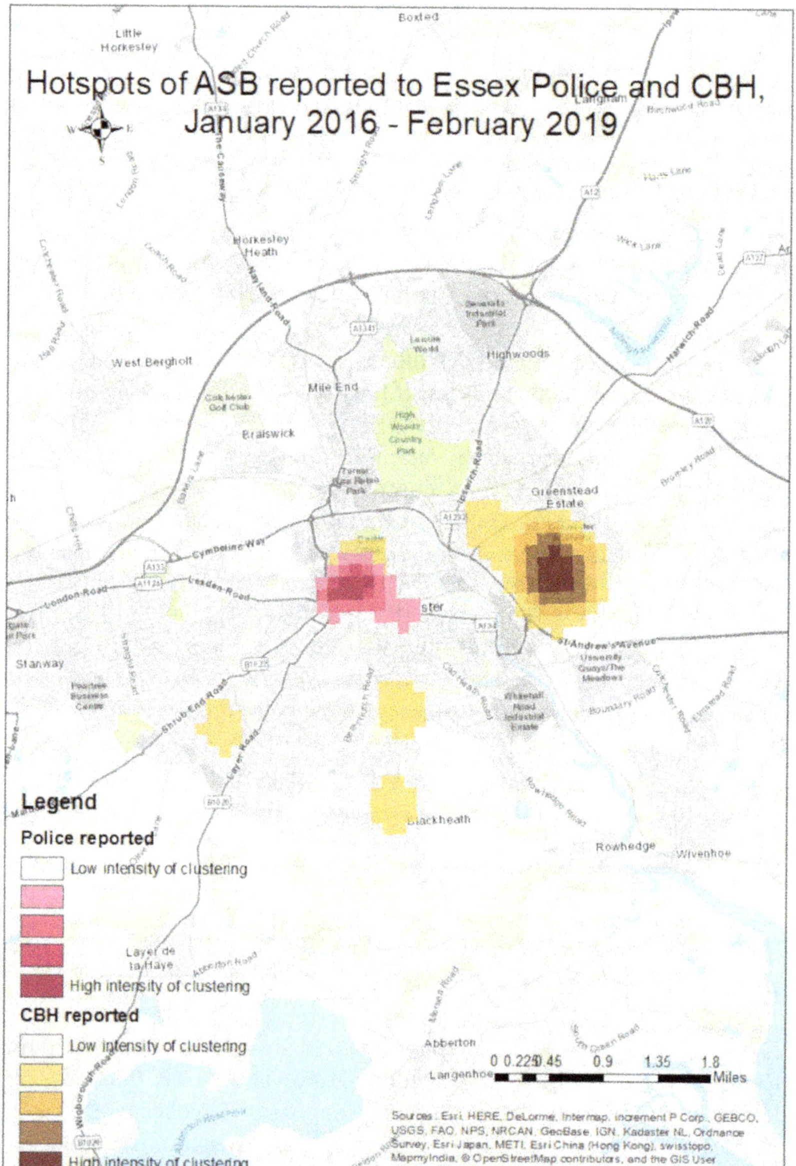

Health

Like housing, the NHS offers a first point of contact for many victims experiencing domestic abuse; however, with the vast array of services the opportunities for disclosure and the recording of domestic abuse are variables. A systematic review of victims' perceptions and experiences of accessing services by domestic abuse found that victims experienced a number of difficulties. These included the following: inappropriate responses by healthcare professionals; discomfort with the healthcare environment; perceived barriers to disclosing domestic violence; and a lack of confidence in the outcomes of disclosure to a health professional (Robinson and Spilsbury, 2008). Patient confidentiality also means that a trade-off between trust between the patient and the practitioner and the disclosure leaving the consulting room is often based on whether the practitioner has to report the abuse. One of the main reasons that abuse would need to be disclosed to other agencies would be if there are safeguarding concerns for a child or vulnerable adult.

The National Institute for Health and Care Excellence (NICE) set out guidelines aimed to help identify, prevent, and reduce domestic abuse. Whilst the guidelines are not mandatory, they encourage health staff to remove obstacles to people disclosing domestic abuse. One of the key ways they suggest to do this is to ask patients if they think that they have might have been abused and to make sure that formal referral pathways are in place. The guidelines also encourage partnerships between health services and local authorities, which will include local safeguarding boards for adults and children (NICE, 2016). What is aspirational as opposed to what is going on in practice is however not clear, but what is apparent are variations within and across organisations (Department of Health, 2015).

Independent Domestic Violence Advisors (IDVAs) were first introduced to support victims during their involvement in the CJS. They predominantly support high-risk victims who are at the greatest risk of death or serious harm and work with a number of agencies, the perpetrator, and any children on a short- to medium-term basis (Howarth et al., 2009). IDVA services are now being used in other settings outside the CJS, such as in A&E and maternity services.

Victim support

Another agency where help may be sought, or victims referred to, is Victim Support. The independent charity supports over 35,000 victims of domestic abuse a year and offers IDVA services and outreach services in local communities. In 2016/17 around 30% of victims of domestic abuse who were referred to Victim Support were aged 25–34. Of those who were referred to Victim Support 77% were female, 66% were White British, followed by Black Caribbean (5%) and the most common crime type was violence with injury (51%) (Victim Support, 2017). Victim Support collect data from their support services, which can be linked to police data. The raw data is not publicly available, but Victim Support does publish several policy reports on their website.

The list of agencies in this chapter is not exhaustive, and there are a range of other organisations where victims may disclose, and these include refuges, charities, and social care services. There are also organisations within the victim's local community where they might build up trust and disclose their abuse (see Box 3.4).

Victims will not always disclose to organisations that specialise in assisting domestic abuse victims but may be more likely to confide in people they know and trust. This was recognised by Women's Aid who has set up a number of "Ask me" projects, which in partnership with communities allows everyday people to become Community Ambassadors. The ambassadors are trained to understand domestic abuse and how to respond to victims (Women's Aid, 2020). There is currently no known data regarding the amount of domestic abuse that is disclosed to community organisations. This therefore makes it very difficult to estimate the scale of abuse that is reported in this way.

BOX 3.4 COMMUNITY ASSET MAPPING – IDENTIFYING OTHER AGENCIES WHERE VICTIMS SEEK HELP

Research in Essex identified several local agencies and organisations where victims were seeking support, but who were unlikely to be recognised in any official statistics. Churches, foodbanks, and community centres, places where residents visited regularly and built up trust, were found to be providing victims with support and in some cases signposting them to other agencies.

In one area the community centre was putting on sessions to raise the awareness of domestic abuse to residents. The sessions had been so well received that they had been asked to run them again.

There were also links between churches and organisations like Victim Support, where counsellors were available to talk to women during their regular coffee morning (Weir, 2020).

Conclusion

This chapter has outlined just how difficult it is to capture the true extent of domestic abuse and to track victims as they move through the range of criminal justice and other organisations, making it a 'wicked' problem (Barrow-Grint, 2016). Our best estimate of the prevalence of domestic abuse is through crime surveys, but the methodology is not without limitations. We can also learn a great deal about victims, perpetrators, and the nature of the abuse from police data, but with only about a fifth of incidents reported to the police we cannot rely on police data alone to identify victims and to design, locate, and fund domestic abuse services. Not everyone seeks a criminal justice intervention and there are a range of other organisations from whom victims will seek support, but data collection in these organisations is limited or non-existent. Furthermore, some victims will remain hidden, never disclosing their abuse to anyone else.

Reflective questions

- What are the strengths and limitations of using crime surveys to measure domestic abuse?
- What issues do you think are created using just police data to understand domestic abuse?
- Why do some victims not want to report their abuse to the police?
- How could we improve our understanding of domestic abuse?

Useful websites

ONS – Domestic abuse in England and Wales overview
https://www.ons.gov.uk/peoplepopulationandcommunity/crimeandjustice/bulletins/domesticabuseinenglandandwalesoverview/november2021

ONS – Domestic abuse findings from the Crime Survey for England and Wales Articles
https://www.ons.gov.uk/peoplepopulationandcommunity/crimeandjustice/articles/domesticabusefindingsfromthecrimesurveyforenglandandwales/previousReleases
Scottish Crime and Justice Survey
https://www.gov.scot/publications/scottish-crime-justice-survey-2019-20-main-findings/pages/20/
Women's Aid – Annual survey
https://www.womensaid.org.uk/womens-aid-annual-survey-reports/
Family Courts – Cafcass and Women's aid domestic abuse research
https://www.cafcass.gov.uk/2017/07/25/cafcass-womens-aid-collaborate-domestic-abuse-research/
DAHA – Domestic Abuse Housing Alliance
https://www.dahalliance.org.uk/about-us/who-we-are-why-we-do-it/
Victim Support – Research reports
https://www.victimsupport.org.uk/more-us/policy-and-research/reports/

References

Barrow-Grint, K., 2016. Attrition rates in domestic abuse: Time for a change? An application of temporal sequencing theory. *Policing: A Journal of Policy and Practice* 10, 250–263.

BBC, 2017. BBC One – EastEnders – Abuse. BBC. https://www.bbc.co.uk/programmes/articles/4nSBsqpS2WRHBnQXYk2sPp9/abuse (accessed 2.17.19).

BBC 2016. What effect has the Archers domestic abuse story had? https://www.bbc.co.uk/news/magazine-35961057 (accessed 7.4.22).

Birchall, J., Choudhry, S., 2018. *Domestic abuse, human rights and the family court.* Women's Aid.

Burman, E., Smailes, S.L., Chantler, K., 2004. 'Culture' as a barrier to service provision and delivery: Domestic violence services for minoritized women. *Critical Social Policy* 24, 332–357.

CAFCASS, 2017. Cafcass and Women's aid collaborate on domestic abuse research. CAFCASS – Children and Family Court Advisory and Support Service. https://www.cafcass.gov.uk/2017/07/25/cafcass-womens-aid-collaborate-domestic-abuse-research/ (accessed 2.9.19).

Christie, N., 1986. The ideal victim, in: Fattah, EA (ed) *From Crime Policy to Victim Policy.* . Basingstoke: Macmillan pp. 17–30.

DAHA, 2018. The facts about domestic violence and housing – DAHA. Wwwdahallianceorguk DAHA. https://www.dahalliance.org.uk/facts (accessed 2.11.19).

Department for Communities and Local Government, 2018. Live tables on homelessness. GOV.UK. https://www.gov.uk/government/statistical-data-sets/live-tables-on-homelessness (accessed 2.11.19).

Department of Health, 2015. Information sharing to tackle violence – Audit of progress. London: Department of Health.

Dobash, R.P., Dobash, R.E., 2004. Women's violence to men in intimate relationships: Working on a puzzle. *The British Journal of Criminology* 44, 324–349.

Douglas, H., 2008. The criminal law's response to domestic violence: What's going on. *Sydney Law Review* 30, 439.

Dutton, M.A., 1993. Understanding women's responses to domestic violence: A redefinition of battered woman syndrome. *Hofstra Law Review* 21, 2.

Family Law, 2017. President issues new PD12J – Child arrangements and contact orders: Domestic abuse and harm. https://www.familylaw.co.uk/news_and_comment/article-details, https://www.familylaw.co.uk/news_and_comment/president-issues-new-pd12j-child-arrangements-and-contact-orders-domestic-abuse-and-harm (accessed 2.11.19).

Farrell, G., Pease, K., 2007. The sting in the tail of the British crime survey: Multiple victimisations. *Crime Prevention Studies* 22, 33.

Felson, R.B., Messner, S.F., Hoskin, A.W., Deane, G., 2002. Reasons for reporting and not reporting domestic violence to the police. *Criminology* 40, 617–648.

Felson, R.B., Pare, P., 2007. Does the criminal justice system treat domestic violence and sexual assault offenders leniently? *Justice Quarterly* 24, 435–459.

Flatley, J., 2016. *Intimate personal violence and partner abuse.* Office for National Statistics.

Flood, M., Pease, B., 2009. Factors influencing attitudes to violence against women. *Trauma Violence Abuse* 10, 125–142.

Gadd, D., Farrall, S., Dallimore, D., Lombard, N., 2003. Equal victims or the usual suspects? Making sense of domestic abuse against men. *International Review of Victimology* 10, 95–116.

Gelles, R.J., Straw, M.A., 1979. *Determinants of violence in the family: Toward a theoretical integration.* Free Press, p. 33.

Gill, A., Sharma, K., 2007. *Response and responsibility: Domestic violence and marriage migration in the UK.* Routledge-Cavendish.

Goodey, J., 2005. *Victims and victimology: Research, policy and practice.* Pearson Education.

Gracia, E., 2004. *Unreported cases of domestic violence against women: Towards an epidemiology of social silence, tolerance, and inhibition.* BMJ Publishing Group Ltd.

Grady, A., 2002. Female-on-male domestic abuse: Uncommon or ignored, in: Hoyle, C. and Young, R. (eds) *New Visions of Crime Victims.* Oxford: Hart Publishing.

Groves, N., Thomas, T., 2014. *Domestic violence and criminal justice.* Routledge.

Harne, L., Radford, J., 2008. *Tackling domestic violence: Theories, policies and practice: theories, policies and practice.* McGraw-Hill Education (UK).

Harris, R.J., Firestone, J.M., Vega, W.A., 2005. The interaction of country of origin, acculturation, and gender role ideology on wife abuse. *Social Science Quarterly* 86, 463–483.

Hester, M., 2013. Who does what to whom? Gender and domestic violence perpetrators in English police records. *European Journal of Criminology* 10, 623–637.

HMIC, 2014. Everyone's business: improving the police response to domestic abuse. Her Majesty's Inspectorate of Constabulary.

HMICFRS, 2021. Police response to violence against women and girls: Final Inspection Report.

Home Office, 2013. Domestic homicide review. GOV.UK. https://www.gov.uk/government/collections/domestic-homicide-review (accessed 3.23.19).

Howarth, E., Stimpson, L., Barran, D., Robinson, A., 2009. *Safety in numbers: A multisite evaluation of independent domestic violence advisor services.* Henry Smith Charity.

Jackson, R., 2013. Domestic abuse and housing in Wales. Cardiff: Chartered Institute of Housing.

Kingsnorth, R.F., Macintosh, R.C., 2004. Domestic violence: Predictors of victim support for official action. *Justice Quarterly* 21, 301–328.

Koffman, L., 1996. *Crime surveys and victims of crime.* University of Wales Press.

Lievore, D., 2003. *Non-reporting and hidden recording of sexual assault: An international literature review.* Commonwealth Office of the Status of Women.

Margolis, D.N., 1998. *Culturally sanctioned violence against women: A look at attitudes toward rape.* Boston College.

Menard, A., 2001. Domestic violence and housing: Key policy and program challenges. *Violence Women* 7, 707–720.

Ministry of Justice, 2017. Practice direction 12j – Child arrangements & contact orders: Domestic abuse and harm. https://www.justice.gov.uk/courts/procedure-rules/family/practice_directions/pd_part_12j (accessed 2.10.19).

Mooney, J., 2000. *Gender, violence and the social order.* Springer.

Myhill, A., 2017. *Measuring domestic violence: Context is everything.* Policy Press. https://doi.org/info:doi/10.1332/239868017X14896674831496 (accessed 6.5.22).

Myhill, A., 2015. Measuring coercive control: What can we learn from national population surveys? *Violence Women* 21, 355–375.

Natarajan, M., 2017. *Domestic violence: The five big questions.* Routledge.

NICE, 2016. Overview|Domestic violence and abuse|Quality standards. https://www.nice.org.uk/guidance/qs116 (accessed 3.24.19).

O'Keeffe, M., Hills, A., Doyle, M., McCreadie, C., Scholes, S., Constantine, R., Tinker, A., Manthorpe, J., Biggs, S., Erens, B., 2007. *UK study of abuse and neglect of older people: Prevalence survey report.* Comic Relief.

ONS, 2020. Domestic abuse prevalence and trends, England and Wales – Office for National Statistics. https://www.ons.gov.uk/peoplepopulationandcommunity/crimeandjustice/articles/domesticabuseprevalenceandtrendsenglandandwales/yearendingmarch2020#crime-survey-for-england-and-wales (accessed 9.7.21).

ONS, 2019. Improving victimisation estimates derived from the Crime Survey for England and Wales – Office for National Statistics. https://www.ons.gov.uk/peoplepopulationandcommunity/crimeandjustice/articles/improvingvictimisationestimatesderivedfromthecrimesurveyforenglandandwales/2019-01-24 (accessed 3.17.19).

ONS, 2018. Domestic abuse in England and Wales – Office for National Statistics. https://www.ons.gov.uk/peoplepopulationandcommunity/crimeandjustice/bulletins/domesticabuseinenglandandwales/yearendingmarch2016#are-there-differences-between-local-areas (accessed 2.17.19).

Pahl, J., 2016. *Private violence and public policy: The needs of battered women and the response of the public services.* Routledge.

Robinson, L., Spilsbury, K., 2008. Systematic review of the perceptions and experiences of accessing health services by adult victims of domestic violence. *Health & Social Care in the Community* 16, 16–30.

Safelives, 2018. Spotlight #5: Homelessness and domestic abuse – Safelives. http://safelives.org.uk/sites/default/files/resources/Safe_at_home_Spotlight_web.pdf (accessed 2.11.19).

Safelives, 2015. Getting it right first time – Complete report. http://www.safelives.org.uk/sites/default/files/resources/Getting%20it%20right%20first%20time%20-%20complete%20report.pdf (accessed 2.11.19).

Sanders-McDonagh, E., Neville, L., 2017. *Too little, too late: Domestic violence policy in the age of austerity.* Discovery Society.

Scott, J., 2013. Charles Saatchi is seen grabbing Nigella Lawson by the throat – Triggering an acrimonious divorce. The Guardian.

Shelter, 2018. What is homelessness? Shelter England. http://england.shelter.org.uk/housing_advice/homelessness/rules/what_is_homelessness (accessed 2.11.19).

St Mungos, 2014. Rebuilding Shattered Lives: the final report. St Mungos. https://www.mungos.org/publication/rebuilding-shattered-lives-final-report/ (accessed 2.11.19).

Straus, M.A., 1979 Measuring intrafamily conflict and violence: The conflict tactics (CT) scales*Journal of Marriage and Family*, 41, 75–88.

Straus, M.A, Gelles, R., Steinmetz, S.K., 1980. Behind closed doors: Violence in America family. US Department of Justice.Stonewall, 2018. LGBT in Britain – Home and communities. https://www.stonewall.org.uk/lgbt-britain-home-and-communities (accessed 16.2.22).

Victim Support, 2017. Victim support policy statement. Victim Support.

Walby, S., Allen, J., 2004. Domestic violence, sexual assault and stalking: Findings from the British Crime Survey. Home Office.

Walby, S., Myhill, A., 2001. Comparing the methodology of the new national surveys of violence against women. *The British Journal of Criminology* 41, 502–522.

Walby, S., Towers, J., 2017. Measuring violence to end violence: mainstreaming gender. *Journal of Gender-Based Violence* 1, 11–31.

Walby, S., Towers, J., Balderston, S., Corradi, C., Francis, B.J., Heiskanen, M., Helweg-Larsen, K., Mergaert, L., Olive, P., Palmer, C.E., 2017. *The concept and measurement of violence against women and men.* Policy Press.

Walby, S., Towers, J., Francis, B., 2014. Mainstreaming domestic and gender-based violence into sociology and the criminology of violence. *The Sociological Review* 62, 187–214.

Walklate, S., 2004. The protective society? Seeking safety in an insecure world. *Safer Communities* 3, 38–48.

Walsh, D., 2018. *Working with domestic violence: Contexts and frameworks for practice.* Routledge.

Ward, R., Bird, R.C., 2005. *Domestic violence, crime and victims act 2004: A practitioner's guide.* Jordans.

Women's Aid, 2020. Ask Me. Women's aid. https://www.womensaid.org.uk/our-approach-change-that-lasts/askme/ (accessed 9.8.21).

Womens' Aid, 2016. Launch of "nineteen child homicides" report and child first campaign. Womens Aid. https://www.womensaid.org.uk/launch-of-nineteen-child-homicides-report-child-first-campaign/ (accessed 2.11.19).

Chapter 4

Assessing risk

KEY POINTS

Having read this chapter, you should be able to:

- Understand the theory of risk assessment and how and why it has been applied to the policing of domestic abuse.
- Identify the risk factors associated with domestic abuse.
- Understand and undertake the current risk assessment tools being used in England and Wales policing services and how to apply them when assessing risk.
- Understand and apply best practice in the completion of risk assessments.
- Understand multi-agency processes for managing and mitigating risk.

Introduction

Assessment of risk is a key concept throughout policing. It is a three-stage process of predicting the likelihood of an event, risk, or hazard occurring; its impact should it occur; and then identifying measures to manage or mitigate its effects (Carson and Bain, 2008). It is not only most used in relation to natural threats such as flooding or pandemics but is also widely applied within workplace health and safety practices. In the late 1990s the concept of risk assessment was introduced across a range of policing areas from major incident and event planning, the deployment of firearms, to child and domestic abuse investigations.

The core role of policing is to prevent crime and keep the peace (Home Affairs Select Committee, 2008). Therefore, in an ideal world police would respond to all calls of domestic abuse. However, the level of domestic abuse recorded by police rose by 42% between 2015 and 2018 (ONS, 2018). This volume of domestic abuse far exceeds the level of policing resources available to respond and deal with the risk it presents, especially given the reductions to policing resources due to the austerity measures and budget cuts policing has experienced in recent years (Almond et al., 2017; Turner

DOI: 10.4324/9781003137412-4

et al., 2019). The process of risk assessment within the policing of domestic abuse has been introduced to identify those cases which are most likely to escalate or cause the most serious harm and align resources to best mitigate that risk. In other words, risk assessment is a process which directs limited police resources to those cases which have the highest need. Risk assessment for domestic abuse concerns the formal application of instruments to assess the likelihood that domestic abuse will be repeated by the same perpetrator (Roehl and Roehl, 2000). Furthermore, the consistent terminology associated with police risk assessments provides a common language recognised by partner agencies in multi-agency forums which is vital in the safety plans put in place to mitigate and manage risks once they have been identified.

As a front-line officer, investigator, or supervisor it is essential to understand the significance of risk assessment, those factors which lead to potential escalation of abuse and how to effectively record decisions. A consistent theme within Domestic Violence Homicide Reviews (See Chapter 8) and the thematic domestic abuse inspections completed by Her Majesty's Inspectorate of Constabularies, Fire Rescue Services (HMICFRS) indicate the importance of early and accurate risk assessment (HMIC, 2014). If risk is misidentified, not considered seriously or not documented correctly, it can lead to fatal consequences for victims and career ending misconduct proceeding for officers and staff (Almond et al., 2017). As quoted by officers in a survey regarding their attitudes towards policing domestic abuse. . . "there have been 'women dying' from the police not doing their job properly" and "at the end of the day you don't want to screw it up because it's someone's life. . . If you are going to lose your job it will be due to a domestic violence case" (Robinson et al., 2016, pp. 12, 14). As domestic abuse is such a priority for policing, there is significant scrutiny over individual staff actions when responding to and investigating allegations. This enhanced scrutiny can create additional pressure within an already pressurised arena of policing as the consequences of getting it wrong can be so severe. Assessing and addressing risk correctly does put a considerable responsibility on police, and therefore, a comprehensive understanding of the process is essential for all staff involved in the policing of domestic abuse.

The theory and process of risk assessment

Risk assessment is now embedded in the practices of many workplaces and regulates much of our daily lives. The process of risk assessment is a three-staged mechanism of identification, assessment, and management (Carson and Bain, 2008). Risks must first be identified, then the likelihood of them occurring, and the potential impact if they do occur is assessed in order to then manage or mitigate those risks. Individually we all evaluate risk, sometimes subconsciously, and make decisions as to whether the cost of an

Table 4.1 Risk rating matrix

Risk Matrix						
Impact	5	Medium/high	Medium/high	High	High	High
	4	Low/medium	Medium/high	Medium/high	High	High
	3	Low/medium	Low/medium	Medium/high	Medium/high	High
	2	Low	Low	Low/medium	Low/medium	Medium/high
	1	Low	Low	Low	Low/medium	Low/medium
		1	2	3	4	5
		Likelihood				

action may be outweighed by the consequences. Each of us will have a different appetite for risk and how we accept it and manage its consequences (Walklate and Mythen, 2011).

The formal process of assessment is generally initiated through some form of 5 by 5 matrix or heat map (see Table 4.1) where once each risk is identified, whether there is a high, medium, or low probability of it occurring and a high, medium, or low impact should that risk occur is calculated (Hardy, 2014). Certain events can be highly unlikely to occur but if they do, they cause devastating impacts such as an earthquake or plane crash. These would be graded as HIGH IMPACT – LOW LIKELIHOOD or given a numerical score of $5 \times 5 = 25$ or shaded dark gray on a heat map.

Other risks may vary slightly but are associated with more minimal consequences. These would be graded as LOW IMPACT – HIGH LIKELIHOOD, scored as $1 \times 1 = 2$ or showing as light gray on a heat map. There can be a whole range of scores and gradings calculated depending on the type and nature of the risk factors being considered. Risk assessment processes are not only applied to events but can also be applied to people and their behaviours (Sebire, 2021, adapted from Stock and Wentworth, 2020).

Once graded and the nature of the risk is understood, decisions can be taken as to how to mitigate against it occurring in the first place or managing the impact if it does occur. The most common assessment methods utilised for this are either actuarial, unstructured clinical, or a hybrid of both formats known as structured professional judgement (Sebire and Barling, 2016). Actuarial assessments apply numerical values and weightings according to set criteria formed from previous representative samples to each risk once identified (Campbell et al., 2005). The total value of each risk will then determine what action and focus are given to manage or mitigate each risk. The higher the value, the more resource potentially will be allocated to managing it. This is a highly structured approach based on the use of mathematical models to provide an objective quantification of the probability and impact of risk. Such an algorithmic approach has been adopted in the assessment of the potential recidivism in sex offenders (Sreenivasan et al., 2000). However, it has been argued that it can be of limited practical value and is too rigid to respond to dynamic and real-world challenges and professional expertise (Robinson and Howarth, 2012).

In contrast, the unstructured clinical approach relies only on the assessor's expertise and judgement to grade risks as to whether their probability and consequences are generally categorised as high, medium, or low. Often used within psychological clinical assessments of patients they are primarily based on interviews with subjects. These gradings then determine subsequent management or mitigating actions. However, whilst this approach is a more flexible methodology results are often very highly caveated and so do not always allow an entirely confident platform on which to base risk management decisions (Robinson and Howarth, 2012).

The practice of structured professional judgement is much less constrained than the actuarial method but less free form than the professional judgement approach. Whilst an identified risk will often have a numerical value assigned, the assessor is not constrained by this. If the assessor believes something is a particular risk or warrants a particular grading but it has failed to reach the required numerical value, they can override the numerical threshold and assign the grade they believe necessary (Robinson and Howarth, 2012). Both the actuarial and structured professional judgement methods are most commonly used by law enforcement and particularly in the field of violence prevention for models such as Spousal Assault Risk Assessment (SARA) in the United States (Hart et al., 2016) and Domestic Abuse, Stalking, Harassment and Honour Based Abuse (DASH) in England and Wales (Richards, 2009).

It is important to remember that whichever models are being used, no situation is ever static and risk must be continually assessed as conditions and circumstances change. Risk assessment is not an exact science and can be prone to human error (Hoyle, 2008). Even with the most sophisticated algorithms and artificial intelligence processes it is important to remember that risk assessments can only ever provide a hypothesis of what might happen and never what will happen (Walklate and Mythen, 2011). Thus, risk assessment and decision-making can be especially challenging due to the dynamic and spontaneous nature of the policing environment. Front-line officers face any number of diverse and challenging situations from pub fights, suicide interventions, protest activity, and armed robberies. Potentially life-saving decisions and assessments are made on partial information, in quick time, under stress, and in changing circumstances over which officers have no or only limited ability to manage and intervene (Turner et al., 2019).

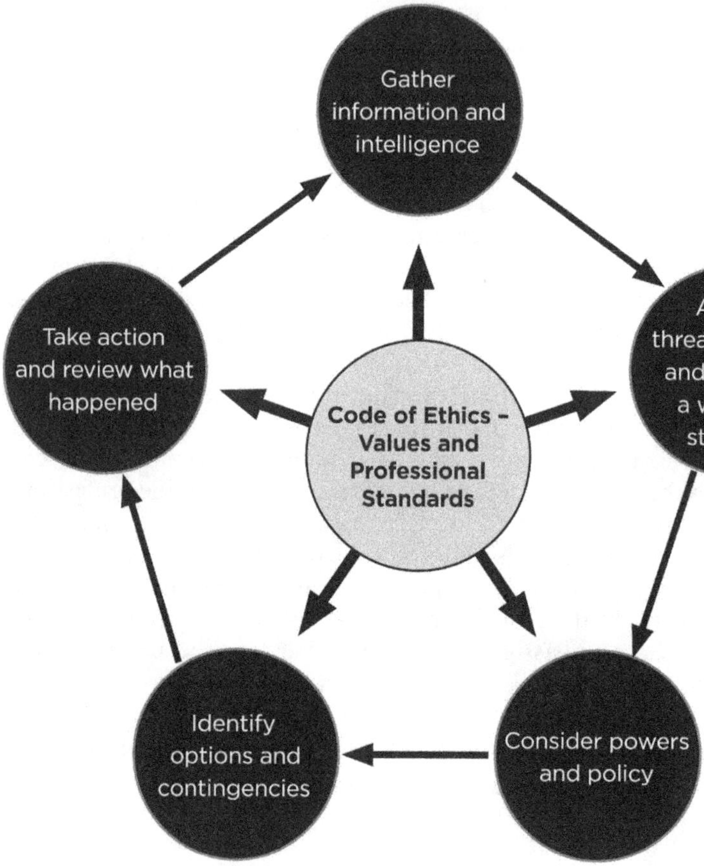

Figure 4.1 National decision-making model.

The term dynamic risk assessment is often used to explain the changing nature of risk and the requirement to continually review assessments and decisions considering new information. The National Decision-Making Model (College of Policing, 2013a) provides an effective tool for decision-making in complex circumstances (Figure 4.1). Assessing risk on the information known at the time is a key element therefore in deciding how to respond appropriately to the prevailing situation.

Whatever form of risk assessment undertaken as summarised in Box 4.1, there are ten principles identified by the College of Policing (2013b) which can be applied to any assessment process to ensure that is both contextual and comprehensive as possible given the prevailing circumstances.

BOX 4.1 TEN PRINCIPLES OF RISK ASSESSMENT

The willingness to make decisions in conditions of uncertainty (i.e., risk taking) is a core professional requirement of all members of the police service	The standard expected and required of members of the police service is that their risk decisions should be consistent with those a body of officers of similar rank, specialism, or experience would have taken in the same circumstances
Maintaining or achieving the safety, security, and well-being of individuals and communities is a primary consideration in risk decision-making	Whether to record a decision is a risk decision which should be left to professional judgement. The decision whether to make a record, and the extent of that record, should be made after considering the likelihood of harm occurring and its seriousness
Risk taking involves judgement and balance. Decision-makers are required to consider the value and likelihood of the possible benefits of a particular decision against the seriousness and likelihood of the possible harms	To reduce risk aversion and improve decision-making, policing needs a culture that learns from successes as well as failures. Good risk taking should be identified, recognised, and shared
Harm can never be totally prevented. Risk decisions should, therefore, be judged by the quality of the decision-making, not by the outcome	Since good risk taking depends on quality information, the police service will work with partner agencies and others to share relevant information about those who pose risk or those who are vulnerable to the risk of harm
Making risk decisions, and reviewing others' risk decision-making, is difficult. This needs to take into account whether they involved dilemmas or emergencies, were part of a sequence of decisions, or might appropriately be taken by other agencies	Members of the police service who make decisions consistent with these principles should receive the encouragement, approval, and support of their organisation

These principles apply to many policing situations and are an acknowledgement that policing has in the past been deemed to be 'risk adverse' and not taking actions for fear of the consequences (Robinson and Howarth, 2012). Police services are providing officers and staff with evidence-based tools which allow them to carry out their duties and aid them to assess risk in the most effective and impactful way. Given the domestic abuse equates to 14% of all crime recorded by police (ONS, 2019) several specific measures have been introduced to assess and manage this risk domestic abuse presents over the past two decades (Hoyle, 2008). However, as outlined at the start of this chapter all risk assessment must start with the identification of risk factors.

Domestic abuse risk factors

As identified in Chapter 2, there are several theories explaining how and why domestic abuse between intimate partners and family members occurs. Whilst there is a lack of consensus within the theoretical understanding of the basis of domestic abuse, research has established that there exists a set of definite behaviours and circumstances associated with perpetrators and victims (Campbell et al., 2005; Robinson et al., 2018; Sebire, 2017; Walklate and Mythen, 2011; Wheller and Wire, 2014). Furthermore, domestic abuse is a crime type that is subject to repetition with the most severe repeat offences often conducted by a small group of offenders (Turner et al., 2019). Because there are such established patterns of behaviours, unlike other crime types, this has allowed evidenced-based measures and tactics to be introduced in order to prevent and manage the ongoing risk of repetition and escalation.

International research within the fields of domestic abuse and, in particular, intimate partner violence has identified common behaviours and risk factors associated with repetitive and/or escalating domestic abuse (Jose Medina Ariza et al., 2016). If such behaviours and factors are identified at an early stage by agencies it allows preventative interventions to then be put in place (Campbell et al., 2005; Robinson et al., 2018; Wheeler and Wire, 2014). Officers and staff responding to calls for service should seek to identify if any of such indicative behaviours or circumstances exist through the investigation of the scene, evidence gathering, and questioning. If any such factors are identified as being present, evidenced-based decisions about the level of risk of further repetition of violence can then be made and prevention activity puts in place to mitigate against further harm taking place. As reflected upon by Robinson et al.:

> Understanding the meaning attached to certain risk factors by relevant practitioners and how they make judgements about risk can be considered a necessary precondition to successful multi-agency partnerships working to reduce domestic abuse, as well as help better understand police responses to domestic abuse.
>
> (Robinson et al., 2018, p. 190)

Identification of the behaviours and risk factors and potentially the motivations behind them are necessary in order to assess the likelihood and impact of future abuse occurring. Table 4.2 represents a collation of individual risk factors and provides an explanation as to how and why they relate to abusive relationships and an association to further repeat victimisation and/or lethality.

Table 4.2 Risk factors associated with domestic abuse

Risk Factor	*Context*
Escalation of abuse	Research has identified that incidents of abuse can escalate over time. Changing patterns of intensity and frequency of abusive is a significant predictive factor of further abusive behaviour (Campbell et al., 2005). The first time a victim calls the police may not be the first incident of abuse they have experienced. A full history of events will assist in more accurate risk assessment.
Relationship breakdown/ separation/ divorce	The ending of a relationship, especially if a unilateral decision, can leave a partner feeling they have lost control (Campbell et al., 2005) adding stain and volatility to the relationship.
Access to a firearm/using a weapon or threatening to use a weapon	There is preventative legislation and police policy in place regarding firearms possession and domestic abuse antecedence in the United Kingdom given the risk access to such weapons presents. However, the spontaneous nature of violence has shown how common household items are also used as lethal weapons. More serious harm and fear can be inflicted upon victims where weapons are involved. The use of weapons is suggestive of clear intent to harm and control. Such behaviours are more likely to persist if they have already reached this level (Robinson et al., 2016).
Making threats to kill	Threats made in the heat of an argument may be difficult to assess as to whether they will be followed through; however, preparatory acts following such comments are highly predictive of malign intent (Campbell et al., 2005).
Strangulation	Given the physical proximity and exertion required previous acts of strangulation have been identified with a propensity for future abuse (Robinson et al., 2016).
Jealousy/ controlling behaviours (controlling/ coercive abuse)	Studies have identified that this can be the most predictive behaviour of repeat and escalating abuse. Coercive control has been recognised as a criminal offence. This ranges from isolating a partner from their friends and family, checking their phones, and making them complete demeaning tasks. It requires sensitive questioning to identify if such activity has taken place, and indeed, victims may not believe they are being coerced or identify these behaviours for what they are. Coercion is founded on the power perpetrators seek to exert over their partners and violence and abuse occurs when they feel this power being diminished or threatened (Robinson et al., 2016).

(*Continued*)

Risk Factor	*Context*
Unemployment/ change to financial position	Changes to financial situations bring added stress to families which can then engender violent and emotionally abusive behaviours. Losing a job can also threaten personal identity and bring about a loss of control that the perpetrator seeks to regain though exerting control over their partner and home environment (Robinson et al., 2018).
Threats of suicide	Suicide ideation is a recognised predictive factor for lethal violence. This is most commonly associated with murder-suicide cases where perpetrators have a proprietorial view of the families killing spouses and children before themselves in 'if I can't have you no one can' scenario (Sebire, 2017). Police officers should ensure Mental Health markers and reports are up to date, and information shared with health providers is vitally important in understanding and assessing this risk factor (Sherman et al., 2017).
Blended family (stepchildren)	The presence of children from other relationships can be threatening as perpetrators feel their partner is still connected to their former partners. Blended families can also add additional stress within the home environment due to divided loyalties within relationships and arguments within the home setting (Campbell et al., 2005; Sebire, 2017).
Spying/stalking/ harassing/ threatening messages	This is associated with the controlling behaviour of perpetrators and is a significant indicator of further and/ or escalating abuse. Officers should ensure they review social media and other means of communication to identify patterns of behaviours and trigger point when considering this particular risk factor (Robinson and Myhill, 2016).
Victim's level of fear	Research indicates that a victim's own judgement of the situation is a predictor of future violence. Victims of abuse are very intuitive towards the nuances of their partners' behaviour and if the threat to them is escalating (Robinson and Howarth, 2012). This is not always the case as other victims however are so traumatised, they may minimise the risk and they cannot objectively assess their situation (Campbell et al., 2005; Wheeler and Wire, 2014).
Physical assault resulting in injury	There is mixed evidence regarding this factor with some studies reporting that previous physical injury incidents are likely to continue if they have taken place within the relationship or family. However, other reports suggest that fatal incidents have occurred where there has been no such prior antecedence (Campbell et al., 2005; Sebire, 2017; Thornton, 2017).
Conflict over child contact	This again adds stress and arguments to family relationships and signifies a lack of control for perpetrators over their family (Campbell et al., 2005).

Risk Factor	*Context*
Victim pregnant or recently had a baby	The risk presented reflects the changing dynamic within the family, and perpetrators may not be the centre of the attention within the relationship which leads to loss of control and strain within partnerships (Wheller and Wire, 2014).
Sexual assault	The fact that a victim has been sexually assaulted by their partner identifies an unbalanced power and control dynamic. Unconsented sexual intercourse is rape, and sensitive questioning will be required to identify the presence of this important factor (Wheller and Wire, 2014).
Mistreatment of an animal or family pet	Pets are often considered family members, a willingness to inflict pain and abuse animal signals a propensity for violence. Abuse of a family pet can also be a controlling and coercive behaviour to threaten and frighten or subdue a partner or family member (McGraw and Jeffers, 2015).
Drug/alcohol abuse	Substance misuse can impact on emotion control and cognition, and whilst not always associated with abusive relationships it is important officers investigate whether there are changes in the patterns of substance use which can be predictive of risk (Wheeler and Wire, 2014).
Bail/injunction/ protection order	The presence of such orders and legal restrictions enforces a loss of control for perpetrator which can provoke violent and abusive responses. Breaches can indicate that perpetrators are unwilling to comply with statutory measures and want to regain control over relationships (Campbell et al., 2005).
Criminal history for prior domestic or sexual violence	Research has identified that there are a cohort of offenders who will engage in abusive relationships within multiple partners and are responsible for a high percentage of overall violence. It is important that police are aware of these individuals and assess their risk and consider Clare's Law and other disruptive measure as appropriate (Turner et al., 2019).

These factors do not operate in isolation, and many are interdependent and can change overtime (Wheller and Wire, 2014). Robinson et al. suggest, "Every risk factor is or can be important depending on the situation, whereas others may be less important when considering context because of the relationship between the risk factors" (Robinson et al., 2018, p. 197). For instance, not every blended family will have experienced abuse, however; where this is associated with increased substance misuse or a change in financial situations this elevates the potential for further and escalating abusive behaviours. Once the risk factors have been identified the next step in the process is to assess it.

Risk assessment tools for domestic abuse

The risk assessment process for domestic abuse is multifaceted. Different assessment tools will be completed by different units at various times throughout the process of investigation and safety planning. Whilst there are some differences between individual force practices, in general, the assessment begins on receipt of a call for service received by the force control room or station front counter. Further assessment will then take place on direct attendance at scene and contact with the victim and then at various times throughout the investigation, criminal justice process, and multi-agency partnership response. Common to all assessments employed is the identification of any risk of harm to the victim and deployment of the most appropriate police or multi-agency support under the circumstances based upon the information known at that time.

On average the police receive a domestic abuse-related call every 30 seconds (HMIC, 2014). Thus, the risk assessment process most commonly is initiated with a call for service received by the force control room through 999 emergency or 101 phone system. Whilst individual force terminology may vary, all calls for service, regardless of whether they are related to a domestic abuse incident, will be graded to manage demand to available resources and ensure the right level of resource/response is dispatched to resolve the incident. Calls will be graded as requiring an immediate fast response, a prompt or standard attendance, or a fixed appointment depending on the threat to life perceived by the call handler. THRIVE (Table 4.3) is a tool commonly used by force control rooms. It is a professional judgement tool which guides the call operator through an assessment of the level of risk and vulnerability associated with all incidents and manages the policing response according to the victims' needs rather than crime type (HMIC, 2015). If not utilising THRIVE, other similar tools are used by forces, and

Table 4.3 THRIVE

Threat	Who or what is subject to the threat and what is the threat
Harm	The likely level and seriousness of the harm
Risk	The risk of it occurring
Investigation	Purpose of investigation – to either preserve life, preserve scenes, secure evidence/ identify victims or witnesses, or identify suspects
Vulnerability	A person is vulnerable if, because of their situation or circumstances, he or she is unable to take care or protect themselves, or others, from harm or exploitation
Engagement	The needs of the caller or circumstances of the incident may represent an opportunity for an engagement, particularly if the caller is from a hard-to-reach group or would benefit from a reassurance visit

whilst not exclusive to domestic abuse THRIVE will often be the first point of risk assessment. The caller hander will seek to answer each element of the THRIVE question set and make a dispatch decision.

Once a domestic abuse call has been assessed and response required graded, officers will be dispatched to deal with the situation and take a full report of the incident. On attendance in response to a call of domestic abuse (of whatever grading) all officers are required to complete a detailed risk assessment. Most forces use the Domestic Abuse, Stalking, Harassment and Honour Based Violence (DASH) risk identification assessment and management tool (Richards, 2009).

Domestic Abuse, Stalking, Harassment (DASH) risk assessment tool

In 2009, the Association of Chief Police Officers (ACPO) (now known as National Police Chiefs' Council (NPCC), along with a leading domestic abuse charity, Co-ordinated Action Against Domestic Abuse (CAADA) (now known as SafeLives), introduced the DASH risk assessment tool to policing. Its main purpose was to identify those at high risk of serious harm in order that interventions to be put in place to prevent homicide and repeat victimisation. The DASH assessment tool uses structured professional judgement and is the mechanism through which high harm victims are identified. This standardisation of the process across forces using DASH encouraged an increased focus on this crime type, effective management of resources, and introduced a common language of risk between police and multi-agency partners (Almond et al., 2017; Robinson et al., 2016). The DASH question set is based upon a review of 30 domestic homicide cases and 394 sexual and domestic abuse crimes as well as discussion with victims and advocacy services (Richards, 2004; Robinson, 2006). The review identified common and potentially causal factors within abusive relationships that were associated with further escalation of abuse or lethality.

Police officers and staff complete the DASH process through asking the victim 27 questions based on their current situation, presence of children and dependants, previous history of domestic abuse, and perpetrators' attitudes and behaviours. The DASH form is completed with either Yes or No answers and free text boxes for further articulation of the situation and context. The format of the DASH forms themselves often varies across forces; however, many are now digitally completed although some forces still utilise hard copy versions which are later transcribed or scanned into digital crime reports. A generalised format is shown in Table 4.4.

Once all the questions have been asked and the risk assessment form completed, the cumulative value of the question set is then considered by the officer to assess whether the risk falls within one of the three gradings:

Table 4.4 Example DASH risk assessment form

DASH Risk Assessment			
Officer Completing		*Date & Time*	
Questions & Answers			
1 Has the current incident resulted in injury? (please state what and whether this is the first injury):			
2 Are you very frightened?:			
Comment:			
3 Are you afraid of further injury or violence? If so, please give an indication of what the abuser might do and to whom. (E.g. Kill themselves or injure the children).:			
Details:			
4 Do you feel isolated from friends/family? (i.e. does the abuser try to stop you from seeing friends/family/Dr or others):			
5 Have you performed a firearms check on PNC/ Intelligence held?:			
6 Are you feeling depressed or having suicidal thoughts?:			
7 Have you separated or tried to separate from the abuser within the past year?:			
8 Is there conflict over child contact? (please state what):			
Details:			
9 Does the abuser constantly text, call, contact, follow, stalk, or harass you? (Please expand to identify what and whether you believe that this is done deliberately to intimidate you? Consider the context and behaviour of what is being done. Ask 11 additional stalking questions):			
Details:			
Is the victim very frightened?:			
Details:			
Is there previous domestic abuse and harassment history?:			
Has the abuser vandalised or destroyed property?:			
Has the abuser turned up unannounced more than three times a week?:			
Is the abuser following the victim or loitering near the victim?:			
Has the abuser threatened physical or sexual violence?:			

DASH Risk Assessment			
Officer Completing		*Date & Time*	
Questions & Answers			
Has the abuser been harassing any third party since the harassment began (e.g. family, children, friends, neighbours, and colleagues)?:			
Has the abuser acted violently to anyone else during the stalking incident?:			
Has the abuser engaged others to help (wittingly or unwittingly)?:			
Has the abuser been abusing alcohol/drugs?:			
Has the abuser been violent in past? (Physical and psychological. Intelligence or reported):			
9 Are you currently pregnant or have you recently had a baby in the past 18 months?:			
10 Are there any children and step-children that aren't the abusers in the household? Or are there other dependants in the household (i.e. older relative)?:			
11 Has the abuser ever hurt the children/dependants?:			
12 Has the abuser ever threatened to hurt or kill the children/dependants?:			
13 Is the abuse happening more often?:			
14 Is the abuse getting worse?:			
Details:			
15 Does the abuser try to control everything you do and/ or are they excessively jealous? (In terms of relationship, who you see, being 'policed at home', telling you what you wear for example. Consider honour-based violence and stalking and specify the behaviour):			
16 Has the abuser ever used weapons or objects to hurt you?:			
17 Has the abuser ever threatened to kill you or someone else and you believed them?:			
18 Has the abuser ever attempted to strangle/choke/ suffocate/drown you?:			
19 Does the abuser do or say things of a sexual nature that makes you feel bad or that physically hurt you or someone else? (Please specify who and what):			
20 Is there any other person that has threatened you or that you are afraid of? (If yes, consider extended family if honour-based violence.):			

(Continued)

DASH Risk Assessment			
Officer Completing		Date & Time	
Questions & Answers			
21 Do you know if the abuser has hurt anyone else? (children/siblings/elderly relative/stranger, for example. Consider HBV. Please specify who and what):			
22 Has the abuser ever mistreated an animal or the family pet?:			
23 Are there any financial issues? For example, are you dependant on the abuser for money/have they recently lost their job/other financial issues?:			
24 Has the abuser had problems in the past year with drugs (prescription or other), alcohol, or mental health leading to problems in leading a normal life? (Please specify what)?:			
Details:			
25 Has the abuser ever threatened or attempted suicide?:			
26 Has the abuser ever breached bail/an injunction and/or any agreement for when they can see you and/or the children? (Please specify what):			
27 Do you know if the abuser has ever been in trouble with the police or has a criminal history? (If yes, please specify):			

- Standard – the current evidence does not indicate the likelihood of causing serious harm.
- Medium – there are identifiable indicators of the risk of serious harm. The offender has the potential to cause serious harm but is unlikely to do so unless there is a change in circumstances, for example, failure to take medication, loss of accommodation, relationship breakdown, and drug or alcohol misuse.
- High – There are identifiable indicators of the risk of serious harm. The potential event could happen at any time and the impact would be serious.

The risk of serious harm in this grading context is defined as:

> A risk which is life threatening and/or traumatic, and from which recovery, whether physical or psychological, can be expected to be difficult or impossible.
>
> (Richards, 2009, p. 7)

It is important to recognise that it is this specific risk, ***the potential for serious injury – physical and/or physiological*** – which police officers are assessing when conducting the DASH assessment process.

Whilst each force will have its own policy, generally an incident will be graded as high risk if it scores Yes to 14 out of the 27 questions. However, those completing the forms can also use their professional judgement if they have reasonable grounds to believe that significant harm is likely due to the circumstance and their own judgement even if the scores are under 14 (Robinson et al., 2016; Turner et al., 2019).

Forces have different policies regarding who completes each phase of the DASH process. A review of all forces by the College of Policing has identified three different practice regimes for the completion of DASH (Robinson et al., 2016):

1 Both risk factor identification and subsequent grading assessment takes place by the front-line reporting officer and signed off as suitable by their supervisor.
2 Risk factors are identified by the reporting officers but the grading in all cases is competed by a specialist unit.
3 ront-line officers complete the risk identification and grading, and a specialist unit will then review a subset of cases. Usually this will be only those which meet the high-risk threshold, but some forces will also reassess medium risk cases as well.

The situation can be made more complicated where there are cross allegations made between parties. In such cases a separate DASH should be completed with each victim and their own individual risk be assessed. However, it is good practice to also consider cumulatively the risk within the relationship. Whilst criminal offences may have been committed by both parties, further investigation may reveal the issues of self-defence and coercive control. Where counter allegations are made, officers are advised to bring this to the attention of a supervisor, seek specialist advice, and consult force policy.

There is no doubt that the introduction of DASH in 2009 and the national acceptance of the significance of risk assessment fundamentally changed the way police responded to allegations to domestic abuse. As identified by Turner et al.: “There is no question that the introduction of risk assessment in the context of domestic abuse was a landmark moment in the development of responses to this phenomenon” (2019, p. 1028). It introduced a new understanding and focus as well as a consistent language. It provided officers with a process to follow in an area of crime which has long been described as a private matter within a policing culture which believed that what happened behind closed doors was simply not a matter for police (Robinson, 2000). However, over the last decade as the evidence base and overall understanding of the policing of domestic abuse has increased, concern has been raised about the predictive validity and operational application of the DASH tool.

Predictive validity

In 2014, 38 of 43 forces in England and Wales were using DASH. Although it remains the national tool for police assessment of risk it has never been formally evaluated (HMIC, 2015; Robinson et al., 2016). Studies have identified that it failed to predict high risk accurately (Thornton, 2017) leading to a number of 'false positives' overestimating the numbers within the high-risk cohort. Similarly, it does not provide significant weight to coercive control elements and is more skewed towards physical abuse (Robinson et al., 2016). In response to the lack of any formal evaluation of DASH highlighted by HMIC (2014), the College of Policing has completed a rapid evidence review (Wheller and Wire, 2014) and has piloted a number of different formats of risk assessment including a reduction in the number of questions, enhanced focus on coercive and controlling behaviour, more free text within the format to contextualised professional judgement decisions, and improved guidance and training in how to complete the process (Wire and Myhill, 2018).

Operational application

Concerns have also been identified regarding the operational use of DASH. Research indicates officers self-select those factors they believe are most significant and that give them more weight in the risk assessment. Officers therefore focus only on a small number of criteria rather than examining all 27 areas against which they make their grading decisions (Robinson et al., 2018).

Field tests have indicated there is an inconsistent understanding of the definition of serious harm and the three DASH gradings. Officers are not clear exactly what specific risk they are assessing and do not understand the DASH definition of serious harm. The subjectivity of decision-making created using professional judgement methodology gives rise to inconsistency in gradings by officers when presented with the same circumstances (Sebire and Barling, 2016). The operational use of DASH was also widely considered by HMIC (2014, 2015) who identified several inadequate and inconsistent practices, including a lack of training, poor quality in completing the forms, lack of supervision, and the completion of DASH over the telephone instead of in person.

Further research has identified that police officers and other professionals working within this field, in assessing domestic violence risk will often grade cases as high even where their numerical count of the factor DASH checklist would rate them as medium or low. The higher grade pushes the responsibility for the risk management to a wider number of specialists and away from the reporting officer. In other words, officers may err on the side of caution and push ongoing management and responsibility to other departments, so it becomes someone else 'problem'.

> This is an inevitable way of working in a climate where, following a serious event such as a child death or domestic violence homicide, it is common to look for failure in practice and to hold individual practitioners publicly accountable.
>
> (Robinson and Howarth, 2012, p. 1506)

Finally, there remains a culture in policing that domestic abuse is simply not a police function. It is a futile endeavour, and police perceive that their efforts are wasted when they could be dealing with real, more exciting crime types. Officers will return to the scenes of many repeat incidents and can often feel frustrated that victims will not cooperate with legal proceedings. There is a lack of empathy and understanding where victims return to abusive perpetrators and officers cannot understand 'why doesn't she just leave' (Robinson et al., 2016, 2018). It is not the role of police to judge a victim's decision to remain in abusive relationships or households. Victims may make informed decisions to manage the risk of violence if they stay against the risk of homelessness, loss of financial support, status, and their emotional connections to their abuser if they leave (Walklate and Mythen, 2011). The police role is to keep the peace, protect, and prevent crime. Officers should advise and support and empower victims to make their own informed decisions. As noted by Campbell at al.,

> . . . convincing a victim that it is necessary to leave her home and friends and take her children out of school to enter an emergency shelter or relocate requires her belief that she has no alternative, that staying home is not safe. Convincing a woman to cooperate in having her partner tried on a felony charge and possibly incarcerated, depriving the children of a father, the family of a source of financial support, and treating the person she is emotionally attached to as a criminal may require persuasive evidence.
>
> (2005, p. 4)

So, whilst it may be the third, fourth, or tenth occasion officers attend a report of a domestic between the same partners, if each time the response has been compassionate and professional, and according to policy it may be that is the time when the victim is ready to be supported to take a different decision to end a relationship. Ultimately, despite police and partnership intervention, it is up to each individual to make their own life choices even if some of them turn out to be fatal. Police attitudes to domestic abuse and the issue of compassion fatigue will be examined in more detail in Chapter 9.

Having understood the importance of risk assessment it is helpful to now consider best practice in the application of the risk assessment process.

Best practice in the application of risk assessment

Responding to domestic abuse incidents often within highly charged and febrile atmospheres police officers are required to make objective and professional decisions and communicate effectively with potentially traumatised victims. This is a very complex and complicated area of policing. As noted by Turner et al.,

> responding to a call for service is often rushed and stressful endeavour. . . the officers and citizens involved in these interactions are often encountering each other from very different gender, ethnic, and professional vantage points', which is likely to produce an endless combination of misunderstandings, judgement errors and mistakes.
>
> (2019, p. 1028)

Attached are excerpts from two DASH risk assessment forms completed, following allegations of harassment and stalking. They provide a comparison of certain questions within the form to indicate good and poor practice.

Table 4.5 Example (i) of completed DASH form

DASH Risk Assessment	
Offence(s)	Domestic Abuse Investigation Harassment – Pursue course of conduct in breach of Sec 1 (1) which amounts to stalking Included Classifications – Domestic Abuse Investigation Included Classifications – Harassment – Pursue course of conduct in breach of Sec 1 (1) which amounts to stalking
Risk Rating: High	
Justification	This is a DV high-risk suspect who has shown coercive controlling behaviours, assaulted the victim by beating, and has stalked her whilst being on bail conditions. The relationship was for three years and the suspect has controlled this relationship and has not let the victim leave. If she tried he would say he would kill himself to get her back Dash Risk Assessment authorised by Detective Sergeant XXXXXXXXXXXXX
Questions & Answers	
4 Do you feel isolated from friends/family? (i.e. does the abuser try to stop you from seeing friends/family/Dr or others):	Yes
Details:	I feel like I have to ask his permission to go anywhere and when I do go out he constantly texts me. I barely have any friends because of him.

Questions & Answers	
8 Does the abuser constantly text, call, contact, follow, stalk, or harass you? (Please expand to identify what and whether you believe that this is done deliberately to intimidate you? Consider the context and behaviour of what is being done. Ask 11 additional stalking questions):	Yes
Details:	He constantly calls and texts me and turns up unannounced. He slept outside my house for two days before.
Is the victim very frightened?:	Yes
Details:	He gets so angry and lashes out
Is there previous domestic abuse and harassment history?:	Yes
Details:	I have reported stuff before but I've always dropped charges
Has the abuser vandalised or destroyed property?:	Yes
Details:	He has smashed mobiles and smashed up my stuff.
Has the abuser turned up unannounced more than three times a week?:	Yes
Details:	He will turn up anywhere he knows where I am
Is the abuser following the victim or loitering near the victim?:	Yes
Details:	He has turned up at work before because he knows where I work from. He also turns up outside my dads.
Has the abuser threatened physical or sexual violence?:	Yes
Details:	He threatens to hit me and has said he will kill me before.
Has the abuser been harassing any third party since the harassment began (e.g. family, children, friends, neighbours, and colleagues)?:	No
Has the abuser acted violently to anyone else during the stalking incident?:	No
Has the abuser engaged others to help (wittingly or unwittingly)?:	Yes

(*Continued*)

Questions & Answers	
Details:	He has got his sister and his aunty to contact me on his behalf
Has the abuser been abusing alcohol/drugs?:	Yes
Details:	He smokes weed everyday
Has the abuser been violent in past? (Physical and psychological. Intelligence or reported):	Yes
Details:	I have reported previous times but dropped charges
14 Is the abuse getting worse?:	Yes
Details:	He has a hold on me he keeps buying me things and uses it against me
15 Does the abuser try to control everything you do and/or are they excessively jealous? (In terms of relationship, who you see, being 'policed at home', telling you what you wear, for example. Consider honour-based violence and stalking and specify the behaviour):	Yes
Details:	He always wants to know what I am doing, and if I am going out without him he will kick off and become abusive
18 Has the abuser ever attempted to strangle/choke/suffocate/drown you?:	Yes
Details:	He has strangled me today, has tried to drown me two years ago, and has choked me by shoving his fingers down my throat to stop me screaming. He has also put pillow over my head to suffocate me
27 Do you know if the abuser has ever been in trouble with the police or has a criminal history? (If yes, please specify):	Yes
Details:	I only know of when I have had him arrested

Table 4.5 is a good example of a DASH risk assessment which lead to a charge of coercive control. The answers have been recorded directly as provided by the victim rather than an officer interpreting what they have been told. The officer completed each section in detail which assists those

specialist workers who are reliant on the data quality of the DASH form to understand the context of the situation and the circumstances as perceived by the victim. The officer provides a clear rationale as to how they made their grading decision which has been authorised by their supervising officer.

Example Table 4.6 is more problematic, and there is a lack of crucial detail in the free text. The DASH should be completed using the victim's own words. For instance, it is unlikely that the victim would reply 'see PNC'. The Police National Computer (PNC) is the commonly used abbreviation used by police officers and staff for PNC so it is hardly likely that this answer would have been stated by the victim in those terms. Furthermore, partners and some specialist support workers do not have access to the PNC so they would not be able to access the previous known criminal history or factor that into the ongoing risk assessment.

Table 4.6 Example (ii) of completed DASH form

Risk Assessment	
Offence(s)	Sending letters, etc., with intent to cause distress or anxiety, Malicious Communications Act 1988 Included Classifications – Sending letters, etc., with intent to cause distress or anxiety, Malicious Communications Act 1988
Risk Assessment Name: DASH Risk Assessment V2 – Risk Rating: High	
Justification	High risk IP is terrified of the suspect.
Questions & Answers	
4 Do you feel isolated from friends/family? (i.e. does the abuser try to stop you from seeing friends/family/Dr or others):	Yes
Details:	
8 Does the abuser constantly text, call, contact, follow, stalk, or harass you? (Please expand to identify what and whether you believe that this is done deliberately to intimidate you? Consider the context and behaviour of what is being done. Ask 11 additional stalking questions):	Yes
Details:	Constantly messaged her
Is the victim very frightened?:	Yes
Details:	Has fled the address because she is afraid of him
Is there previous domestic abuse and harassment history?:	Yes

(Continued)

Questions & Answers	
Details:	As per previous logs
Has the abuser vandalised or destroyed property?:	Yes
Details:	Smashed her car window
Has the abuser turned up unannounced more than three times a week?:	No
Is the abuser following the victim or loitering near the victim?:	No
Has the abuser threatened physical or sexual violence?:	Yes
Details:	Threats of physical violence
Has the abuser been harassing any third party since the harassment began (e.g. family, children, friends, neighbours, and colleagues)?:	No
Has the abuser acted violently to anyone else during the stalking incident?:	No
Has the abuser engaged others to help (wittingly or unwittingly)?:	Yes
Details:	Friends
Has the abuser been abusing alcohol/drugs?:	Yes
Details:	Drinks
Has the abuser been violent in past? (Physical and psychological. Intelligence or reported):	Yes
Details:	As per PNC
14 Is the abuse getting worse?:	Yes
Details:	
15 Does the abuser try to control everything you do and/or are they excessively jealous? (In terms of relationship, who you see, being 'policed at home', telling you what you wear, for example. Consider honour-based violence and stalking and specify the behaviour):	Yes
Details:	Very controlling of her
18 Has the abuser ever attempted to strangle/choke/suffocate/drown you?:	Yes
Details:	Historically tried to choke her this was reported at the time
27 Do you know if the abuser has ever been in trouble with the police or has a criminal history? (If yes, please specify):	Yes
Details:	As per PNC

Taking the above into consideration as well as the general research cited regarding the officer's completion of DASH (Almond et al., 2017; Robinson et al., 2016, 2018; Sebire and Barling, 2016), the following guidelines should be considered by all officers reporting and investigating domestic abuse when conducting a risk identification, assessment, and management.

- Identify and understand the factors which signify domestic abuse. Be professionally curious, and ask open questions in order to identify signs of risk and vulnerability.
- Be alert to signs of circumstances where victims may not be able to fully disclose their situation. Victims may be suffering from coercive control, have a fear of authority, believe they may lose their children or financial support, or simply feel they will not be believed.
- Do not be judgmental of people's life choices. Be aware of the potential for unconscious bias in yourself or colleagues.
- When completing the assessment questions with victims ensure that they understand the process and why the questions are being asked. Record clearly and in as much detail as possible their responses. There is no set way to ask the questions. Some officers will work through them as a list, others will weave them into more general conversation.
- Be victim focussed, build a rapport, and create an environment where they feel comfortable so they can discuss detailed personal information, explain all processes to them, check their understanding and empower them in the decision-making process by providing information, options, and support. Ensure you understand the definitions and gradings associated with the risk assessment process, and if you are unsure ask a supervisor.
- Clearly record your rationale, the evidence upon which you have come to the decisions and gradings you have made.

Management of risk

Once risks have been identified and graded, the final stage of the process is risk management.

There are several actions which can individually or collectively be employed to deal with the risks identified. Referred to by the College of Policing as the 'RARA' model, officers dealing with domestic abuse situations should work through the options to:

- **Remove the risk** – such as arresting suspect, remanding in custody, and enforcing existing orders.
- **Avoid the risk** – such as relocating the victim to a new address.
- **Reduce the risk** – such as changing patterns of behaviour by referring the victim and/or perpetrator to counselling or other services, installation of an alarm, and application for a suitable civil order.

- **Accept the risk** – such as continue to monitor to situation, flag the location on force intelligence system, and add victim and perpetrators details on PNC in order to ensure any calls for service are prioritised.

It can be helpful to use this model to articulate the rationale for the measures police and partners have considered and are putting in place.

One benefit associated with the introduction of DASH was the consistent language it created between police and multi-agency partners. As explained fully in Chapter 8, several initiatives and services are provided to the perpetrators and victims of domestic abuse by statutory and voluntary agencies with the intention of managing the identified risks. Provision and allocation of these services are filtered according to the risk grading. The higher the grade and risk level, the more bespoke support mechanisms are made available. Being graded high risk through 14 DASH 'ticks' is a gateway for a victim's case to be heard at a Multi-Agency Risk Assessment Conference (MARAC) (Turner et al., 2019; Wire and Myhill, 2018). Victims classified as high risk as well as having their cases heard by MARAC will often be provided with an Independent Domestic Violence Advisor (IDVA), whose role is to support and advocate for the victim, who also uses a version of the DASH assessment process (Robinson and Howarth, 2012).

The support available for medium and standard risk victims is inconsistent across the country. The availability of services will depend on individual local authority strategies, demands, and resources of the local area where the victim resides. When managing the risk of victims within medium and standard gradings it is important for police officers and staff to be aware of the local support networks available and ensure any appropriate material to signpost victims to what help, and advice, is accessible. Police can assist in the risk management of these cases through the use of orders and legislations (Robinson et al., 2016) such as Domestic Violence Protection orders and Clare's Law information disclosures (see Chapter 5).

The agreed definition of High, Medium, and Standard risk ensures victims receive an appropriate support according to the level and nature of their assessed risk in order to manage any future escalation or repetition. In short, people's lives are impacted both directly and indirectly by the risk identification and gradings made by police and other agencies (Robinson and Howarth, 2012). Therefore, professionalism, communication, and training are so important for all professionals working in this field given the significance of their decision-making.

Victims' perception of risk

Much of this chapter has focussed on the formal tools and police risk assessment process. However, as alluded to in the risk factors section the victim's perception of their own risk is just as important as any structured formalised tool (Wheller and Wire, 2014). In many cases the victim will be attuned to any slight change of behaviours in their partners or abusive family member which signifies they may be at heightened risk. Victims will often have formulated coping strategies to deal with these subtle changes (Walklate and Mythen, 2011). The victim's perception of their own risk and their strategies to manage it are vital for officers to understand and incorporate in their overall policing assessment. Communication with the victim is key in managing and providing support. It is good practice to talk through the risk assessment process with the victim in a safe environment so they can contribute to the assessment process and where possible they feel empowered to make their own decisions. This is not always the case and victims, particularly those in coercive and controlling relationships may minimise risks or not even see them. Other victims may be fearful of the consequences; however, it is vital to gain their trust and support the victim by helping them to identify and manage their own risks. Officers can support and provide information and guidance. Therefore, the risk assessment process is so important as it aids victims in understanding their own risk.

Conclusion

This chapter has outlined the three-stage process of risk assessment: identification, assessment, and management. Because of domestic abuse can be associated with repeat incidents and commonly associated factors within abusive relationships, risk assessment is a tool often used within domestic abuse as it allows for measures to be introduced to prevent continuation and escalation. Internationally, law enforcement agencies have introduced some form of risk assessment tool to assist in the prevention of crime and deployment of limited resources where it can have the most impact (Campbell et al., 2005; Turner et al., 2019). In the United Kingdom DASH has become the most widely utilised risk assessment tool. Officers completing the tool will take victims through a series of questions in order to identify which risk factors they may be experiencing and then grade risk according to standardised definitions.

Whilst there are several challenges regarding the tool and work is ongoing to improve the theory and understanding of what works in preventing domestic abuse, officers have a duty to act in a non-judgemental, compassionate, and professional manner. Often referred to as 'domestics' there can be a culture that attending such incidents will be frustrating and not as 'exciting' as other areas of policing. Dealing with domestic crime can indeed be challenging and frustrating; however, the decisions and actions taken by officers including how they assess the risk presented at such incidents can be life changing for all involved. Risk assessments do not solve society's domestic abuse issues but helps identify those less obvious cases where help is required but would have been previously overlooked (Baldry and

Sebire, 2016). Where risk assessments have been rushed, ill-informed, and miscommunicated, lives have been lost. However, when done with respect, understanding, and professionalism, people's lives have been changed for the better.

Critical thinking questions

- How can you overcome bias?
- What factors do you need to consider when assessing risk within cross allegations?
- How do you balance professional judgement concerns of future abuse occurring with limited evidence of actual abuse?

Useful links and resources

College of Policing, National Decision-Making Model https://www.app.college.police.uk/app-content/national-decision-model/

College of Policing, Understanding risk and vulnerability in the context of domestic abuse https://www.app.college.police.uk/app-content/major-investigation-and-public-protection/domestic-abuse/risk-and-vulnerability/

DASH Risk Model https://www.dashriskchecklist.co.uk

Safe Lives Dash Risk Checklist https://safelives.org.uk/sites/default/files/resources/Dash%20for%20IDVAs%20FINAL_0.pdf

References

Almond, L., McManus, M., Brian, D., Merrington, D.P., 2017. Exploration of the risk factors contained within the UK's existing domestic abuse risk assessment tool (DASH): Do these risk factors have individual predictive validity regarding recidivism? *Journal of Aggression, Conflict and Peace Research* 9(1), 58–68.

Baldry, A.C., Sebire, J., 2016. Policing and domestic abuse: Challenges and ways to go. *Policing: A Journal of Policy and Practice* 10, 323–327.

Campbell, J.C., O'Sullivan, C., Roehl, J., Webster, D., 2005. Intimate partner violence risk assessment validation study, final report. National Institute of Justice.

Carson, D., Bain, A., 2008. *Professional risk and working with people: Decision-making in health, social care and criminal justice.* Jessica Kingsley Publishers.

College of Policing, 2013a. *National decision making model.* College of Policing.

College of Policing, 2013b. *Risk principles.* College of Policing.

Hardy, K., 2014. *Enterprise risk management: A guide for government professionals.* John Wiley & Sons.

Hart, S.D., Douglas, K.S., Guy, L.S., 2016. The structured professional judgement approach to violence risk assessment: Origins, nature, and advances, in: Craig, L., Rettenberger, M. (Volume Eds.) and Boer, D. (Series Ed.), *The Wiley Handbook on the Theories, Assessment, Treatment of Sexual Offending* (pp. 643–666). Oxford: Wiley.

HMIC, 2015. Increasingly everybody's business. London: Her Majesty's Inspectorate Constabulary.
HMIC, 2014. Everyone's business: improving the police response to domestic abuse. Her Majesty's Inspectorate of Constabulary.
Home Affairs Select Committee, Seventh Report, 2008. Expectations of the police. Home Affairs Committee Publications. The Stationary Office.
Hoyle, C., 2008. Will she be safe? A critical analysis of risk assessment in domestic violence cases. *Children and Youth Services Review* 30, 323–337.
McGraw, C., Jeffers, S., 2015. The importance of considering the treatment and care of family pets in domestic violence risk assessments. *Journal of Health Visiting* 3, 483–488.
Medina, J., Robinson, A., Myhill, A., 2016. Cheaper, faster, better: Expectations and achievements in police risk assessment of domestic abuse. *Policing: A Journal of Policy and Practice* 10, 341–350.
ONS, 2019. Domestic abuse prevalence and trends, England and Wales: Year ending March 2019. Domestic abuse prevalence and trends, England and Wales – Office for National Statistics. ons.gov.uk. https://www.ons.gov.uk/peoplepopulationandcommunity/crimeandjustice/articles/domesticabuseprevalenceandtrendsenglandandwales/yearendingmarch2019 (accessed 7.8.22).
ONS, 2018. Domestic abuse in England and Wales – Office for National Statistics. https://www.ons.gov.uk/peoplepopulationandcommunity/crimeandjustice/bulletins/domesticabuseinenglandandwales/yearendingmarch2016#are-there-differences-between-local-areas (accessed 2.17.19).
Richards, L., 2009. *Domestic abuse, stalking and harassment and honour based violence (DASH, 2009) risk identification and assessment and management model.* Association of Police Officers (ACPO).
Richards, L., 2004. *Getting away with it': A strategic overview of domestic violence sexual assault and 'serious' incident analysis.* Metropolitan Police Service.
Robinson, A.L., 2006. Reducing repeat victimization among high-risk victims of domestic violence: The benefits of a coordinated community response in Cardiff, Wales. *Violence Against Women* 12, 761–788.
Robinson, A.L., 2000. The effect of a domestic violence policy change on police officers' schemata. *Criminal Justice and Behavior* 27, 600–624.
Robinson, A.L., Howarth, E., 2012. Judging risk: Key determinants in British domestic violence cases. *Journal of Interpersonal Violence* 27, 1489–1518.
Robinson, A.L., Myhill, A., Wire, J., Roberts, J., Tilley, N., 2016. *Risk-led policing of domestic abuse and the DASH risk model. What works: Crime reduction research.* Cardiff University, College of Policing and UCL Department of Security and Crime Science.
Robinson, A.L., Pinchevsky, G.M., Guthrie, J.A., 2018. A small constellation: Risk factors informing police perceptions of domestic abuse. *Policing and Society* 28, 189–204.
Roehl, J., Roehl, J., 2000. Intimate partner violence: The current use of risk assessments in sentencing offenders. *Justice System Journal* 21, 171–198.
Sebire, J., 2017. The value of incorporating measures of relationship concordance when constructing profiles of intimate partner homicides: A descriptive study of IPH committed within London, 1998–2009. *Journal of Interpersonal Violence* 32, 1476–1500.

Sebire, J., Barling, H., 2016. Assessing the assessors: An analysis of the consistency of risk grading by police when conducting domestic abuse investigations. *Policing: A Journal of Policy and Practice* 10, 351–360.

Sherman, L., Strang, H., O'Connor, D., 2017. *Introduction—Key facts about domestic abuse: Lessons from eight studies.* Springer.

Sreenivasan, S., Kirkish, P., Garrick, T., Weinberger, L.E., Phenix, A., 2000. Actuarial risk assessment models: A review of critical issues related to violence and sex-offender recidivism assessments. *Journal-American Academy of Psychiatry and the Law* 28, 438–448.

Stock, M.J., Wentworth, J., 2020. Evaluating UK natural hazards: The national risk assessment. https://researchbriefings.files.parliament.uk/documents/POST-PB-0031/POST-PB-0031.pdf

Thornton, S., 2017. Predicting domestic murder and serious assaults in the Thames Valley. *Cambridge Journal of Evidence-Based Policing* 1, 64–84.

Turner, E., Medina, J., Brown, G., 2019. Dashing hopes? The predictive accuracy of domestic abuse risk assessment by police. *The British Journal of Criminology* 59, 1013–1034.

Walklate, S., Mythen, G., 2011. Beyond risk theory: Experiential knowledge and 'knowing otherwise.' *Criminology & Criminal Justice* 11, 99–113.

Wheller, L., Wire, J., 2014. *Domestic abuse risk factors and risk assessment: Summary of findings from a rapid evidence assessment.* College of Policing.

Wire, J., Myhill, A., 2018. Piloting a new approach to domestic abuse frontline risk assessment. Evaluation Report for the College of Policing. https://fdocuments.in/document/piloting-a-new-approach-to-domestic-abuse-frontline-risk-abuse-support-worker (accessed 7.8.22).

Chapter 5

The law, policing policy, and the courts

KEY POINTS

- Understand the chronology of the law as it relates to domestic abuse, including an explanation regarding the lack of specific offences of domestic abuse.
- Be able to identify how societal change influences legislation, for example, in instances of marital rape repeal, coercive control, honour-based abuse and stalking.
- Consider strategically how police resources are managed to address domestic abuse, discussing the pros and cons of specialist and generalist units.
- Recognise best practice in responding to calls for service through call handling, initial attendance, golden hour investigative principles, evidence gathering (including body worn video), case building, victim and suspect interviews, and prosecution.
- Understand the civil and criminal law when dealing with domestic abuse.
- Be aware of the impact policy has on decisions, such as absent victim prosecutions, attrition rates, and the impact of the court process.

Introduction

The history of domestic abuse in the United Kingdom is long, and in many respects is much more entwined with historical social injustice and inequality as much as it is about power and control. There may never have been a time when it did not exist (Hague et al., 2005), and indeed, it could be described as a 'Wicked Problem' (Grint, 2010) as it is a problem with no simple solution and one which may never be resolved. As discussed in Chapter 2, violence committed within a domestic home was often viewed historically as a private issue rather than a matter appropriate for criminal justice intervention (Erez, 2002; Fagan, 1996; Hoppe et al., 2020).

DOI: 10.4324/9781003137412-5

Whilst domestic abuse has moved from being a private issue to a social problem (Groves and Thomas, 2014), domestic abuse or domestic violence is not in itself a specific offence. There are no specific civil or criminal remedies for domestic abuse, rather it is an aggravating factor of other crime types, but it is no longer a private matter and one in which the state must intervene to protect life. Of concern, however, is that only a small proportion of domestic abuse cases are reported to the police (Walby et al., 2014) and the 'iceberg of domestic violence' (Gracia, 2004) is significant.

If state intervention to protect and disrupt domestic abuse happens only in the minority of cases, the use of the law and the Criminal Justice System therefore will touch only a scarce number of incidents. This is overlaid with traditional explanations for apparent police ambivalence in relation to domestic abuse, whereby some commentators have cited a lack of sympathy for domestic violence victims rooted in police misogyny and sexist attitudes (Ellison, 2002), leading to few cases being reported, investigated, charged, or prosecuted. A vicious circle of history and culture has existed, which has meant domestic abuse has not been treated as seriously as it ought to have been, and many have died as a result.

The history of domestic abuse

The history of domestic abuse as a criminal concept is frequently debated and often challenged. Hammurabi's code is a collection of 282 rules which Hammurabi used to govern ancient Babylon from 1792 to 1750 BC. This code is the earliest recorded description of domestic abuse – mandating men to commit violence against women should they breach the code of expectations in private family life (Jenkins and Davidson, 2001). Quite the opposite to today's important distinction that such violent acts are classified as crimes. The use of the phrase 'rule of thumb' by Blackstone in 1865 (Jackson, 2007), whilst contested in many respects in terms of veracity, has often been suggested as the precursor of the 19th-century rule that it was legal for a man to beat his wife, providing that the stick he used was no thicker than his thumb. The patriarchal mandate was enshrined legally in 1860 when the Law of Coveture stated that upon marriage, a husband became legally responsible for the actions of both his wife and children; therefore, he could physically and verbally chastise them in order to control their behaviour (Gubi, 2015). Astonishingly, in 1895 a curfew on wife beating was introduced as a City of London Byelaw to prohibit wife beating between the hours of 10 pm and 7am because the noise may keep the neighbours awake (Womens' Aid, 2016).

Whilst a historical peer at the 19th century may seem to be the majority outrageous now in terms of lack of prevention or intervention to stop domestic abuse and even state support for it through legislation, it was not until the 1970s that tackling domestic abuse through the legal system really started to gain traction, but momentum has been slow. The Domestic Violence and Matrimonial Proceedings Act 1976 provided civil litigation in the form of injunctions for spouses (Burton, 2008), but it was not until 1991 that marital rape was made a criminal act, for example (Dressler et al., 2001).

Nationally, 35% of the police-recorded violence against the person offences were domestic abuse-related as well as 16% of the sexual offences in the year ending March 2020 (ONS, 2020).

Domestic abuse definition

The current Home Office (2013) definition of domestic violence and abuse is:

Any incident or pattern of incidents of controlling, coercive, threatening behaviour, violence, or abuse between those aged 16 and over who are, or have been, intimate partners or family members regardless of gender or sexuality. The abuse can encompass but is not limited to the following:

- Psychological.
- Physical.
- Sexual.
- Financial.
- Emotional.

Whilst there is no specific criminal offence of domestic violence or domestic abuse, the term can be applied to a number of offences committed in a domestic environment. The domestic nature of the offending behaviour is an aggravating factor because of the abuse of trust involved (Crown Prosecution Service, 2020a). Whilst physical and sexual crimes are normally associated with domestic abuse, the increase in financial, psychological, and emotional impacts are now more common, and in 2012, the United Kingdom revised the official definition of domestic abuse to include coercive controlling behaviours, highlighting the importance of non-physical and chronic forms of offending (Robinson et al., 2016).

The government also included adolescents under 18 in the definition at this stage, after the British Crime Survey of 2009/2010 found that the 16–19 age group were the group most likely to suffer abuse from a partner. Domestic violence and abuse is therefore not a social problem limited to adulthood, but it is also a problem in the relationships of children and young people (Rogers et al., 2019). Indeed, such is the concern that Young et al. (2021) concluded that the long-term consequences of violence in young people's dating relationships have not been well researched until now and should be examined as a public health issue.

The Domestic Abuse Act 2021

The Domestic Abuse Act 2021 (see Box 5.1) is the most recent piece of legislation introduced to improve the protection afforded to domestic abuse victims. The act was signed into law on the 29th April 2021 and contains some significant updates to previous legislation (Home Office, 2021).

BOX 5.1 THE DOMESTIC ABUSE ACT 2021

- Creating a statutory definition of domestic abuse, emphasising that domestic abuse is not just physical violence but can also be emotional, controlling, or coercive, and economic abuse.
- Establishing in law the office of Domestic Abuse Commissioner and setting out the Commissioner's functions and powers.
- Providing for a new Domestic Abuse Protection Notice and Domestic Abuse Protection Order.
- Placing a duty on local authorities in England to provide accommodation-based support to victims of domestic abuse and their children in refuges and other safe accommodation.
- Prohibiting perpetrators of abuse from cross-examining their victims in person in the civil and family courts in England and Wales.
- Creating a statutory presumption that victims of domestic abuse are eligible for special measures in the criminal, civil, and family courts.
- Extending the controlling or coercive behaviour offence to cover post-separation abuse.
- Extending the offence of disclosing private sexual photographs and films with intent to cause distress (known as the 'revenge porn' offence) to cover threats to disclose such material.
- Creating a new offence of non-fatal strangulation or suffocation of another person.
- Clarifying by restating in statute law the general proposition that a person may not consent to the infliction of serious harm and, by extension, is unable to consent to their own death.
- Extending the extraterritorial jurisdiction of the criminal courts in England and Wales, Scotland, and Northern Ireland to further violent and sexual offences.
- Provide for a statutory domestic abuse perpetrator strategy.
- Enabling domestic abuse offenders to be subject to polygraph testing as a condition of their licence following their release from custody.
- Placing the guidance supporting the Domestic Violence Disclosure Scheme ("Clare's law") on a statutory footing.

The legislation is available to view here:
Domestic Abuse Act 2021 (legislation.gov.uk)

With some significant legal changes to protect those subjected to domestic abuse and to deal with those who perpetrate it, this new legislation closes a number of gaps within and beyond the Criminal Justice System and evaluation of the impact of these improvements will be key moving forward.

The ever-evolving nature and scrutiny of domestic abuse, the impact it has on its victims, and the significant cost to society mean that domestic abuse is now, more than ever, on the national agenda as a criminological and public health issue. Costing the state £66 billion a year (Home Office, 2019a), it cannot be resolved through policing alone, and criminal and civil legislation, whilst becoming more agile, is not the answer to a reduction in domestic violence in families. Education, culture, support, prevention, and deterrence must all be considered to reduce the occurrence and the impact, but a good understanding of the legal history and framework relating to domestic abuse is useful. In particular, the legal changes and societal progression that have occurred in just the last 30 years show how views on domestic abuse can change, and the United Kingdom's current position through the Violence Against Women and Girls Strategy is to ensure no woman should live in the fear of violence (Home Office, 2019b).

Societal change has influenced legislation in a number of key areas involving domestic abuse cases. For example, marital rape, coercive control, honour-based abuse, and stalking are just some of the areas where laws have changed to encompass behaviours and offences that previously would have been considered private family matters or crimes not associated with domestic abuse. These crimes will now be considered in more detail.

Marital rape

The legal and societal acceptance of rape within a marriage that was overturned in 1991 was a significant step in redefining the legitimacy of domestic abuse and sexual assault. For 300 years, rape within the confines of marriage was seen as legal and legitimate. In 1736 Sir Matthew Hale, a former Chief Justice of the Court of King's Bench in England wrote:

> The husband cannot be guilty of rape committed by himself upon his lawful wife, for by their mutual matrimonial consent and contract, the wife hath given up herself in this kind unto her husband, which she cannot retract.
>
> Hale and Dogherty, 1736

In the 1970s, the feminist movement in the United States pushed to make marital rape illegal, and in many states the marital rape exemption was removed from the law books (Finkelhor and Yllö, 1987). England and Wales took much longer to follow. In 1990, a man 'R' was convicted of raping his wife. He appealed the conviction, citing the marital rape exemption but it was upheld in the 1991 judgement in the House of Lords who deemed that it was a 'common law fiction' that by marriage a wife submits herself irrevocably to sexual intercourse in all circumstances (House of Lords, 1991). Westmarland (2004) suggests that the criminalisation of marital rape at this time was controversial within legal circles because it was seen as being criminalised by the courts rather than the elected government.

Lees (2000) suggests there has been very little analysis of marital rape since the legislative change and raises concerns that marital rape is still taken less seriously by the Criminal Justice System than rape by strangers, despite the fact that research suggests that marital rape is linked to life-threatening violence including murder. Russell and Hand (2017) concur, stating there is a lack of research literature regarding marital or spousal rape, and even more specifically, homosexual marital rape is rarely researched at all.

What is clear however is that the changes in legislation around marital rape such as the case of R V R 1992 (Incorporated Council of Law Reporting, 2022) and the Sexual Offences Act 2003 (Sexual Offences Act, 2003; legislation.gov.uk), together with greater understanding by the police around rape in a domestic abuse context, mean this crime is now treated as seriously as it should be.

Coercive control

The introduction of the Serious Crime Act 2015 closed a legislative gap in domestic abuse cases by making coercive or controlling behaviour in intimate or familial relationships a criminal offence. The aim was to better protect victims who might otherwise be subjected to sustained patterns of domestic abuse, which in themselves may not reach the threshold of criminal charge, for instance, extreme psychological or emotional abuse. The offence of coercive control carries a five-year prison sentence, or a fine, or both on indictment.

The government definition of coercive and controlling behaviour is as follows (Crown Prosecution Service, 2017a):

- Coercive behaviour is an act or a pattern of acts of assault, threats, humiliation and intimidation, or other abuse that is used to harm, punish, or frighten their victim.
- Controlling behaviour is a range of acts designed to make a person subordinate and/or dependent by isolating them from sources of support; exploiting their resources and capacities for personal gain,; depriving them of the means needed for independence, resistance, and escape; and regulating their everyday behaviour.

For the offence to apply, the controlling or coercive behaviour must take place repeatedly or continuously; The pattern of behaviour must have a serious effect on the victim, the perpetrator must know or ought to know this, and the victim and perpetrator must be personally connected (Home Office, 2015).

Coercive control is much more about power and control than it is about physical abuse. Stark (2007) introduced the concept into the domestic abuse arena, categorising it as the way a perpetrator (generally male) goes about micromanaging and controlling their partner's (generally female) activities, thereby undermining the victim's ability to make independent decisions and inhibiting any ability to leave the relationship. Research by Myhill (2015) found that women were far more likely to experience coercive control than men and that victims of coercive controlling abuse also appear to have experienced more severe and more frequent physical violence, and more emotional problems and physical injuries as a result. Stark (2020) reiterates this further describing the entrapment of the victim leading to significant physical, material, and spatial constraints on a victim's options.

As a relatively recent piece of legislation in policing domestic abuse, the evidence base around the police response to the new coercive control offence is relatively limited. Barlow et al. (2018) found that there was low use of the law, indicating issues with police understanding and recording of coercive control, as well as missed opportunities in terms of identifying, prioritising, and evidencing coercive control. This led to low arrest rates and officers often not recognising the extent of the risk in domestic abuse cases with a coercive control element to the offending.

There were 9,053 offences of coercive control recorded by police in the year ending March 2018, but only 960 or 10% of these offences led to a prosecution commencing at magistrates' courts in the year ending March 2018 (ONS, 2019). By the year ending March 2020, 24,856 offences had been recorded, a clear indication of an increasing use of the legislation, as well as perhaps of better recording (ONS, 2020). Tolmie (2018) suggests that offences of coercive control require complex analysis that the criminal justice system is not equipped to provide, which leads to significant risks such as the minimisation of the offending and invalidation of the victims' experiences in court and may therefore account for low prosecution rates.

Ultimately however, this is an additional useful instrument in the battle to improve how domestic abuse is policed, moving away from domestic abuse being seen as a physical event only. Indeed, Wiener (2017) suggests that if the police have an improved understanding of the impact of coercive control on victims, this could help them better understand the challenges that survivors face as they engage with the criminal justice process and have to explain how their life enveloped in domestic abuse rather than just a violent act on a particular occasion. This is particularly important at court where a reframing of domestic abuse to introduce the concept of coercive control can be significant, ultimately leading to more successful prosecutions in the longer run.

Honour-based abuse, forced marriage, and female genital mutilation

There is no statutory definition of honour-based abuse and no specific crime. Honour-based abuse (HBA) or honour-based violence (HBV) is a term used to describe a collection of practices which are used to control behaviour within families or other social groups to protect perceived cultural and religious beliefs and/or honour (Crown Prosecution Service, 2020b).

The Crown Prosecution Service elucidates the formal definition of domestic abuse with the following addition "this definition, which is not a legal definition, includes so called 'honour' based violence, female genital mutilation (FGM) and forced marriage, and is clear that victims are not confined to one gender or ethnic group" (Crown Prosecution Service, 2017a). There is often discomfort around the term 'honour' when there is no honour in committing human rights abuses against another individual, there is only dishonour and shame (National Police Chiefs Council, 2015). There is less consensus about whether honour-based abuse should be intrinsically linked to domestic abuse, especially when often the perpetrators are not intimate partners or family members, although may be linked to them. Indeed, Gill et al. (2018) suggest that Honour Based Violence and Abuse can be distinguished from domestic abuse because it is often committed with some degree of approval and/or collusion from family members in response to perceived immoral or shameful behaviour on the part of the victim.

Each of these areas are significant topics in themselves and should be studied carefully when examining the wide umbrella of the domestic abuse definition. The intention here is to highlight the key pieces of legislation and ensure those working in policing and the domestic abuse arena have an overview of such crimes. The National Police Chief's Council are committed to eradicating these forms of abuse but recognise that it is not up to policing alone to do so, and continue to work with victims, survivors, communities, and statutory partners to work towards this objective (National Police Chiefs Council, 2015).

Forced marriage is now a specific offence under s121 of the Anti-Social Behaviour, Crime and Policing Act 2014. Civil remedies such as Force Marriage Protection Orders (FMPO) have been available for some time, but only in 2014 did a breach of a FMPO become a criminal offence. A forced marriage is one in which one or both spouses do not consent to the marriage, and violence, threats, or any other form of coercion is involved (Home Office, 2020).

Honour-based crimes, and in particular forced marriage, often have an international dimension making investigation difficult but not impossible. In essence, the safeguarding of the victim is paramount and should usurp all other considerations, as attrition due to family or cultural pressure is often common. The Forced Marriage Unit (FMU) is a joint Foreign,

Commonwealth and Development Office (FCDO) and Home Office unit which leads on the government's forced marriage policy, outreach, and casework. It operates both inside the United Kingdom and overseas (FCO, 2013). The FMU gave advice or assistance in 1355 cases in 2019 (Home Office, 2020). Of note, 363 cases (27%) involved victims below 18 years of age and 80% of the total number of cases involved female victims. The unit is able to provide specialist knowledge and advice to police investigators dealing with forced marriage cases.

Female Genital Mutilation (FGM) has been a specific offence in the United Kingdom since the Prohibition of Female Circumcision Act 1985. The 1985 Act was replaced by the Female Genital Mutilation Act 2003. FGM, or Female Genital Cutting, is a criminal act defined as any procedure where a person "excises, infibulates or otherwise mutilates the whole or any part of a girl's labia majora, labia minora or clitoris" (Crown Prosecution Service, 2019). FGM comprises all procedures that involve partial or total removal of the external female genitalia, or other injury to the female genital organs for non-medical reasons (World Health Organisation, 2020). It has no health benefits, often leads to significant medical complications both at the time of the cutting and in later life, particularly around childbirth, and is mostly carried out on young girls from infancy up to the age of 15. There were 5391 new cases of FGM recorded in England and Wales from April 2016 to March 2017 (Malik et al., 2018). Simpson et al. (2012) confirm that like other forms of domestic abuse, there are many barriers to both investigation and prosecution of FGM. Most notably, attrition of victims occurs, as many do not wish to go to court to give evidence against their parents or community members. The FGM is often alleged to have occurred prior to the victim becoming a resident in England and Wales as per the legislation, and more generally, there is still a lack of knowledge around FGM by police and medical professionals. Indeed, the first conviction for FGM only occurred in 2019, when the mother of a three-year-old female was found guilty of failing to protect a person from FGM under Section 3a of the Female Genital Mutilation Act 2003 (Crown Prosecution Service, 2019).

Reframing the links between FGM and domestic abuse is discussed in the work of Salihu et al. (2012) who looked at the connection between those who had undergone FGM as a child and were then subjected to intimate partner violence as an adult. The research found that women with FGM were at heighted risk of domestic abuse and the odds of intimate partner violence increased with ascending FGM severity.

There is clearly a requirement to bring honour-based abuse, forced marriage, and FGM under the auspices of domestic abuse as the very nature of the control, power imbalances, and sustained abuse of all kinds associated with these crimes is indicative of that seen across the domestic abuse landscape. The argument relating to the lack of intimate partner violence or even close family members committing these crimes is valid, but the

Governmental Strategy concerning Violence Against Women and Girls is clear that by necessity, these issues are part of the domestic abuse umbrella, and supporting victims and bringing perpetrators to justice are of utmost importance (HM Government, 2016).

Stalking

There is no precise legal definition of stalking. However, the police and CPS have adopted the following description: "a pattern of unwanted, fixated and obsessive behaviour which is intrusive. It can include harassment that amounts to stalking or stalking that causes fear of violence or serious alarm or distress in the victim" (Crown Prosecution Service, 2020c). Stalking does not comprise a single distressing episode but incorporates a sequence of events in succession over a period of time that may appear harmless in isolation (Sheridan and Davies, 2001). The majority of stalking incidents are perpetrated by someone known to the victim (Scott et al., 2014).

In 1997, legislation was introduced under the Protection from Harassment Act to deal with criminal offences associated with stalking activity. The distinction between what is legally 'reasonable' and 'unreasonable' behaviour is much debated (Dennison, 2007) but essentially comes down to the reasonableness test –– what a reasonable person would think of such behaviour. Critically, the legislation proved tricky to deal with the nuances of stalking and in 2012 the Protection of Freedoms Act created two new offences of stalking by inserting new sections 2A and 4A into the Protection from Harassment Act 1997. Further still, the creation of the Stalking Protection Act 2019 introduced a new Stalking Protection Order (SPO) which can be made on application to the Magistrate's court by the Police. This civil order can be made in particular when the threshold to commence criminal proceedings for the commission of an offence has not yet been or will not be met. This allows for early police intervention in stalking cases but is still a relatively new piece of legislation having only been introduced in January 2020 with limited evaluation as yet.

From a domestic abuse perspective, ex-partner stalkers are more persistent and dangerous than stranger stalkers but are less likely to be convicted of an offence (Scott and Sheridan, 2011; Scott et al., 2014). Of concern, research by Harris (2000) on the impact of the Protection of Harassment Act found that the Crown Prosecution Service was more likely to drop cases where the harassment was conducted by an intimate partner compared to an unknown perpetrator.

In the United States, the work by Klein et al. (2009) suggests that the police grossly under-identify stalking cases from reported domestic violence cases and often only identify stalking offences if they have attended a domestic incident previously where they have arrested the perpetrator. Training front-line police officers to recognise stalking behaviour is therefore paramount and any prevention work that can be undertaken to safeguard the intended victim should be taken at the earliest opportunity, utilising the full benefits of the new legislation where possible, particularly as a breach of an SPO is a criminal offence.

A relatively contemporary concept is that of cyberstalking, and in particular, the role technology plays in the escalation of domestic abuse even to the point of homicide. The work of Todd et al. (2021) explore this relatively new phenomenon finding that technology often plays a key role in domestic abuse, yet the digital footprints of the victim and perpetrator are often overlooked by policing. By considering offences such as stalking in the cyber sphere, there may be an opportunity to address behaviours without them escalating to homicide. This is clearly an important finding, and one which must be considered thoroughly as we move into an increasingly digital age. Digital enquiries should be a routine part of any case investigation, and behaviours identified as concerning as a result should be reviewed as part of the risk assessment. Moreover, investigators should be agile in their considerations of new technology that may be being utilised to stalk or harass victims and the assistance of Digital Media Investigators should always be requested in these circumstances. The digital world is changing at such a pace it is difficult for policing to keep up in order to protect victims and preempt criminal activity in any sphere, let alone one linked to domestic abuse. A lack of capability and capacity by policing to respond to cyberstalking and other technology-assisted crimes is of significant concern, with consideration of more resources to investigate digital domestic violence vital for the future (King-Ries, 2010).

The recognition that domestic abuse is now much more than a physical assault is so important. Whilst physical harm will always be at the forefront of the investigator's mind, the fact that there have been significant legislative changes over the past decade, as well as a continual evolvement of political, academic, and operational thinking to reframe and reflect on the different guises domestic abuse takes, means that the police are now much more adept and equipped to recognise domestic abuse in all its forms.

Policing domestic abuse

This section will consider how police resources are arranged within forces to address domestic abuse as well as the benefits and concerns of specialist domestic abuse units compared to dealing with domestic abuse in a more generalist fashion across uniform and investigation teams. The pervasiveness of domestic abuse means it is an everyday occurrence for policing across England and Wales with the most recent data from the Office for National Statistics (ONS, 2020) detailing the volume and extent of its omnipresence.

BOX 5.2 POLICING DOMESTIC ABUSE

- In the year ending March 2020, an estimated 2.3 million adults aged 16–74 years experienced domestic abuse in the last year.
- The police recorded 758,941 domestic abuse-related crimes in the year ending March 2020, an increase of 9% from the previous year.
- The police made 33 arrests per 100 domestic abuse-related crimes in the year ending March 2020.
- The charging rate in the year ending March 2020 was 73%, a small decrease compared with the previous year (74%).
- Over three-quarters of domestic abuse-related CPS prosecutions were successful in securing a conviction in the year ending March 2020 (78%), a similar level to the previous year.

With two women a week dying in the United Kingdom at the hands of someone with whom they have been intimately connected (Walby and Allen, 2004), the term homicide prevention could be used to describe why the police response to domestic abuse and violence is so important (Box 5.2). Jaffe et al. (2020) describe how domestic homicides are the most preventable of all homicides and lay out a critical evaluation of the factors drawn from numerous domestic homicide reviews to support this. It is therefore significant that there is police intervention at domestic abuse incidents, and with the additional assistance of multi-agency safeguarding attempts can be made to try and protect victims and their families and deal appropriately with perpetrators.

Yet worryingly, HMIC (2014) found significant weaknesses nationally in the police response to domestic abuse with limitations in the service provided to victims and domestic abuse a poor relation to acquisitive crime and serious organised crime. A concerted effort by Chief Constables and forces throughout England and Wales saw substantial improvements over the following years with domestic abuse critically being seen as a priority, and following the 2016 Police Effectiveness, Efficiency & Legitimacy (PEEL) inspections, the HMICFRS (2017) reported that progress was being made, albeit many forces still had much to do.

Forces saw a 60% increase in domestic abuse cases over the three years up to 2016 with it being presented as an unrelenting and increasing demand for the police (HMICFRS, 2017) with domestic abuse accounting for 35% of all violence against the person (ONS, 2020). It is a significant demand on policing and its stretched resources, but leaders are clear in the message that safeguarding the most vulnerable is the key priority for policing and police officers and staff must do everything they can to support victims of domestic abuse and deal appropriately with perpetrators.

There are, however, many differences in how individual police force areas deal with domestic abuse – from variations in the proportion of recorded crimes classified as domestic abuse, through to varying arrest rates, charges, and attrition, as well as the use of Clare's Law and Domestic Violence Protection Notices (HMICFRS, 2017). These civil powers will be discussed in more detail later in this chapter.

With varying levels of standardised practice throughout England and Wales it is the job of HMICFRS to identify and encourage improvement, but for victims of such crimes they should be confident in receiving a professional service at the point at which they contact the police.

Specialist vs generalist units

Domestic abuse is a large proportion of the police's work. It is a priority for all forces and is scrutinised regularly by HMICFRS and other bodies to ensure that responding effectively to domestic abuse is viewed as everybody's business not just that of specialists, with a positive culture embedded throughout policing to ensure victim safety is paramount and offenders are brought to justice. Officers are now much better equipped to deal with the nuances of domestic abuse through better training and improved understanding of the dynamics of domestic abuse and coercive control. Additionally, the impact on staff welfare of dealing with domestic abuse is now more recognised and support made routinely available, particularly through the Police Wellbeing Service Oscar Kilo (2021) (See Chapter 9).

From response policing through to homicide investigation, domestic abuse affects all policing departments. Many forces have specialist domestic abuse investigation units of some sort, whether they are standalone or part of wider public protection teams. Some forces however devolve domestic abuse according to crime type – so lower-level criminality stays with frontline response officers, whilst more serious offending is dealt with by the Criminal Investigation Department (CID). Whatever the make-up of the forces, the main priority should be clear lines of responsibility for victim care and risk assessment in every case, and also good supervision, training, co-ordination, and oversight of trends and intelligence. The Authorised Professional Practice (APP) for Domestic Abuse (College of Policing, 2020) and HMICFRS (2017) suggest that specialist teams are seen as providing a better quality of service because of their greater understanding of context, and therefore, the majority of police forces do focus on this crime type utilising specialist officers and staff.

Rumney et al. (2019) researched the performance of specialist units versus non-specialist units investigating rape offences and found that the specialist unit outperformed the non-specialist investigative approach in many, though not all, performance measures, including charging and 'reached court' rates in rape cases, as well as accuracy of crime recording. Whilst the research is not domestic abuse-specific, the findings reflect those found by HMICFRS (2017) in the United Kingdom and Regoeczi and Hubbard (2018) who conducted an examination of specialist domestic abuse units in the United States. They found that specialist provision has a significant positive impact on the number of domestic violence cases progressing through the criminal justice system, particularly due to the quality of provision to victims, and therefore should be considered when debating domestic abuse investigation (see Box 5.3).

BOX 5.3 SPECIALIST DOMESTIC ABUSE UNITS

In Thames Valley Police high risk Domestic Abuse investigations and all medium risk domestic abuse risk management are dealt with by the Domestic Abuse Investigation Unit (DAIU). These teams, placed in Local Police Area's throughout the force, work under the Protecting Vulnerable People Command. Led by a Detective Chief Inspector and Detective Inspector, a team of Detective Sergeants and Constables and suitable qualified Case Investigators work with the most vulnerable victims of domestic abuse. They engage closely with Independent Domestic Abuse Advisors and statutory and third sector partners to safeguard the victim and their family, obtain the best possible evidence for court from the victim and witnesses, and deal with the perpetrator appropriately. Many forces take this approach, but some forces share this work within their criminal investigation departments rather than having a bespoke unit.

Identification of best practice

Domestic abuse is core police business. The starting point begins at the initial call to the police. Call handling in domestic abuse cases is critical. The police receive a domestic violence-related call every 30 seconds, yet it is estimated that less than 24% of domestic violence crime is reported to the police (HMIC, 2014; Walby and Allen, 2004). Invariably domestic abuse victims are likely to have been subject to many incidents of abuse before seeking the courage to contact the police for the first time, as discussed in the research of Jaffe and Burris (1984) and Strang et al. (2014).

This may therefore be the first time a victim has had the courage to contact the police and an effective response will not only reassure them that they have made the right decision but potentially affect the criminal justice outcome in the long term. Ensuring the safety of the caller and other family members is paramount. Sending officers to the scene if required, either immediately or in slower time, and gathering the first pieces of the investigative puzzle are key activities. In most forces, police staff call takers rather than police officers answer the calls and are trained by the force using the College of Policing Authorised Professional Practice on Domestic Abuse (College of Policing, 2020) to complete the following initial assessment:

- Assess the nature, gravity, and circumstances of the call and the impact on the caller and any children.
- Consider what evidence may be lost if attendance is delayed and whether the victim is particularly vulnerable or likely to disengage.
- Consider any previous risk grading and any other information about further risk to the caller, such as pregnancy, Honour Based Abuse, recent separation, stalking, or escalating behaviour.
- Review the wishes of the victim and seek to maximise their safety and engagement.
- Initiate the completion of the DASH risk management form.

Initial attendance and the activity that follows will determine not only the trust of the victim in the police but also the likelihood of their engagement and ultimately their safety. The College of Policing Authorised Professional Practice on initial attendance and domestic abuse should be key guides for officers in this arena (College of Policing, 2020).

Identification of vulnerable adults and children at risk is of paramount importance, together with safeguarding the victim as appropriate. Often officers arrive at a scene to find both parties stating they are the victim. This can make it difficult in the initial stages to unpick the circumstances and any offences that have occurred, but as with all aspects of policing, the ultimate focus should be the independent gathering of evidence and the safety of all parties involved. Minimisation of what has occurred by the victim can also be a concern, particularly if children are present and they wish to hide or conceal the true impact of the abuse from them. A child who witnesses or is subject to domestic abuse themselves can suffer significant harm, and child protection procedures under Section 47 of the Children Act 1989 can be instigated if necessary to safeguard children subject to such abuse either physically or vicariously (Children Act, 1989).

Completion of the DASH risk assessment form must then take place to assess a number of issues from previous domestic abuse through to honour-based violence, sexual assault, firearms access of the perpetrator, and many other factors (see Chapter 4).

Conversations around the Domestic Violence Disclosure Scheme and Clare's Law, which allow the police to disclose information about a partner's previous history of domestic violence, or violent acts to a new partner, may also be relevant. Safety planning and working out together with the victim how they can keep themselves and their family safe both in the immediate aftermath and also in the longer term are critical. Consideration of

Domestic Violence Protection Notices and the signposting of statutory and third sector support is also necessary. These civil protections are discussed later in this chapter.

Discussions at this early stage with a victim around the collation of evidence and the practical impact of police involvement and the criminal justice system must be completed sensitively and carefully. Victim attrition is significant in domestic abuse cases (Barrow-Grint, 2016; Hester et al., 2006), and the factors affecting such attrition may already be present in the victims mind. Domestic abuse victims are eligible for special measures, and it is vitally important that the police use these measures to enable the victim to give their evidence in the best manner for them. Special measures are available at court for vulnerable and intimidated witnesses. This includes all children under the age of 18 and victims of domestic abuse. Within a court trial, special measures can be requested to support the victim or witness to give their evidence. They include measures such as giving evidence from behind screens or via video link, having access to an intermediary, and by the removal of wigs and gowns.

A clear explanation of special measures should always be given to a victim at the earliest opportunity. The possibility of utilising Section 28 of the Youth Justice and Criminal Evidence Act 1999 to allow a victim to have their evidence pre-recorded to negate attendance at trial is a relatively new special measure to be instigated and domestic abuse victims should be made aware of the provisions and implications. Whilst it may not be possible to discuss this with the victim on initial attendance, such support measures should be discussed at the earliest and most appropriate opportunity.

However, Hall (2007) suggests that some domestic abuse victims who choose to support the criminal justice process and attend court, often do not want to utilise many of the special measures available to them and often feel forced to do so leading to negative implications. Some victims, having made the decision to 'go to court' may want to physically see, and be seen, by the perpetrator, perhaps in order to recover some of the power and control lost during the violent episodes or relationship.

The collation of evidential material from the victim through witness statement and testimony should be supported by the accumulation of evidential material from all available areas. House to house, CCTV, forensics, medical evidence, digital investigation, and witness enquiries may elicit circumstantial or actual evidence of the abuse. Recently, though, body worn video has been utilised more frequently in domestic abuse cases. The benefits of new technology cannot be overestimated, and body worn video is an area which has developed significantly over the past decade in policing. Increased legitimacy and accountability, de-escalating conflict, and improved evidence capture are all advantages (Lister et al., 2018; Morrow et al., 2016). In relation to domestic abuse the outcomes are positive for criminal justice and victims alike where body worn video is utilised. Hester and

Westmarland's (2004) research suggests that photographic evidence is associated with higher arrest rates, victims more willing to give witness statements, and being less likely to subsequently withdraw their statements. The ability of the camera to capture not only the physical and emotional distress of the victim but also the destruction of domestic surroundings is significant in assisting the prosecution case (Nelson, 2013), particularly where the victim later retracts their support and an absent victim or evidence-based prosecution takes place.

Safeguarding victims and charging suspects outweighed the technical impact and organisational cost for police officers, with the added assistance of capturing evidence both from victims and scenes, making them a highly useful tool (Lister et al., 2018). The introduction of Digital Evidence Management Systems across policing will make the transfer of such material to stakeholders such as the CPS and Courts a simpler process going forward and can only be beneficial in terms of criminal justice impact.

Case building

Case building in domestic abuse investigations is paramount, as with any criminal prosecution. The speed at which the police can build the file and take the case to court can only be positive, particularly in terms of reducing victim disengagement. When building a domestic abuse case file, it is important to comply with the current guidelines in relation to content which are provided by the joint National Police Chiefs' Council & Crown Prosecution Service Evidence Gathering Checklist. This is for use by Police Forces and the Crown Prosecution Service in Cases of Domestic Abuse and is a useful document to guide an investigator through the key issues.

An in-depth secondary investigation of all parties involved should be completed, ensuring the investigation is intelligence led and enabling the identification of similar fact cases where similar offending has been alleged, and bad character evidence which pertains to a defendant's bad character being evidence of, or of a disposition towards, misconduct on his part under part 11 of the Criminal Justice Act 2003 (Crown Prosecution Service, 2021a). Other incidents that may not have been recognised as crimes previously, that now, in the context of the current investigation provide opportunities for additional charges to support the case should also be reviewed.

Aggravating factors (Box 5.4) should also be considered when requesting charging advice for a domestic-related crime such as abuse of trust, proven history of violence in domestic relationships, and the vulnerability of the victim. These factors have been identified by the Sentencing Council as having a particular bearing when a court is sentencing perpetrators of domestic abuse offences. Early identification and inclusion within the prosecution file is therefore paramount. Aggravating factors apply to all offenders aged 16 and older, regardless of the date of the offence (Sentencing Council, 2018).

BOX 5.4 AGGRAVATING FACTORS

- Any abuse of trust and abuse of power by the perpetrator.
- Any steps taken by the perpetrator to prevent the victim reporting an incident or obtaining assistance.
- Any proven history of violence or threats by the offender in a domestic context.
- Any history of disobedience to court orders.
- Any conduct or incident which has a particularly adverse impact on children.
- Any use of contact arrangements with a child to instigate an offence.
- Or in cases where the victim is especially vulnerable.
- Victim was forced to leave home, or steps had to be taken to exclude the offender from the home to ensure the victim's safety.

Even if the victim is fully supportive of the police investigation initially, victim attrition is still likely to be significant in many cases, and investigators should ensure they capture the best evidence to support an absent victim prosecution should the victim remove themselves from the criminal justice process at a later stage. This includes activity that could be deemed as 'hearsay' evidence as per the Criminal Justice Act 2003, whereby evidence is used to prove something at trial from a witness who is not in court to give that evidence themselves (Crown Prosecution Service, 2021b), but also all relevant digital and witness materials available.

Evidence led or absent victim prosecutions

Often so-called victimless prosecutions, an evidence-led or absent victim prosecution occurs when there is sufficient evidence to prosecute a criminal case, but the victim refuses to provide a statement, or having provided a statement, refuses to support police investigation or court proceedings.

There is much academic debate on whether evidence led, or absent victim prosecutions are beneficial or positive for the victim or not, but they are becoming more numerous and it is important to consider the implications. Complainant withdrawal in the context of domestic violence appears to have an almost singular effect, namely discontinuance, as police and prosecutors historically have rarely proceeded without victim engagement (Ellison, 2002). Hoyle (1998) also found that complainant withdrawal was crucial in the police decision-making around charge, and cases were unlikely to be taken forward for prosecution without a victim's support.

The complainant-reliant approach to prosecution (Ellison, 2002) meant that despite evidential or public interest grounds, many cases would fall if the victim refused to give evidence or support proceedings. The reasons for victim's withdrawal are discussed later in this chapter but it must be noted that in this context, progressing to prosecution without the complainant's support could be negative or positive for the victim. It could be argued that by taking the decision to proceed to court with a case against the victim's wishes is a further attack on any control they had obtained having disclosed the domestic abuse, and a powerful challenge to a victim's capability to make their own decisions. The impact on the victim is key to this (Ellison, 2002). However, it could also be suggested that the ability to proceed with absent victim prosecutions often allows the victim to portray an inability to stop events to the perpetrator, ensuring as much as possible their own safety as they give evidence against their will.

The concern for policing, however, must primarily be that investigators gather sufficient evidence at the initial stages of investigation to allow absent victim prosecutions to take place in the first instance. Police and prosecutors must then weigh up the impact of proceeding with a victimless prosecution on the victim themselves, particularly if they are ordered to give evidence at court by warrant and the long-term impact this may have not only on their trust in the authorities, in particular the police, but also on their mental health.

BOX 5.5 CASE STUDY – ABSENT VICTIM PROSECUTION

Victim Jenny, a female in her late 60s, had been married to Steven for over 40 years. Throughout that time she had been subject to domestic abuse but had never contacted the police because she 'thought too much' of Steven and didn't want to be alone. On one occasion, Steven subjected Jenny to a significant assault, breaking her eye socket and arm and causing severe bruising across her body. Jenny was in so much pain and she called a neighbour for help. The neighbour called police and Steven was arrested and charged with Grievous Bodily Harm. Jenny refused to go to court, but the evidence of her injuries, the neighbours witness statement, and Body Worn Video footage meant an absent victim prosecution could take place. Jenny's adult children withdrew from Jenny's life as she refused to go to court. They wanted her to take action having lived with domestic abuse all their lives. Steven pleaded guilty and was sentenced to eight years imprisonment. Without Steven and without the support of her children, Jenny had no one left. She was angry at the Police for 'ruining her life' and tried to commit suicide. Fortunately, this was unsuccessful, and Jenny received mental health support, but the impact the criminal justice intervention had on her life was significant and should not be underestimated, even when the evidence is overwhelming.

The case study in Box 5.5 emphasises the impact domestic abuse has on the mental health of victims. One third of female suicides are believed to be linked to domestic abuse (Walby, 2004), and the association between suicidal thoughts and prosecution (absent victim or otherwise) is explored in-depth by Munro and Aitken (2020). Their qualitative research suggests suicidal thoughts could be as high as 80% amongst domestic abuse victims. It is imperative therefore that police officers and critical partners reflect on the benefits and also the risks associated with pursing a court process without the victim's support.

Where a victim contacts the officer in the case to request an investigation or prosecution is dropped the following options should be explored:

- The case should be discontinued with an appropriate safety plan to support the victim.
- The case should continue as an absent victim prosecution because of other supporting evidence. The suspect faces a stiff penalty, the risks are grave, and the case can rely on other hearsay evidence.
- The case can continue to proceed but it is both necessary and appropriate in the circumstances for a witness summons to be obtained. Detail how the victim is likely to respond to this and consider the overall impact on the safety and well-being of the victim and their family before taking this option.

These options are only available however if, right from the start of a domestic abuse investigation, the collation of evidence is completed with the view that the case may have to be presented at court without the support of the victim. With this mindset, investigators can use all the tools at their disposal, from body worn video, hearsay evidence, and other evidential building blocks to ensure there is sufficient evidence to take the case through the court process, so perpetrators are brought to justice, with or without the victim's support. A consideration by the officer in the case in relation to the personal impact on a victim should be part of the decision-making process, with attempts to mitigate any risks raised through tailored victim support.

Specialist Domestic Abuse Courts

The court process is daunting for any victim or witness, but for those that have been subject to domestic abuse, reliving the crime in front of a magistrate or jury is not just about a recollection of events. The perpetrators' power and influence over the victim continues into the courtroom, and often the pressure of giving evidence is too much to bear given the underlying control factors in an abusive relationship. Recognising this issue, and the significant attrition rates associated with domestic abuse cases, Specialist Domestic Abuse or Violence Courts (SDVCs) were set up in 2005. This followed an evaluation of the initial pilot by Cook et al. (2004) which found that 'clustering' and 'fast-tracking' domestic violence cases enhanced the effectiveness of the court and support services for victims, it made advocacy and information-sharing easier to accomplish, and saw victim participation and satisfaction improve.

The Centre for Justice Innovation (2014) found that SDVCs increase successful prosecutions, speed up justice for victims, and keep them safe, but currently such courts are only available in the Magistrates court in England and Wales. Whilst seen as beneficial, SDVCs are limited by the fact that the principles of such a court are not being delivered consistently and differ widely from court to court, depending on the collaborative working of local partnerships. Eley (2005) goes further than this suggesting that the specialist domestic violence courts are less about process and more about people – they allow relationships and knowledge to build up to be able to best support the victim and indeed the alleged perpetrator, but this depends entirely on the people involved.

Synnott and Ioannou (2019) identify the impact of individuals on the success of specialist courts in their preliminary evaluation of a pilot scheme in Aylesbury Crown Court to introduce a specialist domestic abuse court in the Crown arena. Whilst SDVCs are relatively common in the Magistrates court, they are rare in the Crown Court. This pilot saw significant benefits, including the fast tracking of domestic abuse cases which fitted the pilot criteria, so they were heard within 14 days, an increase in guilty pleas and less victim attrition as well as an estimated significant reduction in criminal justice costs across all agencies.

Given the benefits of specialist courts at all levels in the domestic abuse arena, it is paramount that partnerships continue to advocate their use to ensure swift and fair justice is achieved. However, as Robinson and Cook (2007) discuss, even with such innovative courts and strong multi-agency partnerships, over half of all domestic abuse victims choose to retract from the criminal justice system, and this attrition issue will now be discussed in more detail.

Attrition rates

The Criminal Justice System continually develops how it deals with domestic violence, with a plethora of policy initiatives aimed at increasing prosecutions and convictions. CPS data on domestic abuse cases shows that in 2016–2017, unsuccessful outcomes due to victim issues reached 54%, with attrition mainly due to non-attendance at court (Crown Prosecution Service, 2017b). Whilst reducing attrition in domestic violence cases may be a key desire for all stakeholders, there are few studies which delve deeply into victim withdrawal or retraction from the criminal justice process (Hester et al., 2006; Robinson and Cook, 2007).

With estimates that only 24% of domestic violence crime is reported to the police (HMIC, 2014; Walby & Allen, 2004), reasons for not reporting often include feeling that the abuse suffered was too trivial or not worth reporting, believing that it was not the business of the police to interfere as it was a private matter, or even thinking that the police could not help. For cases that did not go to court, 37% of the respondents stated that they, the victim, decided not to take further action. Gracia (2004) suggests there are six key reasons why domestic abuse goes unreported, three of which are personal – embarrassment, fear of retaliation, and economic dependency – and three of which are societal – imbalanced power relations for men and women in society, privacy of the family, and victim blaming attitudes.

Once the hurdle of these factors is overcome and a victim reports to the police, the next challenge is keeping that victim on board during the investigation and any consequential criminal justice proceedings. Ellison (2002) delves into the rationales for withdrawing support from a prosecution, citing that victims may withdraw through:

- Fear of retaliatory violence.
- The controlling nature of the abuser.
- A desire to reconcile the relationship.
- Worrying about the economic and financial impact of a breakup.
- A perception that arrest will be sufficient to make the perpetrator change.
- A desire for the perpetrator to be treated rather than criminalised.

Similar themes are also drawn out by Barrow-Grint (2016) who also introduces the concept of temporal sequencing as a way of explaining attrition. When victims see time in a cyclical rather than linear fashion, they are more likely to remain in an abusive relationship and withdraw from any criminal or court proceedings as a result. Remaining in a cycle of abuse is common rather than being able to psychologically determine that by following the passage of time and seeing the criminal justice process through, the abuse is more likely to stop.

When considering attrition in domestic abuse cases, Hester (2006) found two key themes affecting attrition –victims contacted the authorities when they just wanted the immediate violence to stop, and they needed longer-term protection. So, for some victims, once police attended and stopped the ongoing attack, they did not want to progress to a police investigation or prosecution. This was verified in the qualitative findings of Barrow-Grint (2016, p. 10) where this was highlighted in the words of one victim who stated, "The Police were supportive, I needed help there and then, that's it".

Hester's (2006) second finding confirmed that many victims did want a longer-term solution, but frequently left the Criminal Justice Process due to frustrations at the length of time cases took. Bennett et al. (1999) concluded that misperceptions of the court process and fear of keeping themselves and family safe whilst awaiting a court process or believing that rehabilitation was required rather than criminal punishment also led to increased attrition in domestic abuse cases.

The 2018 Government Consultation into transforming the response to domestic abuse recognised the need to speed up court proceedings to improve victims' experiences and reduce attrition, by avoiding delays likely to cause victims to retract their statements (HM Government, 2018). Indeed, the work of Synnott & Ioannou (2019) in the fast tracking of domestic abuse cases into the Crown Court has shown the positive impact speed can have on reducing victim attrition, as well as the added benefits of cost savings for the criminal justice system as a whole.

What is clear is that every case will have different circumstances. Every victim will be at a different stage of capability in feeling strong enough to proceed to court where required, and police and other agencies must provide as much support as possible, as quickly as possible, to limit attrition in domestic abuse cases.

The civil law & domestic abuse

The civil law is a useful consideration when dealing with domestic abuse and can often complement the criminal law or be utilised to good effect when the criminal thresholds are not met or are not appropriate.

The Crime and Security Act 2010 introduced in England and Wales Domestic Violence Protection Notices (DVPNs) and Domestic Violence Protection Orders (DVPOs) which are short-term police-initiated protection measures, allowing victims time to consider their options when faced with a domestic abuse relationship. Despite being available since 2014, there is relatively little research regarding their use and effectiveness (Blackburn and Graca, 2020). They will be replaced in future by Domestic Abuse Protection Notices (DAPNs) and Domestic Abuse Protection Orders (DAPOs), but a review of their use and impact is worthy of debate here.

For a DVPN, evidence must suggest (including hearsay) that violence has been used or threatened but the threshold for a criminal prosecution is not met as there is not a realistic prospect of conviction as per the codes Crown prosecutors use to make this decision (Crown Prosecution Service, 2018). The alleged perpetrator must not be charged, bailed, or released under investigation in relation to the offence. A DVPN can only be sought where no further action is to be taken. A DVPN must be authorised by an officer of the rank of Superintendent to safeguard against any infringements of the alleged perpetrators' human rights (Burton, 2015) and the police must then make an application to the Magistrates court for a DVPO within 48 hours. If the Magistrates are satisfied on the balance of probabilities that a DVPO is required, one can be instated for between 14 and 28 days.

Restraining Orders under Section 5, Protection from Harassment Act 1997, and Non-Molestation Orders and Occupation Orders under the Family Law Act 1996 are other pieces of civil legislation that are useful to utilise in the domestic abuse environment. They are quite different to DVPNs and DVPOs however in a number of ways, for example, they can be requested for a much longer time period and a breach of a Restraining Order, Non-Molestation Order, or Occupation Order is a criminal offence, whereas breaches of DVPNs and DVPOs are not and are treated as contempt of court under s63 of the Magistrates' Court Act 1980 (Blackburn & Graca, 2020). The new DAPNs and DAPOs will change the position of all previous civil orders and are likely to become very beneficial once available. Benitez et al. (2010) found that although protection orders are not a 'panacea', they can serve a useful role in 'threat management' (managing the threat of violence posed by the perpetrator).

In 2014, Clare's Law or the Domestic Violence Disclosure Scheme (DVDS) was introduced giving members of the public the 'right to ask' the police about a new partner's history of domestic abuse and violence. The scheme was established after the murder in 2009 of Clare Wood by her former partner in Greater Manchester. Utilising common law powers, the DVDS scheme allows police to disclose information about a person's known history of violence or abuse to the public, where there is a pressing need for the disclosure of the information in order to protect and safeguard any individual who may be at risk of harm of domestic abuse of violence (Davies and Biddle, 2018; Home Office, 2016). Hadjimatheou and Grace (2021) raise significant concerns however over the lack of empirical research into the Domestic Violence Disclosure Scheme and a current 'postcode lottery' in terms of the response individuals get from different police forces across the country. They call for more regulation and better sharing of best practice to improve consistency and outcomes for victims.

Such concern about outcomes for victims has also been raised in a police super-complaint by the Centre for Women's Justice (2019) which focussed on a lack of use of protective measures such as civil orders and bail conditions. A joint investigation by HM Inspectorate of Constabulary and Fire & Rescue Services (HMICFRS), the Independent Office for Police Conduct (IOPC), and the College of Policing (2021) found that the police should change their approaches to using protective measures to safeguard women and girls as they are not always utilised effectively. The ramifications of this investigation are still being understood, but clearly policing must continue to review, reflect, and continuously improve upon how it deals with domestic abuse.

Conclusion

This chapter focussed on domestic abuse and the criminal justice system, reviewing how societal culture has changed over time to now view domestic abuse as a crime rather than a private family matter, and the importance of this transformation of views in order to utilise the law effectively to safeguard victims which in turn ensures murder prevention.

Criminal legislation has been slow to change, with the example of marital rape not being repealed until the early 1990s, yet 30 years later the Domestic Abuse Act 2021 is much more agile to deal with the detrimental impact domestic abuse has not only on the victim but also on society as a whole.

The use of legislation to deal with domestic abuse was the main focus of this chapter, with a look at the different methodologies forces use to investigate domestic abuse, the necessity for the finest case building to ensure success at court, the importance of evidence gathering when there is highly likely to be victim disengagement, and the requirement to speed up the whole of the criminal justice process, but particularly in the courts, to reduce attrition at each and every stage.

It is important to recognise that domestic abuse is one of the largest crime types policing must deal with. There will be an impact on the well-being of the officers and staff having to deal with such cases. There will be fatigue about the misconception that victims should just leave, there will be police officers who have been victims or witnesses to domestic abuse in their own lives, and there will be victims and perpetrators from every walk of life. What is important is that when a victim decides to contact the police, they are supported throughout the criminal justice process and given the best possible service to try and prevent them from becoming the next homicide victim.

Reflective questions

- How valuable are civil orders in cases of domestic abuse – what are the benefits and concerns?
- How much consideration should be given to the victims' viewpoint in terms of absent victim prosecutions?
- Should honour-based violence, forced marriage, and FGM be considered as domestic abuse or not?
- Is domestic abuse a wicked problem?

Useful websites

College of Policing – Approved Professional Practice
https://www.app.college.police.uk/app-content/major-investigation-and-public-protection/domestic-abuse

Domestic Abuse Act 2021: Domestic Abuse Act 2021: overarching factsheet – GOV.UK
www.gov.uk

Home Office: The economic and social costs of domestic abuse
https://www.gov.uk/government/publications/the-economic-and-social-costs-of-domestic-abuse

National Police Chiefs Council & Crown Prosecution Service Evidence Gathering Checklist for use by Police Forces and the Crown Prosecution Service in Cases of Domestic Abuse
https://www.cps.gov.uk/sites/default/files/documents/publications/npcc_cps_joint_evidence_gathering_checklist_2015.docm

References

Barlow, C., Walklate, S., Johnson, K., Humphreys, L., Kirby, S., 2018. Police responses to coercive control. Published online N 8, 76. https://documents.manchester.ac.uk/display.aspx?DocID=56477

Barrow-Grint, K., 2016. Attrition rates in domestic abuse: time for a change? An application of temporal sequencing theory. *Policing: A Journal of Policy and Practice* 10, 250–263.

Benitez, C.T., McNiel, D.E., Binder, R.L., 2010. Do protection orders protect? *Journal of the American Academy of Psychiatry and the Law Online* 38, 376–385.

Bennett, L., Goodman, L., Dutton, M.A. 1999. Systemic obstacles to the criminal prosecution a battering partner: A victims perspective. *Journal of Interpersonal Violence* 14(7), 761–772.

Blackburn, K. & Graca, S. 2020. 'A critical reflection on the use and effectiveness of DVPNs and DVPOs' in *Police Practice and Research: An International Journal* Published Online: https://doi.org/10.1080/15614263.2020.1759059

Burton, M., 2015. Emergency barring orders in domestic violence cases: What can England and Wales learn from other European countries. *Child and Family Law Quarterly* 27, 25.

Burton, M., 2008. Legal responses to domestic violence. Routledge-Cavendish.

Centre for Justice Innovation, 2014. A snapshot of specialist domestic violence courts. https://justiceinnovation.org/publications/snapshot-specialist-domestic-violence-courts (accessed 11.6.21).

Centre for Women's Justice, 2019. Police Super Complaint – Police failure to use protective measures in cases involving violence against women and girls. Centre for Women's Justice.

Children Act, 1989. Children act 1989. Statute Law Database.

College of Policing, 2020. Authorised professional practice on domestic abuse. https://www.app.college.police.uk/app-content/major-investigation-and-public-protection/domestic-abuse/ (accessed 11.6.21).

Cook, D., Burton, M., Robinson, A., Vallely, C., 2004. *Evaluation of Specialist Domestic Violence Courts/Fast Track Systems.* London: Crown Prosecution Service. http://www.cps. gov.uk/publications/docs/specialistdvcourts.pdf

Crown Prosecution Service, 2021a. Bad character evidence | The Crown Prosecution Service. cps.gov.uk (accessed 6.3.22).

Crown Prosecution Service, 2021b. Hearsay. The Crown Prosecution Service (cps.gov.uk).cps.gov.uk (accessed 6.3.22).

Crown Prosecution Service, 2020a. *Domestic abuse guidelines for prosecutors.* Crown Prosecution Service.

Crown Prosecution Service, 2020b. *Honour based violence and forced marriage.* Crown Prosecution Service.

Crown Prosecution Service, 2020c. *Stalking protection orders.* Crown Prosecution Service.

Crown Prosecution Service, 2019. *Female genital mutilation guidance.* Crown Prosecution Service.

Crown Prosecution Service, 2018. *The code for crown prosecutors.* Crown Prosecution Service. cps.gov.uk (accessed 6.3.22).

Crown Prosecution Service, 2017a. *Controlling or coercive behaviour in an intimate or family relationships.* Crown Prosecution Service.

Crown Prosecution Service, 2017b. *Violence against women and girls crime report: Tenth edition.* Crown Prosecution Service.

Davies, P.A., Biddle, P., 2018. Implementing a perpetrator-focused partnership approach to tackling domestic abuse: The opportunities and challenges of criminal justice localism. *Criminology & Criminal Justice* 18, 468–487.

Dennison, S.M., 2007. Interpersonal relationships and stalking: Identifying when to intervene. *Law and Human Behavior* 31, 353–367.

Dressler, J., Strong, F.R., Michael Moritz, E., 2001. *Understanding criminal law.* Carolina Academic.

Eley, S., 2005. Changing practices: The specialised domestic violence court process. *The Howard Journal of Criminal Justice* 44, 113–124.

Ellison, L., 2002. Prosecuting domestic violence without victim participation. *The Modern Law Review* 65, 834–858.

Erez, E., 2002. Domestic violence and the criminal justice system: An overview. *Online Journal of Issues in Nursing* 7, 4.

Fagan, J., 1996. *The criminalization of domestic violence: Promises and limits.* US Department of Justice, Office of Justice Programs, National Institute of Justice.

FCO, 2013. *Forced marriage.* Foreign and Commonwealth Office.

Finkelhor, D., Yllö, K., 1987. *License to rape: Sexual abuse of wives.* Simon and Schuster.

Gill, A.K., Cox, P., Weir, R., 2018. Shaping priority services for UK victims of honour-based violence/abuse, forced marriage, and female genital mutilation. *The Howard Journal of Crime and Justice* 57, 576–595.

Gracia, E., 2004. *Unreported cases of domestic violence against women: towards an epidemiology of social silence, tolerance, and inhibition.* BMJ Publishing Group Ltd.

Grint, K., 2010 Wicked problems and clumsy solutions: the role of leadership, in: *The New Public Leadership Challenge.* Springer, pp. 169–186.

Groves, N., Thomas, T., 2014. *Domestic violence and criminal justice.* Routledge.

Gubi, P.M.E., 2015. *Listening to less-heard voices: Developing counsellor's awareness.* University of Chester Press.

Hadjimatheou, K., Grace, J., 2021. 'No Black and White answer about how far we can go': Police decision making under the domestic violence disclosure scheme. *Policing and Society* 31, 834–847.

Hague, G.M., Malos, E.M., Wilton, T., 2005. *Domestic violence: Action for change.* New Clarion Press.

Hale, M., Dogherty, T., 1736. The history of the pleas of the crown, in: *Two Volumes – Volume 1: Sollom Emlyn.* Printed by E. Rider, Little Britain. https://books.google.co.uk/books?id=2HfVyAEACAAJ&printsec=frontcover&source=gbs_ge_summary_r&cad=0#v=onepage&q&f=false

Hall, M., 2007. The use and abuse of special measures: Giving victims the choice? *Journal of Scandinavian Studies in Criminology and Crime Prevention* 8, 33–53.
Harris, J., 2000. An evaluation of the use and effectiveness of the protection from Harassment Act 1997. Home Office Research, Development and Statistics Directorate.
Hester, M., Westmarland, N., 2004. *Tackling street prostitution: Towards a holistic approach.* Home Office Research, Development and Statistics Directorate.
Hester, M., Westmarland, N., Gangoli, G., Wilkinson, M., O'Kelly, C., Kent, A., Diamond, A., 2006. Domestic violence perpetrators: Identifying needs to inform early intervention. Northern Rock Foundation.
HM Government, 2018. Transforming the response to domestic abuse: Government consultation. HM Government.
HM Government, 2016. Ending violence against women and girls (VAWG) strategy 2016–2020. HM Government, p. 44.
HM Government, 2022. A duty to protect: Police Use of protective measures in cases involving violence against women and girls. HM Government (www.gov.uk).
HMIC, 2014. *Everyone's business: Improving the police response to domestic abuse.* London: Her Majesty's Inspectorate of Constabulary.
HMICFRS, 2017. Progress report on the police response to domestic abuse. HMICFRS.
Home Office, 2013. New government domestic violence and abuse definition (Home Office Circular No. 0032). Home Office.
Home Office, 2015. Controlling or coercive behaviour, statutory guidance. Home Office.
Home Office, 2016. Domestic violence disclosure scheme (DVDS) guidance. Home Office.
Home Office, 2019a. The economic and social costs of domestic abuse. https://www.gov.uk/government/publications/the-economic-and-social-costs-of-domestic-abuse (accessed 11.6.21).
Home Office, 2019b. Ending violence against women and girls 2016–2020 strategy. Home Office.
Home Office, 2020. Forced marriage unit statistics 2019. Home Office.
Home Office, 2021. Domestic abuse act 2021. Overarching factsheet. GOV.UK. www.gov.uk (accessed 11.6.21).
Hoppe, S.J., Zhang, Y., Hayes, B.E., Bills, M.A., 2020. Mandatory arrest for domestic violence and repeat offending: A meta-analysis. *Aggression and Violent Behavior* 53, 1359–1789.
House of Lords, 1991. R v R. Retrieved from: http://www.bailii.org/uk/cases/UKHL/1991/12.html (Accessed 22.9.20).
Hoyle, C., 1998. *Negotiating domestic violence: Police, criminal justice, and victims.* Claredon Press.
Incorporated Council of Law Reporting, 2022. Index card R v R (Rape: Marital exemption) – ICLR (accessed 6.3.22).
Jackson, N., 2007. *Encyclopaedia of domestic violence.* Routledge.
Jaffe, P., Scott, K., Straatman, A.-L., 2020. Future directions on promoting domestic homicide prevention in diverse populations, in Jaffe, P. Scott, K. & Straatman, A. (eds), *Preventing Domestic Homicides.* Elsevier, pp. 281–297.

Jaffe, P.G., Burris, C.A., 1984. An integrated response to wife assault: A community model. Ministry of the Solicitor General of Canada Ottawa.

Jenkins, P.J., Davidson, B.P., 2001. *Stopping domestic violence: How a community can prevent spousal abuse.* Springer Science & Business Media.

King-Ries, A., 2010. Teens, technology, and cyberstalking: The domestic violence wave of the future. *Texas Journal of Women and the Law* 20, 131.

Klein, A., Salomon, A., Huntington, N., Dubois, J., Lang, D., 2009. Statewide study of stalking and its criminal justice response. US Department of Justice Report.

Lees, S., 2000. Marital rape and marital murder, in: Hanmer, J. & Itzen, C. (Eds), *Home Truths About Domestic Violence: Feminist Influences on Policy and Practice: A Reader*, pp. 57–74.

Lister, S., Burn, D., Pina-Sanchez, J., 2018. Exploring the impacts of police use of body-worn video cameras as incidents of domestic abuse. N8 Policing Research Partnership.

Malik, Y., Rowland, A., Gerry, F., Phipps, F.M., 2018. Mandatory reporting of female genital mutilation in children in the UK. *British Journal of Midwifery* 26, 377–386.

Morrow, W.J., Katz, C.M., Choate, D.E., 2016. Assessing the impact of police body-worn cameras on arresting, prosecuting, and convicting suspects of intimate partner violence. *Police Quarterly* 19, 303–325.

Munro, V.E., Aitken, R., 2020. From hoping to help: Identifying and responding to suicidality amongst victims of domestic abuse. *International Review of Victimology* 26, 29–49.

Myhill, A., 2015. Measuring coercive control: What can we learn from national population surveys? *Violence Against Women* 21, 355–375.

National Police Chiefs Council, 2015. *Honour based abuse, forced marriage, and female genital mutilation: A policing strategy for England, Wales and Northern Ireland – Eradicating honour based abuse, Forced Marriage, and female genital mutilation.* National Police Chiefs Council.

Nelson, E.L., 2013. Police controlled antecedents which significantly elevate prosecution and conviction rates in domestic violence cases. *Criminology & Criminal Justice* 13, 526–551.

ONS, 2020. Domestic abuse prevalence and trends, England and Wales – Office for National Statistics. https://www.ons.gov.uk/peoplepopulationandcommunity/crimeandjustice/articles/domesticabuseprevalenceandtrendsenglandandwales/yearendingmarch2020#crime-survey-for-england-and-wales (accessed 9.7.21).

ONS, 2019. Improving victimisation estimates derived from the Crime Survey for England and Wales – Office for National Statistics. https://www.ons.gov.uk/peoplepopulationandcommunity/crimeandjustice/articles/improvingvictimisationestimatesderivedfromthecrimesurveyforenglandandwales/2019-01-24 (accessed 3.17.19).

Oscar Kilo, 2021. Evidence base & best practice for emergency services wellbeing. *Oscar Kilo.* https://oscarkilo.org.uk/ (accessed 8.5.21).

Regoeczi, W.C., Hubbard, D.J., 2018. The impact of specialized domestic violence units on case processing. *American Journal of Criminal Justice* 43, 570–590.

Robinson, A., Cook, D., 2007. *Understanding victim retraction in cases of domestic violence: Specialist courts, government policy, and victim-centred justice.* Contemporary Justice Review.

Robinson, A.L., Pinchevsky, G.M., Guthrie, J.A., 2016. Under the radar: Policing non-violent domestic abuse in the US and UK. *International Journal of Comparative and Applied Criminal Justice* 40, 195–208.

Rogers, M., Rumley, T., Lovatt, G., 2019. The change up project: Using social norming theory with young people to address domestic abuse and promote healthy relationships. *Journal of Family Violence* 34, 507–519.

Rumney, P.N., McPhee, D., Fenton, R.A., Williams, A., 2019. *A police specialist rape investigation unit: A comparative analysis of performance and victim care.* Policing and Society.

Russell, K.J., Hand, C.J., 2017. Rape myth acceptance, victim blame attribution and just world beliefs: A rapid evidence assessment. *Aggression and Violent Behavior* 37, 153–160.

Salihu, H.M., August, E.M., Salemi, J.L., Weldeselasse, H., Sarro, Y.S., Alio, A.P., 2012. The association between female genital mutilation and intimate partner violence. *BJOG: An International Journal of Obstetrics & Gynaecology* 119, 1597–1605.

Scott, A.J., Gavin, J., Sleath, E., Sheridan, L., 2014. The attribution of responsibility in cases of stalking. *Psychology, Crime & Law* 20, 705–721.

Scott, A.J., Sheridan, L., 2011. 'Reasonable' perceptions of stalking: The influence of conduct severity and the perpetrator–target relationship. *Psychology, Crime & Law* 17, 331–343.Sentencing Council, 2018. Domestic abuse sentencing guidelines. Sentencing Council.

Sexual Offences Act, 2003. legislation.gov.uk (accessed 6.3.22)

Sheridan, L., Davies, G.M., 2001. What is stalking? The match between legislation and public perception. *Legal and Criminological Psychology* 6, 3–17.

Simpson, J., Robinson, K., Creighton, S.M., Hodes, D., 2012. Female genital mutilation: the role of health professionals in prevention, assessment, and management. *BMJ* 344: e1361. doi:10.1136/bmj.e1361

Stark, E., 2020. The 'coercive control framework': Making law work for women, in: McMahon, M., McGorrery, P. (Eds.), *Criminalising Coercive Control: Family Violence and the Criminal Law.* Springer, pp. 33–49.

Stark, E., 2007. *Coercive control: How men entrap women in personal life.* Oxford University Press.

Strang, H., Neyroud, P., Sherman, L., 2014. Tracking the evidence for a 'mythical number': Do UK domestic abuse victims suffer an average of 35 assaults before someone calls the police? *Policing: A Journal of Policy and Practice* 8, 222–228.

Synnott, J. & Ioannou, M., 2019. An Evaluation of the 'Protocol for the Handling of Domestic Abuse Cases at Aylesbury Crown Court'. University of Huddersfield Research Portal.

Todd, C., Bryce, J., Franqueira, V.N., 2021. Technology, cyberstalking and domestic homicide: Informing prevention and response strategies. *Policing and Society* 31, 82–99.

Tolmie, J.R., 2018. Coercive control: To criminalize or not to criminalize? *Criminology & Criminal Justice* 18, 50–66.

Walby, S., 2004. The cost of domestic violence. Women and Equality Unit.

Walby, S., Allen, J., 2004. Domestic violence, sexual assault and stalking: Findings from the British Crime Survey. Home Office.

Walby, S., Towers, J., Francis, B., 2014. Mainstreaming domestic and gender-based violence into sociology and the criminology of violence. *The Sociological Review* 62, 187–214.
Westmarland, N., 2004. Rape law reform in England and Wales. School for Policy Studies Working Paper Series – Paper 7.
Wiener, C., 2017. Seeing what is 'invisible in plain sight': Policing coercive control. *The Howard Journal of Crime and Justice* 56, 500–515.
Womens' Aid, 2016. Launch of "Nineteen Child Homicides" report and child first campaign. *Womens Aid.* https://www.womensaid.org.uk/launch-of-nineteen-child-homicides-report-child-first-campaign/ (accessed 2.11.19).
World Health Organisation, 2020. *Female genital mutilation.* WHO.
Young, H., Long, S.J., Melendez-Torres, G.J., Kim, H.S., Hewitt, G., Murphy, S., Moore, G.F., 2021. Dating and relationship violence victimization and perpetration among 11–16 year olds in Wales: A cross-sectional analysis of the School Health Research Network (SHRN) survey. *Journal of Public Health* 43, 111–122.

Chapter 6

Victims

KEY POINTS

- Homelessness is a key issue for domestic abuse victims.
- Understanding different inequalities, such as gender, race, ethnicity, and disability, identifies vulnerable victims.
- Victims of domestic violence include those over the age of 60 as well as those under the age of 16.
- Men can also be victims of domestic violence.
- Children can be adversely affected by living in a violent household.

Introduction

This chapter considers the victims of domestic abuse. It highlights the needs and vulnerabilities of victims and how abuse can be hidden under other social variables. For many years victims were stereotyped as hysterical women but as detailed below domestic abuse is spread across all sections of society, and it is essential that police and other professionals recognise that there is not a singular 'victim' type where domestic abuse is concerned.

It is important to appreciate the multifarious problems that can result from violence in the household, especially where other inequalities or social locations are present. Identifying victims and managing risk are far from straightforward, and many victims are not highlighted by the police but by other partnership agencies. The Crime Survey in England and Wales (CSEW) found that 73% of victims confide in family and friends, only turning to police and official agencies when this support mechanism fails (Weir, 2020). So many victims never come to the attention of the criminal justice system but are managed by various support groups – at least until a major crisis occurs. Even then not every victim wants their abuse resolved by a criminal justice approach but may choose to seek an alternative pathway to support.

For example, within health there are several places where victims may disclose abuse or seek support. The CSEW found that of those who received medical attention as a result of their abuse the majority (83.1%) were seen

DOI: 10.4324/9781003137412-6

at a GPs surgery, 36.4% at a specialist mental health or psychiatric service, and 12.2% had gone to accident and emergency departments (the figures add up to more than 100% because some victims sought support from more than one service). As pregnancy has been found to be a risk factor, maternity services proactively ask pregnant women if they are experiencing abuse. Independent Domestic Violence Adviser (IDVA) (see Chapters 3 and 8) services are available in some health settings both to counsel the victim and to initiate appropriate support mechanisms. Another areas of health where domestic abuse may be disclosed or reported are through health visitors who work in the community and are well placed to guide victims to specialist organisations for expert advice.

The COVID-19 pandemic has seen a move to virtual health appointments either online or on the telephone. Although NICE (2016) provides full guidance to health professionals and others when dealing with domestic abuse, SafeLives (2020) have developed some practical tools including the five Rs, particularly useful when discussing domestic abuse with clients remotely – Recognise (and ask), Respond, Risk assess, Refer, and Record.

Since only 21% of victims report to the police (CSEW), other agencies have contact with the vast majority and this can present some issues for local provision and support.

First, it begs the question why don't victims report to the police? The CSEW found a quarter of respondents felt police were unable to help or support them. Many feared stories would be disbelieved or their crime 'downgraded' (HMIC, 2014).

Second, there is no 'joined up' data collection between the various agencies involved. Therefore, estimating the extent, or indeed types, of domestic abuse in any area is problematic and indeed, there is the danger that victims will become lost in the system. Data is collected in some agencies and not particularly well in others, and it is not always measured in the same way. The information is often not shared between agencies, unless victims are under multi-agency arrangements, such as a Multi-Agency Risk Assessment Conference (MARAC) (see Chapter 8 for further discussion). Therefore, it is difficult to tell the number of agencies that an individual victim might be engaged with or if they are known to any at all (Weir, 2020).

Third, there is also a danger of assuming that the iceberg of 'unknown victims' have the same or similar profile to those identified in official data. This presents further difficulties for those who must select and commission services. We do know that there is no set victim type and the stereotype of the 'ideal victim' often assumed in social and some professional circles is not helpful. Recently this myth has been partly eroded by the inclusion of stories concerning domestic violence on the Archers, EastEnders, and the #MeToo campaign. It is social changes such as these that support difference and work towards acknowledging the problems that individual victims encounter.

Understanding victims

The issues and concerns that arise for victims of domestic abuse sometimes get side-lined or forgotten if an intersectional approach is not used. An intersectional approach makes sure that multiple inequalities are considered together including race, gender, class, sexuality, and immigrant status (UN Women, 2020) and it recognises that the way in which women are marginalised through these characteristics leads to considerable variation in their experiences (Groves and Thomas, 2014). Strid et al. (2013) believe that recognising intersectionality is particularly important in producing good quality policy that reaches all women and ensures all can access support services.

Strid et al. (2013) found three ways to ensure that inequalities are visible. First, by the naming of multiple inequalities, as Day and Gill confirm,

> . . . the threat of violence from an intimate partner remains one form of oppression among many for numerous survivors and failing to take account of these various oppressions place such survivors at further risk.
>
> (2020, p. 847)

Second, acknowledgment by professionals of the effect that numerous inequalities have on victims is crucial. Again, as Day and Gill suggest, domestic abuse victims who are faced with several structural inequalities encounter ". . .additional issues and pressures" (2020, p. 831) sometimes negating or at the very least blurring the level of risk they face unless the multiple intersections are recognised.

Third, including the victims' voices – and especially ". . .minoritised women" in the policy-making process creates the ". . . strongest form of visibility and inclusion" (Strid et al., 2013, p. 559) and can challenge both policy and practice.

Victims are often affected by multiple inequalities, and this in turn impacts their visibility to others, their reaction to domestic violence, and their response to professionals and Non-Governmental Organisations (NGOs). Some of these factors are considered below alongside what pathways are required in order to ensure they are better protected. Agencies working together (see Chapter 8) offer a more holistic approach to understanding, for instance, the impact of homelessness and the implications of extra social inequalities such as age, ethnicity, gender, sexuality, and disability. As Robinson and Payton point out:

> Many models of multi-agency practice are likely to be in operation even within a single geographical area, involving different combinations of professionals, each with their own aims and objectives. Many of these interagency networks will focus specifically on domestic violence victims as clients whilst others will provide a different type of service that touches on their experience in some way.
>
> (2016, p. 254)

Housing and homelessness

Domestic abuse is one of the key causes of homelessness, particularly for women (Menard, 2001; St Mungos, 2014). In 2018 domestic abuse contributed to homelessness for at least one in ten people who required local authority support (Department for Communities and Local Government, 2018). Temporary emergency housing may be provided by refuges (see Box 6.1), but ideally local authorities try to seek longer term solutions.

BOX 6.1 REFUGES

There are over 500 refuges in the United Kingdom. Some victims may contact a refuge directly if they need urgent support, whilst others may be referred from another agency. Refuges provide emergency accommodation for those fleeing abuse, but they also undertake outreach work in the community to keep victims safe within their own homes. At the national level there are two main organisations, Women's Aid and Refuge. There are also local organisations providing shelters as well as those that offer specialist support to victims experiencing certain types of abuse or requiring culturally specific services. Women's Aid has a directory of refuges run by local authorities, which include those that offer specialist support for men and women with children.

Refuge also hosts the 24-Hour National Domestic Abuse Helpline.

Housing providers are key partners in Multi-Agency Risk Assessment Conferences (MARAC – see Chapter 8) providing shelter to victims. The Housing Act 1977 gave housing departments of district and borough councils the statutory responsibility to house all victims fleeing domestic abuse. This legislation was updated to become the Housing Act 1996 and Homelessness Act 2002, and these acts require somebody to be treated as homeless if they are seen to be at risk of domestic violence or abuse (Shelter, 2018).

A possible link has been identified between reports of anti-social behaviour and domestic abuse, as 40% of tenants who have suffered domestic abuse have had complaints made against them for anti-social behaviour (Jackson, 2013). But domestic abuse remains an entrenched problem with victims experiencing abuse for an average of three years before engaging with support services (Safelives, 2015). This places housing providers in an ideal position to identify any domestic abuse acting early as a first point of contact. For instance, this could be the maintenance officer raising concerns after discovering a door has been kicked in, or an investigation by a housing officer into a noise nuisance complaint made by a neighbour. Key to pushing this work forward has been the Domestic Abuse Housing Alliance

(DAHA), which is a partnership formed between three agencies: Gentoo, Peabody – both are housing associations – and Standing Together, which is a national domestic abuse charity. The aim of the partnership is to improve responses of the housing sector to domestic abuse (DAHA, 2018). Given the strategic position of housing providers they are often invited to Community Safety Partnerships (CSPs), which are made up of responsibility authorities (police, local authorities, fire and rescue services, health and probation services). The CSPs have a responsibility to work together to protect local communities from crime and make people feel safer. Although housing providers are not responsible authorities, they are often members of CSPs as they form an important link between social housing and victims of domestic abuse. Box 6.2 gives an example of how the CSP in Colchester is structured.

BOX 6.2 SAFER COLCHESTER PARTNERSHIPS

SAFER
COLCHESTER
PARTNERSHIP

The Safer Colchester Partnership (SCP) is the Community Safety Partnership for the Colchester Borough Council area of Essex. The partnership produces an annual strategic assessment of crime, using a risk matrix and analysis of hidden harm areas and partnership data to identify its priorities. Membership of the SCP comprises six statutory representatives from the responsible authorities which are Colchester Borough Council, Essex County Council, Essex County Fire and Rescue Service, Essex Police, and NHS including the East of England Ambulance Service and the National Probation Service. There are also four other organisations that are members who are not responsible authorities, these are Colchester Borough Homes, Colchester Garrison, Community 360, and the University of Essex. From April 2019 to March 2020 there were three priorities that SCP focussed on, one of these was to increase confidence in identifying and reporting hidden harms, which included domestic abuse (Safer Colchester Partnership, 2021).

Gender and sexuality

Despite the academic and policy focus on females, men and boys can also be victims of domestic abuse, in both heterosexual and gay relationships. In 2018 25% of all domestic abuse recorded by police forces in England and Wales involved male victims (Mankind, 2020) and 13.8% of men reported to the CSEW that they had been a victim of domestic abuse at least once since the age of 16, compared to 27.6% of women (ONS, 2020a). Figure 6.1 shows that whilst there were fewer male victims of domestic homicide, there are very similar proportions of male and female suspects (53% and 47%, respectively), which differs from female victims, where 85% of suspects are male. The relationship between the victim and the suspect also differs when both are male, 86% of suspects revealed as either a parent or other family member. When the male victim is killed by a female suspect 85% are partners or ex-partners.

It can be difficult for men to identify themselves as a victim or survivor of the crimes framed with the VAWG Strategy, which remain largely hidden. Harmful gender norms, shame or honour, and stereotypes of masculinity and sexuality can act as barriers for male victims and survivors to seek support and can impact on reporting. For example, some male victims have found that harmful gender stereotypes around masculinity prevent them from discussing these issues or 'reaching out for help until they're in crisis' (HM Government, 2019, p. 2).

There are fewer services for male victims of domestic abuse and those that do exist tend to be largely helpline based. In the United Kingdom the ManKind Initiative is a specialist charity that focusses on male victims.

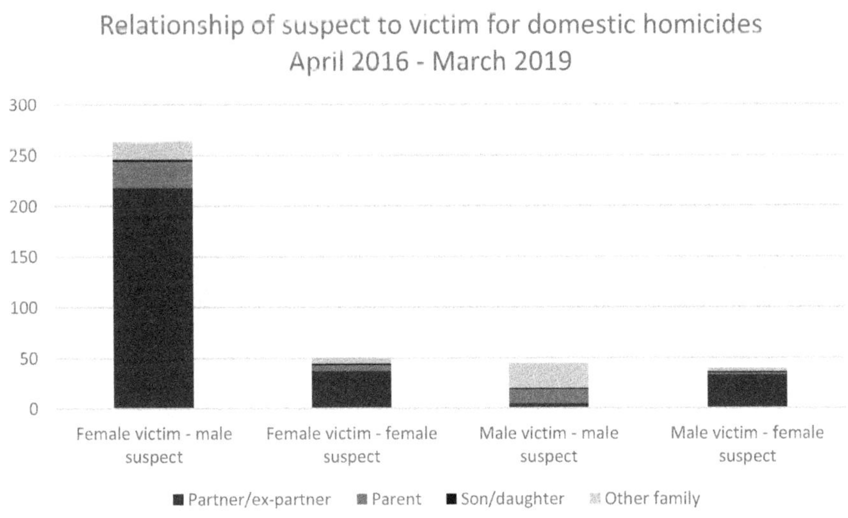

Figure 6.1 Relationship of suspect to victim for domestic homicides.

The charity works in partnership with other organisations to provide support and has three main activities: first, it provides a national helpline; second, it campaigns for better support, recognition, and understanding of male victims; and finally, it aims to give male victims a voice by engaging with stakeholders including the government, statutory agencies, and the media (ManKind, 2020). Another specialist service is the Respect Men's Advice Line. This organisation provides a confidential helpline, email, and webchat service for male victims of domestic abuse (Respect Men's advice line, 2020). There are only a small number of organisations that offer refuge or safe house provision for male victims of domestic abuse, and ManKind estimates that there are only 78 spaces in the whole of the United Kingdom (ManKind, 2020).

Most of the published data on domestic abuse focusses on heterosexual relationships. However, as can be seen in the domestic homicide data above (Figure 6.1), abuse also takes place in Lesbian, Gay, Bisexual, and Transexual (LGBT) relationships. There are currently no published CSEW reports on sexual orientation and the prevalence of abuse, but the US National Intimate Partner and Sexual Violence Survey found that lesbian and gay men had equal or higher levels of intimate personal violence than those of heterosexual men and women. Bisexual women had significantly higher prevalence of rape, physical violence, and/or stalking by an intimate partner, when compared to heterosexual and lesbian women (Black et al., 2011). Research by the Scottish Trans Alliance found that 80% of transgender people had experienced some form of emotional, sexual, or physical abusive behaviour by a partner or ex-partner. However, only 60% named this as domestic abuse. Of the different types of abuse the most frequent was transphobic emotion abuse, with 73% of respondents having experienced at least one form of transphobic emotional abuse (Scottish Trans Alliance, 2010).

Some elements of abusive behaviour have been found to follow similar patterns for heterosexual and LGBT victims; however, there are also some unique aspects to LGBT domestic abuse. These specific issues include the following:

- Threats of disclosure of sexual orientation and gender identity,
- Controlling the access to spaces and support networks for coming out,
- Belief by the abused person that support services or the criminal justice system is homo/bi/trans phobic,
- Increased isolation because of a lack of family support, and
- Accusations that a survivor may not be a real lesbian or gay man (Donovan et al., 2006; Galop, 2020).

As with all victims, recognising behaviour as abusive and being believed by others are particular concerns for those experiencing abuse in same sex relationships. This has been found to be very acute for those experiencing emotional rather than physical abuse (Donovan et al., 2006). For those who did seek help, Donovan et al. found it was more likely to be from friends, family, a counsellor, or therapist. As in heterosexual relationships, those under the age of 25 years are more likely to report their abuse (Donovan et al., 2006).

There is a range of specialist support for LGBT victims of domestic abuse. The charity Galop runs the National LGBT Domestic Violence Helpline, and it also hosts a survivors' forum on its website (Galop, 2020). The Bi Survivors Network engages in community advocacy as well as providing a space where survivors can talk to each other, and The Survivors Network offers a range of resources for LGBTQ+ survivors (The Survivors Network, 2020).

National and international data suggest that women suffer more frequent and more severe domestic violence throughout their lives. However, the figures above indicate that there are numerous issues around sexuality and gender to be considered when dealing with victims of domestic abuse.

Ethnicity

Another important intersection to recognise in terms of the prevalence, level of reporting, and nature of domestic abuse is ethnicity. One of the difficulties of understanding the scale of domestic abuse in terms of ethnicity is the lack of reliable data. The CSEW does not offer a great deal of insight into the ethnicity of victims, as the results reported in the published analysis are only broken into two categories of white or non-white. The proportions of victims are higher in the white group for both men and women. The North London Domestic Violence Survey (NLDVS) did however have a more comprehensive analysis of responses by ethnicity, and the results found that there was considerable variation in the prevalence, reporting, and understanding of domestic abuse amongst different groups. When asked about the different categories that they recognised as abuse, such as rape, emotional, physical, and psychological abuse, those from African-Caribbean ethnic groups recognised all types of abuse as domestic violence more than any other group. Those of African ethnicity exhibited the lowest levels of recognition for most types of abuse, particularly rape, where only 55% regarded it as a form of domestic violence compared to 85% amongst African-Caribbean (Mooney, 2000).

Both prevalence and underreporting is also thought to be high amongst women with insecure immigration status who are reliant on being married to stay in the country (Erez and Harper, 2018). This includes the so-called 'Mail Order' brides and women from Thailand and the Philippines who marry UK 'sex tourists' (Harne and Radford, 2008; Narayan, 1995). Their insecure immigration status is used by the perpetrator as an element of control, leaving the woman to fear deportation if the marriage fails (Erez and Harper, 2018).

Another group who are known to underreport are those from travelling communities. There are a number of reasons for not disclosing including conflicts of loyalties between the travelling communities and the authorities (Harne and Radford, 2008). Other reasons include more severe and longer suffering of abuse for those who report (Equality and Human Rights Commission, 2009) and ostracisation within communities for those getting divorced, therefore deterring victims from separating from their partner. Abuse can also be normalised, with those living in closed communities not receiving education about domestic abuse or being aware that this behaviour is neither acceptable nor normal (Clark, 2009). An intersectional approach to understanding travelling communities is needed, to support these women whose attitudes to domestic abuse are beginning to change (Hamilton, 2018).

Across different ethnicities the context in which abuse is perpetrated may also vary; for example, reported domestic abuse may include forced marriage, Honour Based Violence and Abuse (HBVA), or Female Genital Mutilation (FGM) (Women's Aid, 2014). The role that the so-called honour, the shame brought upon a family, plays in this type of abuse and distinguishes it from other types of domestic abuse, and it is thought to be even less likely to be reported or reporting delayed, putting victims at more risk than other forms of domestic abuse (Harrison and Gill, 2017; Mulvihill et al., 2019). In some communities the cultural norm is that problems at home should be resolved within the family or the community. This type of abuse can involve more than one perpetrator, most likely to be the victim's male blood relatives or in-laws (Stewart, 1994; Wikan, 1984). Older women may also be involved in the perpetration of abuse, although it usually the men who carry out the violence (Ertürk and Purkayastha, 2012). HBVA can be perpetrated against young men as well, for instance, for refusal to enter into an arranged marriage (Chesler, 2010; Oberwittler and Kasselt, 2011) or those coming out as gay (Bilgehan Ozturk, 2011; Jaspal and Siraj, 2011). Victims who do seek help from the police have reported an increased feeling of vulnerability and risk of serious harm (Gill et al., 2018). The government has tried to address this by raising the priority given to victims of HBV/A, FGM, and forced marriage in the Victim's Code of Practice (VCOP) in 2015. But recent research has found that more work is still needed to recognise perpetrators and hear (and listen) to the voices of the victims (Gill et al., 2018). Variations in the honour system are found according to location, ethnicity, regional culture, and economic status (Dobash and Dobash, 2000) which may influence the levels of abuse perpetrated and reported. Any interaction with the victim requires a thoughtful understanding of the intersecting factors of gender, ethnicity, and the immigration status any of which can create barriers to reporting abuse or in some cases put the victim in further danger. Mulvihill et al. (2019) found that of those who did overcome the hurdle of disclosing only 25% were happy with their reporting experience.

One of the reasons more broadly why underreporting is higher amongst Black and minority communities highlights conflicting loyalties when it comes to seeking help in a society where racism continues to be a problem. The victim may be fearful of exposing themselves or the perpetrator to racism when reporting to what may be perceived as 'white authorities' (Walklate, 2004). There are also other barriers including language, although all police forces have access to translation services either face to face or online for victims, witnesses, and suspects, so theoretically this should not be a practical barrier.

There are a number of support services for Black and Marginalised Communities. These include specialist by and for Black and Minoritised Communities, VAWG agencies (services provided by and for the community they serve), support services for migrant survivors with No Recourse to Public Funds (NRPF), forced marriage support, FGM support, and immigration support.

Disability

Surveys and other research studies have found that adults with disabilities are at increased risk of domestic abuse, with disabled women twice as likely to experience domestic abuse as non-disabled women (Hughes et al., 2012; ONS, 2019; Public Health England (PHE), 2015; Refuge, 2020; SafeLives, 2017a). The CSEW suggested that 15.7% of women and 7.3% of men with a long-standing illness or disability had experienced domestic abuse in the last year, compared with 6.2% of women and 3.9% of men with no disability (ONS, 2017). The amount of time that victims experience abuse for has also been found to be longer. Furthermore, SafeLives (2017a) identified that disabled clients were typically experiencing abuse for 3.3 years compared to 2.3 years for non-disabled clients and that disabled clients were twice as likely to have planned or attempted suicide. As highlighted in Box 6.3, disabled victims may have difficulty leaving if the perpetrator acts as their carer and as many as 37% of disabled clients remained living with an abusive partner, compared with 28% of their non-disabled clients (SafeLives, 2017a).

BOX 6.3 DISABLED VICTIM EXPERIENCE

Sarah (not her real name), who did eventually escape from her perpetrator, described her experiences of being a disabled domestic abuse victim.

> "He'd say that I ruined his life with my disability, that I couldn't cope on my own." Throughout their marriage, she was reliant on

> him to be her carer; a setup that became part of the abuse. He typically withdrew "care" – even food or water – if she broke one of his many rules and threatened to call mental health services to get her sectioned if she didn't do as he said. He was regularly violent, forcing her to stop taking antidepressants and other medication, while getting "angry with me for getting sick so much". It was easy to isolate her: he would take away her Motability car, keeping her housebound for days or even weeks on end.
>
> Even after escaping the abuse, Sarah continued to face difficulties, with the refuge she was accommodated in not being accessible. Her room is upstairs, but there is no lift, so it is a big effort for her to get downstairs and she has lost weight because he has eaten very little due to not being able to get to the kitchen. She has also fallen down the stairs twice.
>
> (Guardian, 2019)

Domestic abuse has been found to be particularly prevalent amongst those with mental illness, with one in three people with mental illness having experienced domestic abuse in the last year (PHE, 2015). Men with post-traumatic stress disorder (PTSD) were found to be seven times more likely to be experiencing domestic abuse than those without PTSD and women with anxiety disorder four times more likely than those without anxiety (PHE, 2015).

Perpetrators target those who are vulnerable, and there are parallels between those victims who experience domestic abuse, disability hate crime, and 'mate' crime. 'Mate' crime is the "befriending of people perceived to be vulnerable for the purposes of taking advantage of them, exploiting or abusing them" (McCarthy, 2017, p. 596). However, despite the similarities in victimisation, the responses to domestic abuse and mate crime are quite different. If somebody moves next door and commits 'mate' crime they would be prosecuted using the Anti-Social Behaviour, Crime and Policing Act, 2014, whereas those moving in with the victim and engaging in domestic abuse are treated differently (McCarthy, 2017).

In addition to the abusive behaviour experienced by all domestic abuse victims, disabled victims may also be experiencing abusive behaviour linked to their particular disability. For instance, the abuser may remove mobility and sensory devices that the victim needs for independence. The abuser may be financially controlling the victim by claiming state benefits in order to care for the victim and using the victim's disability to degrade and control. If physically vulnerable the victim may find it more difficult to escape from the abuse and thereafter become more socially isolated. Furthermore, opportunities to disclose abuse to healthcare and social care professionals is made more complicated if the perpetrator is always present at medical appointments (Women's Aid, 2020). A disabled victim may be regarded as a vulnerable adult. If this is the case, then multi-agency policies and procedures for safeguarding and protection for vulnerable adults will apply. The safeguarding responsibilities of social services also extend to vulnerable adults who have care and support needs that sometimes prevent them from protecting themselves. If a vulnerable adult is experiencing abuse, they need to be supported to access a choice of specialist domestic abuse services. More details on this can be found in the 'No Secrets Guidance' (GOV.UK, 2015). There are a range of specialist support services for disabled victims. Some services are linked to specific disabilities, such as sight or hearing loss, whereas others offer support to all disabled victims.

Older people

Data from police statistics and surveys alone would indicate that young people are more likely to be victims of domestic abuse. The CSEW finds that respondents between the ages of 16 and 24 have experienced the highest rate of abuse in the last 12 months (Flatley, 2016). It must, however, be remembered that until 2017 personal violence questions on the CSEW were only directed at 16–59 year olds, so the extent of abuse in respondents aged over 60 was not covered (Walby and Towers, 2017). The CSEW has now been extended to age 74. But there remains a significant gap in our understanding of both younger (under 16) and a lack of national data concerning older victims' experiences of abuse.

The small amount of research that has been conducted on older victims has found the abuse to be even less likely to be reported (McGarry et al., 2011). Research from the National Centre for Social Research and King's College London (O'Keeffe et al., 2007) found that 1% of people aged 65 and over living in private households experienced interpersonal abuse in the past year. The proportion of over 65 reporting to the police was, however, only 4%, a figure considerably lower than 21% of younger victims in the CSEW. In contrast, 29% reported to their GP and 30% to friends or family, which highlights the need to consider a variety of data sources in addition to the CSEW and police reports. The NLDVS found that whilst the prevalence of domestic abuse diminished after the age of 45, older people's recognition of abuse was narrower than younger respondents, particularly concerning the emotional and psychological elements of abuse (Mooney, 2000). This is hardly surprising given the generational differences. For instance, early advice to housewives includes:

> Don't ask him questions about his actions or question his judgement or integrity. Remember, he is the master of the house and as such will always exercise his will with fairness and truthfulness. You have no right to question him. A good wife always knows her place.
>
> (Housekeeping Monthly, 1955)

A narrower definition of abuse and generational issues are thought to be key contributing factors to older people not reporting their abuse. With domestic abuse only becoming an issue for public concern in the 1970s, many older victims will have been brought up with traditional attitudes towards marriage and gender roles (Scott et al., 2004), as the excerpt above from Housekeeping Monthly demonstrates. Furthermore, the perception was that violence in relationships belonged in the private sphere and that police did not get involved in 'domestics'. In some long-standing relationships, violence is a routine part of marriage. This coupled with a stigma around divorce and separation, and other factors such as dependency on the perpetrator in later life have created barriers for older women wanting to report or escape from abusive relationships. Brandl and Meuer (2000) found that people who are victims of violence perpetrated by strangers like the perpetrator to be punished, but those abused by someone, especially an intimate relationship, would like the abuse to stop but the relationship to continue. There is a desire to seek services to help the perpetrator reform, rather than seeking support for themselves as a victim (Brandl and Cook-Daniels, 2002). Shame and embarrassment were cited as the main reasons for not telling anyone; of particular concern was the reaction that older children might have. Some women who have left their partner have been estranged by their children, who they feel found the situation embarrassing (Scott et al., 2004). Older women may also find it more difficult to leave an abusive relationship as they are more financially dependent on the perpetrator than many younger women. Lack of careers or work experience make it more difficult to find employment and to build sufficient resources for retirement (Phillips, 2000; Scott et al., 2004). SafeLives insight data found that only 27% of victims aged 61 and over attempted to leave their perpetrator in the year before accessing help, compared with 68% of those aged 60 and under (SafeLives, 2016).

The problem for some is not the embarrassment for their children, but the fact that the children are the perpetrators of the abuse, with intergenerational abuse a recognised issue for older people (Brandl and Meuer, 2000; Young, 2014). The figures are stark with 44% of victims aged 61 and above experiencing abuse from an adult family member, compared with only 6% aged 60 and under (SafeLives, 2016). Research conducted in Canada found that whilst spouses were more likely to be physically abusive, adult children were more likely to perpetrate financial abuse. There are debates concerning an intergenerational cycle of abuse, with some suggesting those who have been victims of child abuse potentially retaliating against their parents when they become adults (Brandl and Cook-Daniels, 2002; Buchanan, 2002) and others suggesting such links are far from certain (Rezmovic et al., 1996).

There is also confusion around the differences between domestic abuse and elder abuse (Kilbane and Spira, 2010; Straka and Montminy, 2006), which can contribute to this age group being overlooked (Blood, 2004). Most domestic abuse services are targeted at those aged 18–44, and protection services for adults are aimed at the frail elderly and vulnerable victims. The result is a gap in service provision, and the people in between are lost in the cracks (Brandl and Cook-Daniels, 2002). Older victims may not be aware of services available (Beaulaurier et al., 2007), services are always not appropriate for their needs, and in rural areas seeking help without people knowing is difficult (Blood, 2004). As highlighted by the case study in Box 6.4 it is quite often private organisations, rather than statutory services, that become aware of older people experiencing domestic abuse.

BOX 6.4 EXPERIENCE OF A CARE PROVIDER

Research in an English coastal town with a high population of older people found that very low numbers of victims reported their abuse to the police. An interview with a care provider, who visited clients in their own homes, highlighted the hidden nature of the abuse and the hesitancy in reporting.

> I have seen quite a lot of abusive behaviour between my clients, but it is very unlikely that it would be reported, unless it was very serious. . . Most victims don't want to leave the perpetrator, especially as they are often caring for them as well, they just wanted the perpetrator to stop the abuse and get help. Often warring couples are having to cope with the fact that one of them has Alzheimer's. My clients don't want to speak to the police, in the serious cases I encourage victims to contact an advocacy charity instead or I try to speak to adult Social Care. The service is just too slow though.
>
> I have come across several victims who were being abused by their children. Most of the abuse had been financial, but there was a murder in the area where a daughter strangled her mother.
>
> Weir (2020, p. 203)

The need to take an intersectional approach is supported by Grossman and Lundy (2003) who found that abuse in older people is not uniform and the types of abuse varied and interacted with other factors such as ethnicity and disability (SafeLives, 2016). With the experiences of older victims being very different from younger victims and given the ageing population, the need for this research is particularly pertinent and relates to provision of resources.

Sibling abuse

One form of abuse that is highly prevalent, but less likely to be reported or researched is sibling abuse. Incidence rates of sibling abuse range from 60%

to 80% of young people experiencing some form of sibling maltreatment (Goodwin and Roscoe, 1990; Hoffman and Edwards, 2004). In England and Wales, from the end of March 2017 to the end of March 2019, there were 13 domestic homicides where the victim and perpetrator were siblings (ONS, 2020b). Unlike other forms of domestic abuse, sibling abuse tends not to be gendered, with equal levels of victimisation between males and females (Duncan, 1999; Goodwin and Roscoe, 1990). Research by Hoffman and Edwards (2004) proposed that sibling abuse can be modelled by combining three theoretical models: feminist theory, conflict theory, and social learning theory. Due to the familial nature of sibling abuse and cultural norms it is believed that parents are unlikely to call the police unless the violence is particularly bad (Fitz Gibbon et al., 2018). With children increasingly living at home for longer the largely unexplored issue of sibling violence in adolescence and adulthood is an issue that warrants further exploration.

Adolescent domestic abuse

Domestic abuse between adolescents is an often neglected and overlooked topic for research and policy, with teenage victims and perpetrators often falling through the gaps between child protection procedures and domestic abuse protocols in many agencies. In the United Kingdom and internationally, teenage domestic violence victims appear to be absent from domestic violence legislation (Brown, 2007). Whilst there is significant research on the impact of domestic abuse on adults and the consequential impact on children who witness it (Holt et al., 2008), there is very little known about teenage experiences of partner violence in intimate relationships (Barter et al., 2013).

Women aged 16–19 years are more likely to experience domestic abuse than all other age groups (ONS, 2020b). Despite the high prevalence for this age group, the rate of referrals into support services and MARACs is lower than the percentage they make up of the population (SafeLives, 2017b). The impact of domestic abuse on the lives of younger teenagers is not fully known, and the help and support available to them extremely limited. This is important as US studies of self-reported offending have suggested that the peak age for perpetrating domestic abuse may be as young as 16 years of age (Nocentini et al., 2010).

In 2013 domestic abuse legislation in England and Wales was changed to include those aged 16 and over (Home Office, 2013), but many relationships start in the early teenage years and the consequences of domestic violence and the impacts of coercive control are being seen in younger children who are in intimate partnerships. Whilst the IDVA role is embedded in the government's violence against women and girls' strategy (Home Office, 2019), the Youth Domestic Abuse Advisor (YDVA) or Children and Young People IDVA (CYPIDVA) role is not. Roles such as these have been created to provide high-risk children and young people aged 13–17 with domestic abuse support, offering age-appropriate awareness and safety planning with the intention to provide advice and mitigation around the very different risks posed to children and young people in today's multi-media society (SafeLives, 2017b).

There is also a real difference in how perpetrators of domestic abuse are treated depending on age, with adolescents dealt with in juvenile or youth criminal justice arenas, where the focus is more significantly on restorative justice and rehabilitation, whilst adult perpetrators are more likely to have a court or custodial criminal justice outcome. Zosky (2010) suggests this may lead to child perpetrators being held less accountable for their actions, increasing the risk of repeat and more significant violence, as there are very limited interventions available for youth perpetrators. Suarez (1994) describes how until laws change to acknowledge that violence is not confined to adults; teenagers will learn that the state will rarely prevent or punish abuse; and therefore, the implications for future behaviour are concerning. This view is challenged however by Travis (2011) who states that teenagers' brains are not yet fully formed so they are unable to make rational decisions and should not be treated equally to adult abusers when considering punishment for domestic abuse offences.

Proliferation

The impact for those under 16 engaged in dating/relationship violence can be devastating leading to a wide range of mental health and social impacts, such as teenage pregnancy, self-harm, and violent behaviour (Young et al., 2021). SafeLives (2017b) research found that less than half (45%) of young people in an abusive intimate relationship were known to children's social services, so more hidden and with fewer outlets to reach out for support.

Existing UK research produced for the NSPCC suggests that up to 75% of girls and 50% of boys report emotional abuse in intimate relationships (Barter et al., 2009). The NSPCC research of 1377 children aged under 18 also found that 25% of girls and 18% of boys reported some form of physical partner violence. The majority of young people either told a friend or told no one about the violence, and having an older partner, especially a "much older" partner, was a risk factor for girls. Thirty-one per cent of girls and sixteen per cent of boys reported some form of sexual partner violence, and this was even higher for girls where their partner was older than them.

Fox et al. (2014) conducted similar research with the Boys to Men Project. Research was conducted with 1143 pupils aged 13–14 years to assess their experiences of domestic abuse as victims and perpetrators. Overall, 45% of pupils who had been in an intimate or dating relationship stated they had been victimised, with 25% making admissions to have perpetrated abuse.

Data was obtained from 74,908 children from 193 schools as part of a Welsh cross-sectional study into dating and relationship violence in children aged 11–16 years. This research suggests lower levels of violence than other studies previously conducted, but the age range of participants is much lower which may account for this anomaly. Physical violence was experienced more by boys than girls, but emotional victimisation was worse for girls (Young et al., 2021).

Each of these studies gives not only a glimpse of the magnitude of the problem, but also the lack of guidance and interventions available to deal with such a bespoke subject matter. If up to three quarters of girls under 18 have been in an intimate or dating relationship containing emotional abuse and at least a quarter suffering from physical or sexual violence, the question is why is this category of abuse is not discussed or debated as frequently, or indeed treated as a public health issue, compared to adult perpetrated domestic abuse?

Finally, another serious concern is the lack of research on domestic abuse linked to gang violence. Traditional domestic violence research does not account for victims of gang abusers. Young women and girls who are in relationships with gang members find it even more difficult to report any violence and offending, most notably because they face the wrath not only from the perpetrator but also from other members of the gang (Brown, 2007). Relationship abuse and inter-partner violence is common within gangs made up of youths (Ulloa et al., 2012), and girls involved in gangs are more likely to be subject to sexual and domestic abuse than girls not in gangs (Auyong et al., 2018). With over 30,000 children believed to be part of a gang in the United Kingdom (Children's Commissioner, 2019) further exploration is required to understand the extent and impact of domestic abuse between adolescents involved in gangs. Whilst the proliferation of domestic abuse between adolescents is underreported and underresearched, there is a growing body of evidence about the negative effect domestic abuse can have on children witnessing parental conflict and violence which will now be considered.

Children & domestic abuse

Whilst the proliferation of domestic abuse between adolescents is underreported and underresearched, there is a growing body of evidence about the negative effect domestic abuse can have on children witnessing parental conflict and violence. Living in an abusive household has been identified as an adverse childhood experience which can impact upon their behaviours and adult life course (Asmussen et al., 2019). Whilst not all children who witness or experience domestic abuse as a child grow up repeating the cycle as adults, some do. Such childhood experience can also result in the onset of adult mental health challenges and attachment issues if support and assistance are not provided through early intervention by safeguarding agencies.

Where parents have a violent or abusive relationship, they may not be able to adequately protect or parent their children. As such whilst the children may not be at direct risk because of the domestic abuse being perpetuated, they may be subject to suffering from neglect or emotional abuse simply by being present within the household. The Royal College of Psychiatrists (2015) have identified that living within such an environment can impact children's performance at school, their mental health, and their physical and emotion health. It has also been recognised that domestic abuse within the home is associated with gang membership as children seek role models, support, and time away from the home environment increasing their vulnerability to exploitation. Young offenders associated with gangs are 39% more likely to be living in homes experiencing domestic abuse (Children's Commissioner, 2019).

Police have statutory child safeguarding responsibilities under multi-agency safeguarding arrangements under the Children's Act 2004 and the Children's and Social Work Act 2017 (HM Government, 2018). Where children are within the household even if they were not present at the time of the police response to a domestic incident, officers must ensure appropriate referrals or reports are made through force safeguarding mechanisms to ensure any risk to them can be further identified and specific support put in place. The College of Policing's Approved Professional Practice regarding child protection has a specific section containing information and guidance as to actions police should take where children are found to be living within households experiencing domestic abuse. Not only should the presence of children be seen as a potential risk factor in terms of DASH but the risk to the children themselves must be considered. Where the child is reasonably believed to be a risk of significant harm, police have an emergency power under Section 46 The Children Act 1989 to take that child into Police Protection. This allows the police to remove that child to a suitable accommodation or prevent the child being removed from a hospital or other accommodation. The power can last up to a maximum of 72 hours after which this child is returned, or further court orders are sought to ensure their continuing safety by local social care departments (Box 6.5).

BOX 6.5 SOCIAL CARE SERVICES

Local authority Social Care Services are provided to safeguard both adults and children. For children there are number of ways in which concerns around domestic abuse can be reported. Members of the public can contact their local authority child protection team directly or refer concerns to the police or NSPCC helpline who pass these to the local authority teams. It is an obligation on the police and other professionals to report the presence of children in a household where domestic abuse has been identified. Upon receiving a referral, the local authority must decide within one working day about the action that is to be taken. In some cases, the team will decide that the child has not been harmed and is not at risk or that no further action is necessary. In other cases, further assessment is needed to gather more information. If the initial assessment reveals that the child has suffered or is at risk of suffering significant harm then decisions regarding a section 47 enquiry are needed, involving a core assessment led by a social worker gathering significant information from the child, parents, family members, and other professionals. If a section 47 enquiry upholds the concerns, then the local authority must make provision for the child and a child protection plan is drawn up (UK Parliament, 2012).

Many areas now have a Multi-Agency Safeguarding Hub (MASH), where a number of agencies work together and share information in an integrated way to act as a single point of entry for all notifications related to safeguarding. The aim of the MASH is to triage referrals and facilitate early intervention by managing cases through co-ordinated interventions. The agencies involved in the MASH vary across different areas but could include adult and children's social care, police, health, education, probation, housing, and Youth Offending Service (YOS) (Home Office, 2014).

Social care services

Whether or not children are removed from the household by police, on every occasion of police contact at an incident of domestic abuse, a safeguarding risk assessment should be undertaken and a referral made to the relevant children's social care authority. Many police forces will have a Multi-Agency Safeguarding Hub (MASH) where referrals are processed, and information is exchanged between other partners such as health, education, and social care so a full picture of that child's experience can be drawn together and the threat to them can be better assessed. Several forces have schemes where following police attendance at any domestic incident a referral is made to the child's school within 24 hours (Box 6.6). This allows teachers to monitor any immediate adverse impact as well as provide support to that child as necessary. In such situations it is good practice to seek the advice of a supervisor or child safeguarding specialist.

BOX 6.6 EDUCATION

Another place where domestic abuse in a family may be identified is in schools. As part of schools' safeguarding policy, all staff need to be aware of the systems that support safeguarding and there should be a designated safeguarding lead who they can speak to should they suspect abuse. In terms of partnership Operation Encompass operates in most police forces in England helping police and schools to work together to provide practical and emotional support to children. When police are called to an incident of domestic abuse where children have been witnesses they will inform the designated safeguarding lead in the school before the child or children come to school the following day. If police forces have not signed up to Operation Encompass they need to have their own arrangements in place.

(Department for Education, 2021)

Research indicates there are devastating and long-term impacts on many children who grow up witnessing and living within abusive households. Living within an abusive household has been identified as an adverse childhood experience which can impact upon their behaviours and adult life course (Asmussen et al., 2019). Whilst not all children who witness or experience domestic abuse as a child grow up repeating the cycle as adults, some do. Such childhood experience can also result in the onset of adult mental health challenges and attachment issues if support and assistance are not provided through early intervention by safeguarding agencies.

One theory (Box 6.7) which has recent currency within policing is the impact of Adverse Childhood Experiences (ACEs) on the inter-general cycle of domestic abuse within families. Whilst in no way suggesting that all children who grow up witnessing domestic abuse will go on to be abusers in adulthood, there is evidence to indicate that many children who witnessed and experienced abuse within the home can have difficulties in forming adult relationships in later life because of an increased propensity for violence, antisocial behaviour, and lack of trust. More and more police forces are becoming ACE aware, and trauma informed in how they manage family violence and safeguarding issues.

BOX 6.7 TRAUMA INFORMED PRACTICE

There is not a formally agreed definition of what trauma informed policing is. However, trauma-informed practice principles recognise the short- and long-term impact of traumatic experience and how it can influence victims and suspect witnesses and staff behaviours. Trauma-informed policing also seeks not to retraumatise people with whom it engages with. For instance, constantly asking a rape victim to provide detailed accounts of their experience. Of recognising children being groomed may be loyal to their groomers. Or domestic abuse victim who despite evidence to the contrary do not provide truthful accounts of how they received injury. Such practices are most commonly found in policing vulnerability, child and adult sexual abuse, and domestic abuse.

(Gillespie-Smith et al., 2020)

Conclusion

This chapter has highlighted the need to look at the problem of domestic violence across different social locations to appreciate who are the victims and how victims might need support. It emphasises that domestic abuse is not a simple crime with simple solutions for police officers on the front-line or the criminal justice service more generally. Cross cutting all aspects of diversity, with differing implications in terms of current and future harm, practitioners and academics alike should consider individual need in order to ensure victims receive the best possible service and are supported whether or not a criminal justice outcome is obtained.

Reflective questions

- Who is most likely to be a victim of domestic abuse and why?
- Domestic abuse amongst adolescents is not as gendered as with adults. What is the reason for this?
- Intersectionality is often overlooked when considering domestic abuse. How can you assure a multifaceted approach to victims' needs?
- How would you assess the impact on children living within an abusive household?

Useful websites

Domestic Abuse Housing Alliance (DAHA): https://www.dahalliance.org.uk/
Galop: https://galop.org.uk/
Mankind: https://www.mankind.org.uk/
No Secrets Guidance: https://www.gov.uk/government/publications/no-secrets-guidance-on-protecting-vulnerable-adults-in-care
Respect Men's Advice Line: https://mensadviceline.org.uk/
SafeLives: https://safelives.org.uk/

Specialist services for Black and minority ethnic women: https://www.womensaid.org.uk/information-support/useful-links/#1448368625673-5cc06085-f0aa

Survivors Network: https://survivorsnetwork.org.uk/

Women's Aid Domestic Abuse Directory: https://www.womensaid.org.uk/domestic-abuse-directory/

References

Asmussen, K., McBride, T., Waddell, S., 2019. The potential of early intervention for preventing and reducing ACE-related trauma. *Social Policy and Society* 18, 425–434.

Auyong, Z.E.G., Smith, S., Ferguson, C.J., 2018. Girls in gangs: Exploring risk in a British youth context. *Crime & Delinquency* 64, 1698–1717.

Barter, C., McCarry, M., Berridge, D., Evans, K., 2009. *Partner exploitation and violence in teenage intimate relationships.* NSPCC.

Beaulaurier, R.L., Seff, L.R., Newman, F.L., Dunlop, B., 2007. External barriers to help seeking for older women who experience intimate partner violence. *Journal of Family Violence* 22, 747–755.

Bilgehan Ozturk, M., 2011. Sexual orientation discrimination: Exploring the experiences of lesbian, gay and bisexual employees in Turkey. *Human Relations* 64, 1099–1118.

Black, M.C., Basile, K.C., Breiding, M.J., Smith, S.G., Walters, M.L., Merrick, M.T., Chen, J., Stevens, M.R., 2011. National intimate partner and sexual violence survey 2010 summary report. Atlanta, GA: National Center for Injury Prevention and Control.

Blood, I., 2004. *Older women and domestic violence. Help the Aged.* https://equation.org.uk/wp-content/uploads/2012/12/Older-women-and-Domestic-Violence.pdf (accessed 7.10.22)

Brandl, B., Cook-Daniels, L., 2002. *Domestic abuse in later life.* Applied Research Forum, National Electronic Network on Violence Against Women.

Brandl, B., Meuer, T., 2000. Domestic abuse in later life. *Elder Law Journal* 8, 297.

Brown, V.A., 2007. Gang member perpetrated domestic violence: A new conservation. *The University of Maryland Law Journal of Race, Religion, Gender & Class* 7, 395.

Buchanan, A., 2002. *Cycles of child maltreatment: Facts, fallacies and interventions.* Wiley.

Chesler, P., 2010. *Worldwide trends in honor killings.* Middle East Quarterly.

Children's Commissioner, 2019. *Childhood vulnerability in numbers.* Children's Commissioner.

Clark, J., 2009. On the road to change: Dealing with domestic violence in gypsy and traveller groups. *The Guardian.*

DAHA, 2018. The facts about domestic violence and housing. *DAHA.* https://www.dahalliance.org.uk/facts (accessed 2.11.19).

Day, A.S., Gill, A.K., 2020. Applying intersectionality to partnerships between women's organizations and the criminal justice system in relation to domestic violence. *The British Journal of Criminology* 60(4), 830–850.

Department for Communities and Local Government, 2018. Live tables on homelessness. GOV.UK. https://www.gov.uk/government/statistical-data-sets/live-tables-on-homelessness (accessed 2.11.19).
Department of Education, 2021. *Keeping children safe in education 2021*, https://assets.publishing.service.gov.uk/government/uploads/system/uploads/attachment_data/file/1014058/KCSIE_2021_Part_One_September.pdf (accessed 7.10.22)
Dobash, R.E., Dobash, R.P., 2000. The politics and policies of responding to violence against women, in: Hanmer, J., Itzin, C. (Eds.), *Home Thruths About Domestic Violence. Feminist Influences on Policy and Practices: A Reader.* Routledge, pp. 187–204.
Donovan, C., Hester, M., Holmes, J., McCarry, M., 2006. *Comparing domestic abuse in same sex and heterosexual relationships.* University of Sunderland and University of Bristol.
Duncan, R.D., 1999. Peer and sibling aggression: An investigation of intra-and extra-familial bullying. *Journal of Interpersonal Violence* 14, 871–886.
Equality and Human Rights Commission, 2009. *Inequalities experienced by gypsy and traveller communities: A review (No. 12).* Equality and Human Rights Commission.
Erez, E., Harper, S., 2018. Intersectionality, immigration, and domestic violence, in: Martinez, R., Hollis, M.E., Stowell, J.I. (Eds.), *The Handbook of Race, Ethnicity, Crime, and Justice.* Wiley, pp. 457–474.
Ertürk, Y., Purkayastha, B., 2012. Linking research, policy and action: A look at the work of the special rapporteur on violence against women. *Current Sociology* 60, 142–160.
Fitz-Gibbon, K., Elliott, K., Maher, J., 2018. *Investigating adolescent family violence in Victoria: Understanding experiences and practitioner perspectives.* Monash University.
Flatley, J., 2016. *Intimate personal violence and partner abuse.* Office for National Statistics, London.
Fox, C.L., Hale, R., Gadd, D., 2014. Domestic abuse prevention education: Listening to the views of young people. *Sex Education* 14, 28–41.
Galop, 2020. Support for victims of abuse. Galop. https://galop.org.uk/resource/support-for-victims-and-survivors-of-domestic-abuse-and-honour-based-violence/ (accessed 11.29.21).
Gill, A.K., Cox, P., Weir, R., 2018. Shaping priority services for UK victims of honour-based violence/abuse, forced marriage, and female genital mutilation. *The Howard Journal of Crime and Justice* 57, 576–595.
Gillespie-Smith, K., Brodie, Z., Collins, K., Deacon, K., Goodall, K., 2020. *Moving towards trauma-informed policing: An exploration of police officers' attitudes and perceptions towards Adverse Childhood Experiences (ACEs).* Teesside University.
Goodwin, M.P., Roscoe, B., 1990. Sibling violence and agonistic interactions among middle adolescents. *Adolescence* 25, 451.
GOV.UK, 2015. No Secrets: Guidance on protecting vulnerable adults in care. GOV.UK. https://www.gov.uk/government/publications/no-secrets-guidance-on-protecting-vulnerable-adults-in-care (accessed 4.16.21).
Grossman, S.F., Lundy, M., 2003. Use of domestic violence services across race and ethnicity by women aged 55 and older: The Illinois experience. *Violence Against Women* 9, 1442–1452.
Groves, N., Thomas, T., 2014. *Domestic violence and criminal justice.* Routledge.

Hamilton, P., 2018. School books or wedding dresses? Examining the cultural dissonance experienced by young Gypsy/Traveller women in secondary education. *Gender and Education* 30, 829–845.

Harne, L., Radford, J., 2008. *Tackling domestic violence: theories, policies and practice: Theories, policies and practice.* McGraw-Hill Education.

Harrison, K., Gill, A.K., 2017. Breaking down barriers: recommendations for improving sexual abuse reporting rates in British South Asian communities. *The British Journal of Criminology* 58, 273–290.

HM Government, 2019. *Position statement on male victims of crimes considered in the cross-Government strategy on ending Violence Against Women and Girls (VAWG).* HM Government.

HM Government, 2018. Transforming the response to domestic abuse: Government consultation.

HMIC, 2014. Everyone's business: Improving the police response to domestic abuse. Her Majesty's Inspectorate of Constabulary.

Hoffman, K.L., Edwards, J.N., 2004. An integrated theoretical model of sibling violence and abuse. *Journal of Family Violence* 19, 185–200.

Holt, S., Buckley, H., Whelan, S., 2008. The impact of exposure to domestic violence on children and young people: A review of the literature. *Child Abuse & Neglect* 32, 797–810.

Home Office, 2019. Ending violence against women and girls 2016–2020 strategy. London: Home Office.

Home Office, 2014. *Multi-agency working and information sharing project*, https://www.gov.uk/government/publications/multi-agency-working-and-information-sharing-project (accessed 7.10.22).

Home Office, 2013. *New government domestic violence and abuse definition*Home Office Circular No. 0032.

Housekeeping Monthly, 1955. The good wife's guide. *Housekeeping Monthly.*

Hughes, K., Bellis, M.A., Jones, L., Wood, S., Bates, G., Eckley, L., McCoy, E., Mikton, C., Shakespeare, T., Officer, A., 2012. Prevalence and risk of violence against adults with disabilities: A systematic review and meta-analysis of observational studies. *The Lancet* 379, 1621–1629.

Jackson, R., 2013. *Domestic abuse and housing in Wales.* Cardiff: Chartered Institute of Housing.

Jaspal, R., Siraj, A., 2011. Perceptions of 'coming out' among British Muslim gay men. *Psychology & Sexuality* 2, 183–197.

Kilbane, T., Spira, M., 2010. Domestic violence or elder abuse? Why it matters for older women. *Families in Society* 91, 165–170.

Mankind, 2020. Statistics and research. https://www.mankind.org.uk/statistics/ (accessed 11.29.21).

McCarthy, M., 2017. 'What kind of abuse is him spitting in my food?' Reflections on the similarities between disability hate crime, so-called 'mate' crime and domestic violence against women with intellectual disabilities. *Disability & Society* 32, 595–600.

McGarry, J., Simpson, C., Hinchliff-Smith, K., 2011. The impact of domestic abuse for older women: a review of the literature. *Health & Social Care in the Community* 19, 3–14.

Menard, A., 2001. Domestic violence and housing: Key policy and program challenges. *Violence Against Women* 7, 707–720.
Mooney, J., 2000. *Gender, violence and the social order.* Springer.
Mulvihill, N., Gangoli, G., Gill, A.K., Hester, M., 2019. The experience of interactional justice for victims of 'honour'-based violence and abuse reporting to the police in England and Wales. *Policing and Society* 29:6, 630–656.
Narayan, U., 1995. "Male-order" brides: Immigrant women, domestic violence and immigration law. *Hypatia* 10, 104–119.
NICE, 2016. Overview – Domestic violence and abuse – Quality standards – NICE. https://www.nice.org.uk/guidance/qs116 (accessed 3.24.19).
Nocentini, A., Menesini, E., Pastorelli, C., 2010. Physical dating aggression growth during adolescence. *Journal of Abnormal Child Psychology* 38, 353–365.
Oberwittler, D., Kasselt, J., 2011. *Ehrenmorde in Deutschland – 1996–2005: Eine Untersuchung auf der Basis von Prozessakten.* Luchterhand.
O'Keeffe, M., Hills, A., Doyle, M., McCreadie, C., Scholes, S., Constantine, R., Tinker, A., Manthorpe, J., Biggs, S., Erens, B., 2007. UK study of abuse and neglect of older people: Prevalence survey report. London: Comic Relief.
ONS, 2020a. Domestic abuse prevalence and trends, England and Wales – Office for National Statistics. https://www.ons.gov.uk/peoplepopulationandcommunity/crimeandjustice/articles/domesticabuseprevalenceandtrendsenglandandwales/yearendingmarch2020#crime-survey-for-england-and-wales (accessed 9.7.21).
ONS, 2020b. Domestic abuse victim characteristics, England and Wales – Office for National Statistics. https://www.ons.gov.uk/peoplepopulationandcommunity/crimeandjustice/articles/domesticabusevictimcharacteristicsenglandandwales/yearendingmarch2020#age (accessed 11.30.21).
ONS, 2019. Disability and crime, UK – Office for National Statistics. https://www.ons.gov.uk/peoplepopulationandcommunity/healthandsocialcare/disability/bulletins/disabilityandcrimeuk/2019#domestic-abuse (accessed 11.29.21).
Phillips, L.R., 2000. Domestic violence and aging women. *Geriatric Nursing* 21, 188–194.
Public Health England, 2015. Disability and domestic abuse Risk, impacts and response. Public Health England. https://www.gov.uk/government/publications/disability-and-domestic-abuse-risk-impacts-and-response (accessed 7.10.22)
Refuge, 2020. Support for disabled women. Refuge charity – Domestic violence help. https://www.refuge.org.uk/get-help-now/support-for-women/help-for-disabled-women/ (accessed 4.16.21).
Respect Men's Advice Line, 2020. Domestic abuse helpline for men. Men's Advice Line. https://mensadviceline.org.uk/ (accessed 11.29.21).
Rezmovic, E.L., Sloane, D., Alexander, D., Seltser, B., Jessor, T., Office, U.G.A., Division, G.G., United States of America, 1996. Cycle of sexual abuse: Research inconclusive about whether child victims become adult abusers. US Government Accountability Office General Government Division United States.
Royal College of Psychiatrists, 2015. Domestic violence and abuse – The impact on children and adolescents. RC Psych Royal College of Psychiatrists. https://www.rcpsych.ac.uk/mental-health/parents-and-young-people/information-for-parents-and-carers/domestic-violence-and-abuse-effects-on-children (accessed 12.1.21).
SafeLives, 2020. Five Rs of asking about domestic abuse. https://safelives.org.uk/sites/default/files/resources/Domestic%20abuse%20guidance%20for%20virtual%20health%20settings-%20C19.pdf (accessed 7.10.22)

SafeLives, 2017a. Spotlight #2: Disabled people and domestic abuse – Safelives. https://safelives.org.uk/knowledge-hub/spotlights/spotlight-2-disabled-people-and-domestic-abuse (accessed 11.29.21).
SafeLives, 2017b. Spotlight #3: Young people and domestic abuse – Safelives. https://safelives.org.uk/knowledge-hub/spotlights/spotlight-3-young-people-and-domestic-abuse (accessed 11.2.21).
SafeLives, 2016. Spotlight #1: Older people and domestic abuse – Safelives. https://safelives.org.uk/spotlight-1-older-people-and-domestic-abuse (accessed 11.11.21).
SafeLives, 2015. Getting it right first time. http://www.safelives.org.uk/sites/default/files/resources/Getting%20it%20right%20first%20time%20-%20complete%20report.pdf (accessed 2.11.19).
Safer Colchester Partnership, 2021. The Partnership, https://www.safercolchester.co.uk/safer-colchester/safer-colchester-partnership/ (accessed 7.10.22)
Scott, M., McKie, L., Morton, S., Seddon, E., Wosoff, F., 2004. Older women and domestic violence in Scotland. . . and for 39 years I got on with it. Edinburgh: Health Scotland.
Scottish Trans Alliance, 2010. Out of sight, out of mind?. Scottish Trans Alliance. https://www.scottishtrans.org/resources/abuse-out-of-sight-out-of-mind/ (accessed 11.29.21).
Shelter, 2018. What is homelessness? Shelter England. http://england.shelter.org.uk/housing_advice/homelessness/rules/what_is_homelessness (accessed 2.11.19).
St Mungos, 2014. Rebuilding shattered lives: The final report. St Mungo's. https://www.mungos.org/publication/rebuilding-shattered-lives-final-report/ (accessed 2.11.19).
Stewart, C., 1994. Honour and sanctity: Two levels of ideology in Greece. *Social Anthropology* 2, 205–228.
Straka, S.M., Montminy, L., 2006. Responding to the needs of older women experiencing domestic violence. *Violence Against Women* 12, 251–267.
Strid, S., Walby, S., Armstrong, J., 2013. Intersectionality and multiple inequalities: Visibility in British policy on violence against women. *Social Politics: International Studies in Gender, State & Society* 20, 558–581.
Suarez, K.E., 1994. Teenage dating violence: The need for expanded awareness and legislation. *California Law Review* 82, 423.
The Guardian, 2019. 'I'm tired and desperate' – a disabled victim of domestic violence on her struggle to survive, https://www.theguardian.com/lifeandstyle/2019/sep/19/disabled-victim-of-domestic-violence-on-her-struggle-to-survive (accessed 7.10.22).
The Survivors Network, 2020. Resources. Survivors Network. https://survivorsnetwork.org.uk/resources/ (accessed 11.29.21).
Travis, J., 2011. Reflections on juvenile justice reform in New York. *New York Law School Law Review* 56, 1317.
UK Parliament, 2012. Domestic Violence, Crime and Victims (Amendment) Act 2012, https://services.parliament.uk/bills/2010-12/domesticviolencecrimeandvictimsamendment.html (accessed 2.17.19).
Ulloa, E.C., Dyson, R.B., Wynes, D.D., 2012. Inter-partner violence in the context of gangs: A review. *Aggression and Violent Behavior* 17, 397–404.
UN Women, 2020. Intersectional feminism: What it means and why it matters right now. UN Women. https://www.unwomen.org/en/news/stories/2020/6/explainer-intersectional-feminism-what-it-means-and-why-it-matters (accessed 11.29.21).

Walby, S., Towers, J., 2017. Measuring violence to end violence: Mainstreaming gender. *Journal of Gender-Based Violence* 1, 11–31.

Walklate, S., 2004. The protective society? Seeking safety in an insecure world. *Safer Communities* 3, 38–48.

Weir, R., 2020. *Individuals, families and neighbourhoods: Predictors of domestic abuse in Essex.* University of Essex.

Wikan, U., 1984. Shame and honour: A contestable pair. *Man* 19:4, 635–652.

Women's Aid, 2020. The survivor's handbook: Support for disabled women. Women's Aid. https://www.womensaid.org.uk/the-survivors-handbook/the-survivors-handbook-disabled-women/ (accessed 4.16.21).

Women's Aid, 2014. Women's aid annual survey 2014. London: Women's Aid.

Young, H., Long, S.J., Melendez-Torres, G.J., Kim, H.S., Hewitt, G., Murphy, S., Moore, G.F., 2021. Dating and relationship violence victimization and perpetration among 11–16-year-olds in Wales: A cross-sectional analysis of the School Health Research Network (SHRN) survey. *Journal of Public Health* 43, 111–122.

Young, L.M., 2014. Elder physical abuse. *Clinics in Geriatric Medicine* 30, 761–768.

Zosky, D.L., 2010. Accountability in teenage dating violence: A comparative examination of adult domestic violence and juvenile justice systems policies. *Social Work* 55, 359–368.

Chapter 7

Perpetrators

KEY POINTS

- Understand key theories of perpetration including Violence Against Women, Family Violence perspective, and feminist criminology.
- Review how the police categorise offenders and prioritise them for ongoing action and disruption, through MAPPA, RFGV, and CCHI.
- Develop critical thinking around the Police Management of Offenders thorough effective investigation and criminal justice or out of court disposal.
- Understand the effective treatment of perpetrators by instigating behavioural change through therapeutic methodologies.

Introduction

This chapter reviews and critiques the key theories of domestic abuse perpetration. It also outlines the statutory responsibility of police forces to manage dangerous offenders through partnership arrangements. However, not all perpetrators will be subject to such arrangements and, as previously noted, the capacity of police to manage and prevent abuse outweighs its levels of demand. Police therefore must prioritise offenders and risk assess their levels of 'dangerousness' in order to effectively manage the risk they may present. This is clearly not an exact science, and this chapter considers some of the methods currently in use and the ethical issues in predictive policing. Perpetrators are held to account for their criminal actions through the criminal justice system, and best practice in terms of investigation, interviews, and charging will be presented throughout this chapter. The range of effective treatment options are outlined; however, there is limited research or evidence as to their long-term success in changing offending behaviour.

Theories of perpetration

As outlined in Chapter 2 there are two primary and competing approaches which seek to explain the perpetration of domestic abuse. The Violence

DOI: 10.4324/9781003137412-7

Against Women (VAW) approach is based on research regarding official law enforcement and social agency data of women's experience of violence. It situates abuse as a unilateral, asymmetrical, and gender-specific phenomenon of male violence against women (Dobash et al., 1992). Where women are violent it is only in response to the violence acted upon them by the men. Defined as patriarchal or intimate terrorism this theory is rooted in feminist criminology (Johnson, 1995). The use of violence and abuse perpetrated by men is deliberate and deployed to maintain control and social order over women and their families. For this dominance to be maintained when challenged or simply to act as re-enforcement of the social order, violence and control need to be frequently demonstrated, hence the repeat victimisation and escalation associated with domestic abuse. Such terroristic violence is predominantly the result of feelings of loss of control and the need for reassertion, generated especially by separation, possessiveness, infidelity, and jealousy (Dobash et al., 1992).

The family violence perspective sees violence and abuse as bilateral and symmetrical with men and women being equally responsible for its perpetration. It is based primarily in national survey research and does incorporate the influence of sibling and non-intimate family member violence to a greater extent when considering domestic abuse than that of the feminist perspective (Straus and Gelles, 1990). Violence is described as situational or common couple violence. It is more spontaneous and contextual, triggered through stress and routine conflicts within relationships. Most perpetrators (95%) do not resort to more severe or lethal exertion of violence, and it is often the result of conflicts arising out of finance, division of labour, parenting, and the minutiae of day-to-day life (Johnson, 1995).

What is absent in both theories is the impact of individual circumstances and agency in the perpetration of domestically violent behaviours. Lack of impulse and emotion control and inability to defuse feelings of anger leading to domestic violence and abuse can also be explained through an individual's own personal experience and medical conditions. Brain injury, substance misuse, mental health conditions, adverse childhood experiences (ACEs), and personal trauma have all been identified as potential drivers of domestic abusive behaviour (Bates et al., 2017; Sebire, 2013; Woolford and Wardhaugh, 2019).

The theories regarding domestic abuse perpetrators, particularly those based in feminist criminology, can appear to make arbitrary divisions of roles. People are either victims or perpetrators. Within the policing environment systems and process are also calibrated in such a way as people are given singular status as either a suspect or victim. In reality, such arbitrary classifications are much less apparent (Spivey and Nodeland, 2020). These classifications can be blurred, and the role of victim and offender can seem to overlap. Cross allegations made by both parties against each other can be a common occurrence that reporting officer's encounter. To reemphasise the points made in Chapter 4, careful and objective investigation must take place at the crime scene and within all subsequent enquiries to ascertain the nature of all potential offences and the dynamics of relationships. If perpetrators' behaviours are driven by possessiveness and jealousy and the need to control and dominate their partner any effective management and treatment programmes to address their behaviours will be very different from those treating a perpetrator who may be suffering mental health crisis, brain injury, or substance misuse challenges (Robinson and Clancy, 2020).

Police prioritisation of domestic abuse offenders

It has been estimated that police are only aware of approximately 25% of the overall levels of domestic abuse that takes place (Hester et al., 2006). Even then it is a challenge to successfully manage those who perpetrate such crimes through the criminal justice system. However, as has been found with crime in general and domestic abuse in particular, a small number of offenders are responsible for most of the crime. If they can be identified accurately, it allows for the effective deployment of limited police resources against the 'power few' (Robinson and Clancy, 2020).

Various processes to identify, rank, and prioritise perpetrators for ongoing management or disruption by police and multiagency partners have been introduced. There are statutory guidelines for the identification and management of high-risk sexual and violent offenders under Multi-Agency Public Protection Arrangements (MAPPA) for those who have been convicted of the most serious offences and are to be released into the community following their release from custody. However, MAPPA only account for a very small proportion of domestic abuse offenders. There are no other national or statutory policing guidelines as to best practice process in prioritising or categorising the vast majority of the remaining domestic abuse perpetrators, and local force guidelines should be consulted. However, the most frequently used are RFGV, PPIT, CCHI/CSS, and Kent typology. This next section summarises these approaches to prioritisation.

Multi-Agency Public Protection Arrangements (MAPPA)

MAPPA is a statutory mechanism where 'responsible authorities' of police, HM Probation and Prison services and local authorities, as well as other agencies such as housing and health, have formalised agreements to work together, sharing information and supporting risk management plans for sexual and violent offenders. MAPPA regulations apply to all seriously violent and dangerous offenders who have been convicted of offences in both domestic and non-domestic contexts. MAPPA offenders are categorised into three levels which will be agreed by local MAPPA screening processes. MAPPA Level 1 are low-level offenders and are managed by a single agency. Level 2 have been convicted of more serious offences and require a multi-agency approach to managing risk, and this is coordinated through MAPPA meetings. Level 3 are the most serious and complex and require senior officer representation at meetings as the offender management plans will come with resourcing requirements. For instance, Level 3 cases from a policing perspective could entail the use of covert policing tactics including surveillance teams to be committed to monitoring the offender's behaviour. The plan may also require specific accommodation or treatment programmes to be made available, or the offender may be required to wear an electronic tag to monitor their location. MAPPA meetings will be chaired by an Inspector or Chief Inspector from the local force or National Probation Service equivalent, and each agency will be held to account to ensure all areas of the agreed action plan are adhered to in order to manage the risk presented by the offender.

Common arrangements within police forces will ensure that MAPPA nominals are managed within a specialist offender management team. Intelligence and records regarding MAPPA offenders are maintained on a secure computer system known as ViSOR (Violent and Sexual Offenders Register). Whilst MAPPA 3 offenders do have significant resources committed to them due to their high-risk status, it is good practice for non-specialist officers to familiarise themselves with any MAPPA offenders who may reside within their patrol areas so they can monitor their behaviour and provide up-to-date intelligence on their activities.

There are consequences for offenders should they be found to have breached conditions placed upon them. Should an offender be released on licence and is found to have breached any conditions they can be recalled to prison or have their licence conditions reviewed and amended. However, not all offenders will have been released on licence and therefore recall may not always be an option. Under these circumstances the MAPPA panel will consider what other measures can be put in place to protect the public and manage the risk presented by the individuals' behaviours. This may include arrest for further offences should evidence be available to do so. Consideration should also be given to whether any civil orders (SHPO, Clare's Law, and Non-Molestation as outlined in Chapter 5) are applicable as further means of perpetrator management.

In circumstances where a nominal has been found to have committed serious offences whilst subject to MAPPA arrangements, the commissioning of a Serious Case Review examining the actions and decisions of the relevant partners' agencies will be considered.

However, not all domestic abuse offenders will be subject to MAPPA arrangements and police forces have developed other means to prioritise those who present an ongoing risk.

Recency, Frequency, Gravity & Victims tool (RFGV)

This is an algorithmic tool which mines police crime data and ranks perpetrators with scores between 1 and 100. The scores are weighted according to several factors such as seriousness of the offence(s) escalation and the number of victims they have offended against. The higher the total score, the more likely to perpetrator will be targeted for intervention and/or enforcement. This model was initially introduced in Scotland for focussing on prolific offenders committing anti-social behaviour. Various iterations of the RFG tool have been adopted by a number of forces in England and Wales in order to identify cohorts of the most concerning domestic abuse offenders (Davies and Biddle, 2018). Many of the adaptions to the RFG now include measurements of harm.

Cambridge Crime Harm Index (CCHI) and Crime Severity Scores (CSS)

Whilst used in the wider crime context, both the CCHI and CSS have been increasingly used by forces as a tool to narrow down the groups of high-risk perpetrators for additional actions and oversight. The CCHI is a scoring methodology which focusses on harm. It is founded on the basis that not all crimes are not equal in terms of severity and harm they cause to victims. Therefore, scores should be weighted by their severity. This is calculated by grading the specific offence by the number of days of imprisonment under the sentencing guidelines in England and Wales. The more serious the crime, the higher the CCHI. For instance, murder attracts a score of 5475, assault with intent to cause serious harm a score of 1825 and robbery 365. Where the CCHI process is filtered for domestic abuse perpetrators, those who consistently commit the most harm through amalgamation of the CCHI scores over time can be identified. Further links to the CCHI and CSS can be found in the resources section at the end of this chapter.

The Crime Severity Score (CSS) has been created by the Office for National Statistics (ONS), and again is a weighted scoring system. In this case, rather than use sentencing guidelines it uses average sentencing data to calculate the ranking order of harm/severity. So, in this case murder equates to a score of 7979, serious assault 1919 and robbery 746. Again, once all force perpetrators' offending histories have been scored, they can be filtered to those who perpetrate domestic abuse and then those who generate the most significant demand and harm can be better identified.

Priority Perpetrator Identification Tool (PPIT)

The PPIT is a prioritisation tool which combines the offence and the offender's characteristics to systematically identify and grade perpetrators in order to direct levels of appropriate levels of intervention. It is completed by grading five questions regarding the characteristic of the offence(s) such as escalating levels of violence, number of victims, and five questions relating to the individual themselves including mental health conditions and substance misuse. It was devised in a similar manner to the DASH assessment, in that it can be used within a multiagency approach to have a shared understanding of risk (Robinson and Clancy, 2020).

Typology approach

Innovative data analysis within Kent Constabulary (Robertson et al., 2020) established a typology of domestic abuse perpetrators. The objective being once classified would lead to improved targeting towards those offenders where efforts were more likely to be effective. Perpetrators were classified as being either acute, severe, generic, or chronic. Acute offenders represented a very small percentage of the cohort and were the unpredictable 'out of the blue' offenders who due to the random and spontaneous nature of their behaviour were unlikely be suitable for any form of treatment for their offending behaviour. Severe were the highest risk repeat offenders and therefore, in theory, had predictable behaviours and could be receptive to intervention. Generic offenders are lower-level perpetrators or commit single offences who may be amendable to restorative justice approaches. Chronic offenders are those who exhibit repetitive lower harm behaviours.

Whilst all the above approaches are gaining currency as innovative and evidence-based mechanisms for grading offenders and focussing activity most appropriately against them, the most common mechanism to do this still remains the use of the DASH risk grading (Robertson et al., Forthcoming). The high-risk classification acts a gateway for referral into multi-agency structures of prevention and intervention. Whilst all high-risk victims are referred to, in many cases the associated offender will also be managed through safety plans devised at the conference. There are no better means of keeping a victim safe than managing the danger present by their abuser.

These prioritisation tools evidence that a small proportion of offenders are responsible for a significant proportion of crime. They provide an evidence-based and effective mechanism for identifying the 'power few' and assist police in targeting their enforcement and engagement interventions on those offenders who cause the most harm and who might be most receptive to a form of treatment intervention. Best practice for forces is to have mechanisms to identify and manage those offenders whose behaviour may be serial and/or escalating. This will support victims' safety in an efficient and effective way (HMIC, 2014a).

However, as the use of algorithms and artificial intelligence increases within policing to better utilise data available into identifying and ranking distinct cohorts of victims and offenders, there is some caution needed with these developments (Oswald et al., 2018). There are ethical considerations to how such data is used within these models and the legacy effect or 'data shadow' of having been identified as 'high' risk and the label that follows an individual through their journey around various multiagency partnerships and interventions, especially if the algorithms are found to be built on inaccurate data or ill-founded theories. Police and other agencies hold significant amounts of 'big data' which can be effectively used to understand significant complex social issues such as domestic abuse. Police can harvest such data to build models to assist in effectively managing demand and ensure resources are placed where they can have maximum effect. Any model, however, is only as good as the data it is founded on. Crime recording standards have been found to be strewn with mistaken or missing information largely due to human inputting error (HMIC, 2014b). If someone is mistakenly labelled as high risk and subsequent interventions targeted against them, this can be a breach of their human rights and they may be stigmatised and suffer detriment as a result of these unnecessary actions. Forces will be held liable for such breaches. Such errors of process or judgement suggest that not only were resources ineffectively deployed, but this may also have prevented a genuine subject from receiving intervention or support. Whilst useful and necessary, tools that assist with prioritisation ought to be accompanied by ethical professional judgement and appropriate supervision and scrutiny.

Once they have been identified, how can police and multi-agency partners more effectively manage perpetrators? This can be done in two ways: effective investigation and prosecution through the criminal justice system where they can be held to account for their actions within the criminal justice system and/or through treatments and behavioural change programmes delivered through statutory and non-statutory basis (Davies and Biddle, 2018).

Effective investigation and prosecution

Whilst it is to be expected that all crime investigations and prosecutions are managed in a professional and effective manner by police, any investigation into domestic abuse offences comes with additional complexities due to the safeguarding implications associated with such criminality. The College of Police have produced extensive guidance within the Authorised Professional Practice (APP) on domestic abuse. Of note in relation to the management of perpetrators are the sections regarding investigation, post-arrest suspect management, and case files.

Arrests and interviews

National guidance pertaining to all forces points to a positive arrest or positive action policy following allegations of domestic abuse. The implication of this direction is that arrests should be made where possible and at the earliest opportunity rather than managed through other options such as a voluntary interview. Local force practices will have individual interpretations of this national guidance, and positive arrest should not be confused with mandatory arrest (HMIC, 2014b).

Police forces and academics alike will often discuss the value or otherwise of positive action policies at domestic abuse incidents. This is sometimes confused with a suggestion that a positive arrest policy is in place and a perpetrator should always be arrested where a criminal offence has occurred and the Police and Criminal Evidence Act 1984 allows. The evidence on positive action is mixed (Hoppe et al., 2020; Sherman et al., 1992; Westmarland et al., 2014), and the individual circumstances of a case will always have to be assessed in terms of practical decision-making on the ground. The duty of positive action in domestic abuse cases is well documented in the College of Policing Authorised Professional Practice (APP) on Domestic Abuse (College of Policing, 2020). Positive action in this context should not be confused with the concept of positive action under the Equality Act 2010, and positive action does not necessarily determine whether there should be an arrest made or not, although where an offence is disclosed or identified it is highly likely to be the outcome in most circumstances.

The Human Rights Act 1998 imposes a positive obligation on policing, within their lawful powers, to protect and safeguard individuals from acts that interfere with their rights. This includes Article 2 – the right to life; Article 3 – the right not to be tortured or subjected to inhuman or degrading treatment or punishment, which includes ill-treatment; and Article 8 – the right to respect for private and family life are the key obligations most closely affected by domestic abuse (College of Policing, 2020). These positive obligations lead to a requirement for positive action to protect victims and children who need safeguarding following an incident of domestic abuse. Criminal proceedings where suitable should follow, and the risk of harm from the perpetrator should be managed. In many cases, this will mean an arrest takes place. What needs to be considered is the impact of that arrest, whether arrest is right in every circumstance, and whether arrest can lead to increased attrition of the victim or a likelihood of further harm.

Sherman and Berk (1984) found that offenders who were arrested for misdemeanour domestic violence had lower recidivism rates than those given advice or ordered away from the scene. However, later research suggested the opposite (Sherman et al., 1992). Complexities were identified in which arrest could be helpful in some cases, but not others: for example if the suspect was employed then future violence was likely to decrease with arrest, but if unemployed it would increase. More recently, Hoppe et al. (2020) have conducted a meta-analysis of 11 published studies and concluded that arrest did not limit the likelihood of another offence being committed during the follow-up periods and likely did not have a deterrent effect on domestic violence offenders.

Sherman and Harris (2015) found that in a longitudinal study in the US state of Milwaukee, domestic abuse victims whose perpetrators were arrested 23 years before were more likely to have died than those where no arrest took place. The reason for this increased likelihood of death two decades later for victims where the offender was arrested are unknown, but this was a highly valid randomised-control trial and worthy of further exploration.

Iyengar (2009) identified that mandatory arrest laws increased intimate partner homicides, as well as leading to an increase in retaliations by perpetrators and a decrease in victim reporting of future incidents. Indeed, Iyengar suggests that victims may not report offences if they know that the suspect will be arrested, which is a concerning finding but one which was also found in the qualitative interviews concerning the retraction of allegations by victims following initial reporting conducted by Barrow-Grint (2016).

A positive outcome of mandatory arrest policies however is a likely reduction in unequal arresting practices in relation to perpetrator age, race, or socio-economic status (Hirschel and Buzawa, 2013). Any bias, unconscious or otherwise, towards a perpetrator is removed if officers must make an arrest if a criminal offence is confirmed. However, in England and Wales, the Police and Criminal Evidence Act 1984 Code G must be complied with which provides in law a review of the necessity of arrest when a criminal offence has occurred.

Whilst the evidence based on mandatory arrest at domestic abuse crime incidents fluctuates regularly around the benefits or otherwise of such action, what is clear is that positive action in some form, be it arrest, safeguarding, or mitigating the perpetrator's risk is instrumental in ensuring the police service obligations under the Human Rights Act are fulfilled.

Where officers have powers of arrest under Police & Criminal Evidence Act 1984 (PACE) those powers must be both proportionate and legal. The arrest must be necessary, and all officers are accountable for their actions. Arrests will be deemed as necessary under PACE guidelines to ensure the safety of vulnerable victims or children and allow for a prompt and effective investigation. Swift arrests will allow the victim, and potentially witnesses, time to feel safe, and consider their future option and be provided with support services (Myhill, 2019). Officers should not put the decision as to whether the perpetrator should be arrested or not on the victim. Officers will seek the victims' views asking, "Do you want them arrested". All arrests are at an officer's discretion, and whilst a victim will always be encouraged to support a prosecution, they should not be put in a position as to whether they support an arrest or not. Indeed, victims may not support the perpetrator being arrested (HMIC, 2014a). They may be angry and upset if their partner or family member is arrested and can be verbally or physically aggressive to officers when such arrests are made. Despite such provocation, officers dealing with such incidents must take into consideration that these events are emotionally charged. Victims may be fearful of consequences of the suspect being arrested and then being blamed for police intervention.

If suspects are later charged and convicted there may be considerable financial implications for them and their family.

Offenders who are not arrested at the time can also be invited into police stations for voluntary interview under Code G of PACE as a mechanism to obtain evidence through questioning. Whilst domestic abuse suspect interviews are not materially different from any other interview conducted under PACE, given the intimate or familial context, certain considerations should be taken when planning and undertaking the suspect interviews:

- Ensure there are no conflicts of interest between the suspects, legal advisor, interpreter or appropriate adult, and the victim. It may be the case that in particularly close knit and minority communities those fulfilling such roles may know both victim and suspect. Should this be the case, they cannot complete their roles objectively or impartially and on occasion could take the opportunity to negotiate or speak with both parties outside the boundaries of the roles to resolve the situation.
- Whilst the suspect may ask questions about the location of the victim, this should not be disclosed, especially details regarding the address of any refuge or safe house where the victim has been housed. Whilst such enquiries can be borne out of genuine concern, they can also be manipulative in their attempts to locate and intimidate victims and continue their abusive and coercive behaviour towards them.
- Where separated couples have children, arrangements of child contact can be a particular area of conflict, so it is always helpful to confirm a suspect's intentions in this matter to assist with subsequent safeguarding and risk assessment.
- It is important to ascertain as much detailed relationship information as possible from the suspect, including how they regard the status or perceived status of their relationship with the victim. As noted in Chapter 4, suspect's belief in infidelity or perceived infidelity of a partner or acceptance of separation can be key motivators for abuse and violence. Insightful questioning regarding how the suspect perceives the relationship itself is important. Asking information about how they feel about each other, how it operates on a day-to-day basis, division of labour, finances, and how arguments are generally resolved all helps provide context against which the offences may have taken place and allows of informed risk assessment.
- It is important to record and listen to any counter allegations the suspect may also make. On occasion, adopting the role of the victim may be a manipulative tactic by a coercive offender but in other circumstances there may well be situational conflict within the relationship that will require further investigation.
- Opportunities should be taken where relevant to challenge suspects on their prior 'bad character'. Domestic abusers are known to repeat

patterns of their behaviour and may have several current and or previous partners. Full intelligence database research, including the Police National Database (PND) and Police National Computer (PNC), should be completed to evidence if there is any antecedent history or repeat patterns of behaviour.
- Interviews should not be rushed, even if the suspect is silent or continually makes no comment to all questions put to them. This is an opportunity to put all evidence to the suspect and ask them to account for it.

It is important to always remain objective. However emotive or distressing the allegations, officers should remain impartial. The role of the police is to gather evidence and present it to the courts. It is acknowledged that this can be difficult and distressing in such cases. It is important to remain professional and manage the conflicting emotions such cases can generate. Any concerns regarding impartiality or the impact of an officer's mental health in dealing with domestic abuse investigation should be passed on to a supervisor or occupational health team. These issues are explored further in Chapter 8.

Lines of enquiry

Whilst the victim and suspect accounts will be fundamental elements of any effective prosecution each case will also provide other lines of enquiry for evidence gathering. Time should be taken to review the known facts and set an action plan which is regularly reviewed to ensure all opportunities are taken to gather evidence. The lines of enquiry listed below are no different from those that would be considered in any other type in investigation. Simply because offences are alleged to have occurred within a domestic context does not make them any less worthy of consideration for obtaining relevant evidential material. Again, these are no different from those which would be followed for non-domestic abuse offences, but they should not be discounted simply because the victim and offender know one another or there may be assumption that the victim will withdraw the case at a later stage, so it may not be worth the effort in pursing them. All evidential material, where possible, should be recovered and retained as it may be that an absent victim or victimless prosecution is possible.

House-to-house enquiries may be effective in terms of building up a chronology of what has been witnessed or heard within the home. Enquiries with family members, colleagues, or friends may reveal the information of where victims have previously made disclosures and can again provide situation awareness to provide the contextual dynamics of the relationship.

The timing of photographic evidence should be considered as it may take several days for the full extent of any bruising is visible. Depending on the nature and extent of the injuries and where any sexual offences may have been committed, consultation should take place with a scenes of crime officer or crime scene manager to agree a forensic evidential recovery plan.

Where possible body worn video should always be used to capture evidence of the scene as well as the individuals present within it. The recordings and, if necessary, transcripts of 999 emergency calls should be made available as they can provide background sounds and conversations which may be significant. They are also the first account relating to any subsequent formal allegations. Cyber evidence such as downloads of mobile phone, laptops, and other electric devices should also be considered. They may detail conversations and photographs which assist in building an evidence base of coercion. They may also provide contextual information as well as location-based evidence regarding the movements of victims and offenders.

Charging and bail management

Once available and relevant evidence has been gathered, the next stage in perpetrator management is to approach the Crown Prosecution Service (CPS) for a charging decision in a timely manner. Dependant on the amount of evidence recovered, the length of time the suspect has been in custody, and the potential risk they present to the victim, witness, and themselves, the CPS will make a charging decision on either a threshold or full code test. The threshold test related to circumstance where there is still further evidence to attain but this cannot be achieved within the detention time limits allowed under PACE. For instance, where forensic evidence needs to be processed or further witnesses' statements are required. These time limits in gathering such evidence may also present significant risks to the victims or suspect themselves, and thus, officers will seek to charge based on evidence that is likely to be available in the future. Alternatively, once most of the evidence is available a full code test will be applied by the CPS who will assess whether there is a realistic prospect of a successful prosecution. Whilst there is no difference between domestic abuse and non-domestic abuse cases in this process because of the risks and complexities associated with domestic cases as we have seen at every stage within the investigation process additional checks and balances have been introduced.

As mentioned in Chapter 5, the NPCC and CPS have agreed a Joint Evidence Checklist (2015) which should be submitted with the case file of submission for charging decisions. It prompts investigating officers and reviewing lawyers to consider whether all relevant evidence from the scene, victims, witnesses, forensic, and medical material has been secured. It has prompts for the reviewing lawyers to ensure witness and victim support has been considered and what aggravating and mitigating matters may pertain to the perpetrator.

In addition, the CPS follow a domestic abuse aide memoire in their decision-making which reminds the reviewing lawyers to build a robust and contextual case. Whilst each case is taken on its merits, the lawyers, through the aide memoire, are reminded to consider the strengths of each case, not assume a case cannot be taken to successful prosecution should a victim refuse to provide evidence or attend court. Wider consideration to the context of the relationship in which the offence occurred should be acknowledged.

Should the CPS reviewing lawyer direct that there is sufficient evidence to charge, the alleged perpetrator will be released on post-charge bail pending court proceeding (Section 38 PACE) or remanded into custody. If the threshold has not been met and further evidence is required, the suspect may be released on pre-charge bail (Section 37 PACE). Arrested suspects can also be released 'under investigation' where they are not subject to any form of bail regulation. Given the vulnerability of victims it is preferable to release suspects under some bail so any risk they present can be better regulated. Careful consideration should be given to appropriate measures and risk management using bail conditions. Bail conditions can be granted to mitigate any risk to the victim, children, and the suspect themselves. The most common conditions are non-contact with victims or witness, alternative residence, not to go to specified locations, for example, school or the victim's workplace, and to report regularly to a police station. Should a suspect have been released under conditions on pre-charge bail and then are subsequently charged, the conditions should be reviewed and if required reinstated. Conditions do not automatically translate following any charge. Should bail conditions be imposed they should be clearly explained to the suspect what they are, and the consequences should they breach them. Prior to the suspect being released, the victim must be informed of this and the conditions if any, which may be associated with their release. Furthermore, prior to release officers should ensure that any keys the suspect may have to a property where the victim resides are seized. Arrangements may be required for suspects to attend and collect property from the family home and officers should facilitate this if practicable. Where possible checks should be made to ensure that the suspect is adhering to their conditions, and any reported breaches should be acted upon expeditiously as such non-compliance with a legal duty speaks to a disregard of the criminal justice process and may be an indication that the victim is at increased risk.

Following a charge, the suspect should be sent before the court at the earliest opportunity. It may be that an application for bail is made if a suspect was initially remanded in custody. Officers should liaise with CPS lawyers in the case to make the appropriate application for suitable conditions to be imposed by the court in these circumstances. Further details on pre- and post-charge bail management can be found at APP Domestic abuse and CPS website.

As identified in Chapter 5, other perpetrator management tools such as DVPNs and Non-Molestation orders can also act concurrently with bail conditions to ensure risks are identified and mitigated. Checks should be undertaken to establish whether the perpetrator is a licenced firearms holder.

Due to the additional risk presented of serious injury where there is ready access to a firearm, under Home Office regulations (2015) any involvement of a licence holder in a domestic incident should trigger a review of licence conditions and a referral should be made to the local force firearm licencing unit to undertake such a review.

Following a charge, offenders will then stand trial to answer the charges laid against them. Effective victim management is essential as charging the offender can be a trigger event for further abusive behaviour, and victims will be a heightened pressure to withdraw from proceedings. Whether at Magistrates or Crown Court through the mechanism of a trial, suspects will be provided with an opportunity to account for their behaviour and either plead or be found guilty or not guilty beyond reasonable doubt. However, not all allegations result in a prosecution.

Non-prosecution perpetrator management options

Cautions

Approved Professional Practice (APP) recommends that where possible, charging and putting a matter before the court is the preferred course of action in domestic abuse cases given the added matters of safeguarding and harm associated with offences committed in this context. However, there are occasions that whilst there is sufficient evidence to charge a perpetrator it is not appropriate to do so, and a caution should be considered. The circumstances may be where they have been arrested for a low harm or severity offence and have no previous arrests or convictions or the suspect is a young person. Cautions can be simple or conditional. Simple cautions can be issued if approved by an Inspector independent of the investigation and the suspect has admitted to the offence. There is no power to impose any conditions associated with a simple caution, and therefore, any referrals for support or management of behaviour would be voluntary on the part of the suspect. Conditional cautions do have such requirements attached to them such as attending a treatment programme; however, it is only in very rare cases that they are used for offences committed within domestic relationships and, the authority of the Director of Public Prosecutions (DPP) is required if this is to be the case disposal option.

It should be noted that the APP is emphatic that fixed penalty notices for any offences in the domestic abuse setting should not be issued.

Restorative justice programmes

This is a more contentious method of out of court, non-prosecution disposal options (HMIC, 2014a). Suspects are eligible for such programmes if they have admitted the offence, it is a first-time offence, the victim is supportive, and the offence itself is low harm and severity. There should no evidence of a repeat offending or coercive behaviours within the relationship. The APP is clear that restorative justice programmes are risky because they bring offender and the victim together to talk about the crimes and the impact on the victim for the offender to understand the impact of their behaviour and learn to change as a result. Because of the difficulties with coercion and relationship dynamics this could be seen as potentially damaging to the victim engaging is such a process. This approach is not widely recommended in the APP, and careful consideration should be given to utilising this mechanism. However, there have been several research and pilot programmes which evidence restorative justice programmes can have a positive effect in lowering repeat offending.

Perhaps the most well-known RJ programme is Cautioning and Relationship Abuse (CARA) which is operated by Hampshire Police in a multi-agency partnership arrangement. A randomised control trial where males who had offended against female intimate partners who attended a four-day workshop who were subsequently arrested for a domestic abuse offence was 27% less harmful compared to those males who were rearrested who had not attended the course (Strang et al., 2017).

Force policies should be consulted where an RJ initiative, in relation to domestic abuse offending, is being considered as a means of perpetrator management.

Instigating behavioural change through therapeutic treatments

Whether perpetrators are convicted and sentenced to custody or community orders, are cautioned, are undergoing restorative justice programmes, and are mandated to undertake treatment or are outside the criminal justice process and recognise their behaviours and self-refer, there are several treatment options available.

In general, the therapeutic interventions in the United Kingdom are founded in feminist theories and perspectives of male issues of power, control, and abuse being the causes of violence and abusive behaviour. Therapies are based on confronting these attitudes and assisting in understanding and addressing behaviour change (Bates et al., 2017). As defined by the National Health Service this form of therapeutic approach is known under the umbrella of Cognitive Behavioural Therapy (CBT) and has been applied to the treatment of a number of conditions such as anxiety, depression, and other mental health conditions and addresses the linkage between an individual's thoughts and feelings and how they then manifest into behaviours (NHS, 2021). The position being that if a perpetrator's attitude to their relationship is based on negative feelings of jealousy, possessiveness, superiority, control, and anger this then is linked to their abusive violence and criminal behaviour towards their partner and/or family member. By challenging these thoughts and feelings and their impact, new more constructive behaviours result. Those in such therapies are taught skills and tools to internally challenge themselves when situations arise in order to deflect their thoughts. They learn tactics to diffuse conflict and anger and impulses, leading to more prosocial and less destructive or criminological behaviours. The therapeutic programmes can be delivered within individual, group-based, or family interventions or a blend of each. The interventions often use role plays, challenging conversations, and educational packages in the delivery of their service.

Respect is a government-funded organisation which accredits many of the Domestic Violence Perpetrator Programmes (DVPPs) provided within the United Kingdom. To achieve accredited status the programme and service provider will be subject to checks to ensure their delivery is of a high standard and there are associated measures to ensure victim safety whilst the perpetrator is completing the programme. Once accredited the provider will be audited every three years to ensure compliance with standards continues.

There is mixed and limited evidence as to the long-term success of domestic abuse perpetrator programmes (Bates et al., 2017; Geoghegan-Fittall et al., 2020). Measures of success are often based on levels of recidivism. However, with such low and inconsistent levels of victims reporting abuse to police or other agencies, any measurements of success have to be viewed with caution (Woolford and Wardhaugh, 2019). There are also dangers that manipulative offenders can display 'disguised compliance' with programmes by outwardly completing them but not really learning the lessons the programmes aspire to. Additionally, offenders may simply adapt their behaviours from overt violence to coercive control which are more difficult to detect and to enable them to continue to exert power over their victims.

Those therapies founded in the feminist perspective that all violence is the result of male aggression and coercion of women fail to consider male victims of female perpetrators or address an individual's own agency, history, and characteristics or challenges (Woolford and Wardhaugh, 2019). They assume all violence and abuse are based on unequal power within relationships, and their methodology is based on addressing this. They are, therefore, not appropriate as a means of addressing situational or couple's violence although they may be offered to perpetrators whose behaviour is exhibited in those circumstances. CBT is based on current thoughts and behaviours and does not address previous histories and experiences of the individuals such as substance misuse, financial pressures, housing, or education issues which all contribute to stress and violence in relationships. The final concern about DVPPs is that many of these programmes are based on male intimate partner violence towards women meaning there are very limited therapeutic programmes that address female, family, or LGBT perpetrators of domestic abuse (Bates et al., 2017; Robinson and Clancy, 2020).

Multi-Agency Tasking & Co-ordination (MATAC)

In a similar way to MARAC and MAPPA, MATAC has been piloted in a number of forces as a multi-agency partnership arrangement for the management of domestic abuse perpetrators (Davies and Biddle, 2018). A dedicated team of police and support staff manage the case work of serial domestic abuse perpetrators who have been identified by a prioritisation matrix approach, most typically the RFG matrix. Oversight of the process is lead through representatives of relevant agencies such as police, probation, housing, and health at monthly MATAC meetings. The MATAC process primarily provides bespoke interventions and support for perpetrators who may potentially fall outside other statutory regulations but present an ongoing risk. Where subjects fail to engage then enforcement and disruption activity is pursued against them. The partnership also combine activity with support to any associated victims. Whilst evaluations have found this approach to be successful, they are costly and resource intensive and can duplicate other arrangements such as MAPPA and MARAC.

One hybrid program which has sought to tackle these challenges is DRIVE. This seeks to address individual perpetrator needs and behaviours through one-to-one key work, support to victims and children. Deterrence is facilitated through disruptive consequences if perpetrators do not comply with the programme. Introduced in 2018 in the London Borough of Croydon following several national pilots, it has delivered multi-agency service provision to 170 perpetrators and 203 victim-survivors. The Metropolitan Police Service (MPS) are a partner in the DRIVE programme and contribute through intelligence and information sharing, collaborating in risk assessment decisions as well as managing the disruption and enforcement activity. This is often through Achilles' heel techniques whereby subjects may be arrested or processed for minor offences or breaches, such as road traffic or non-payment of fines, to disrupt their more serious criminal behaviours. At the time of writing the COVID-19 pandemic has impacted on a full evaluation of the results of this more blended intervention programme (Geoghegan-Fittall et al., 2020).

Conclusion

From the late 1980s the focus has turned from victim safety to perpetrator management with an acceptance that offenders should be held to account and change their behaviours. Police services play a vital role in the prevention of crime and ensuring the safety of victims through how they investigate crime and manage offenders. The finding by HMIC (2014a) that police services had better systems to manage prolific shoplifters than repeat domestic abusers has led to an increased focus on offender management. Initiatives to design tools to identify the most dangerous or prolific offenders in order to better target resources are ongoing. Following the recognition of the requirement to improve victim safety through effective perpetrator management, APP was published by the College of Policing so perpetrators could be held to account for their behaviour through the criminal justice system. Whilst there is mixed evidence as to whether perpetrators can truly be reformed, or rehabilitated, programmes are becoming more flexible and evolving. It is important that all efforts are made to ensure that perpetrators are held to account and given the opportunity to reform and rehabilitate to break cycles of violence and abuse.

Reflective questions

- How should victims who commit criminal acts of domestic abuse be treated?
- How would you manage cross allegation of domestic abuse?
- How would you seek to include evidence of previous abusive behaviour within a criminal prosecution case file?
- What are the ethical issues when using police data to predict future offending?

Useful websites

The CCHI can be found at: https://www.cambridge-ebp.co.uk/crime-harm-index

The CSS can be found at: https://www.ons.gov.uk/peoplepopulationandcommunity/crimeandjustice/datasets/crimeseverityscoredata

National Police Chiefs Council & Crown Prosecution Service Evidence Gathering Checklist for use by Police Forces and the Crown Prosecution Service in Cases of Domestic Abuse: https://www.cps.gov.uk/sites/default/files/documents/publications/npcc_cps_joint_evidence_gathering_checklist_2015.docm

References

Barrow-Grint, K., 2016. Attrition rates in domestic abuse: Time for a change? An application of temporal sequencing theory. *Policing: A Journal of Policy and Practice* 10, 250–263.

Bates, E.A., Graham-Kevan, N., Bolam, L.T., Thornton, A., 2017. A review of domestic violence perpetrator programs in the United Kingdom. *Partner Abuse* 8, 3–46.

College of Policing, 2020. Authorised professional practice on domestic abuse. https://www.app.college.police.uk/app-content/major-investigation-and-public-protection/domestic-abuse/ (accessed 11.6.21).

Davies, P.A., Biddle, P., 2018. Implementing a perpetrator-focused partnership approach to tackling domestic abuse: The opportunities and challenges of criminal justice localism. *Criminology & Criminal Justice* 18, 468–487.

Dobash, R.P., Dobash, R.E., Wilson, M., Daly, M., 1992. The myth of sexual symmetry in marital violence. *Social Problems* 39, 71–91.

Geoghegan-Fittall, S., Keeble, C., Wunsch, D., 2020. The Croydon drive project: A 2-year evaluation. Final Report, MOPAC Evidence and Insight, p. 53. https://www.london.gov.uk/sites/default/files/croydon_drive_final_evaluation_report.pdf (accessed 4.6.22).

Hester, M., Westmarland, N., Gangoli, G., Wilkinson, M., O'Kelly, C., Kent, A., Diamond, A., 2006. *Domestic violence perpetrators: Identifying needs to inform early intervention.* Northern Rock Foundation.

Hirschel, D., Buzawa, E.S., 2013. The impact of offenders leaving the scene on the police decision to arrest in cases of intimate partner violence. *Violence Against Women* 19, 1079–1103.

HMIC, 2014a. Everyone's business: Improving the police response to domestic abuse. Her Majesty's Inspectorate of Constabulary. https://www.justiceinspectorates.gov.uk/hmicfrs/publications/improving-the-police-response-to-domestic-abuse/

HMIC, 2014b. Crime recording: Making the victim count. The final report of an inspection of crime data integrity in police forces in England and Wales. HMIC. https://www.justiceinspectorates.gov.uk/hmicfrs/publications/increasingly-everyones-business-a-progress-report-on-the-police-response-to-domestic-abuse/ (accessed 7.8.22).

Hoppe, S.J., Zhang, Y., Hayes, B.E., Bills, M.A., 2020. Mandatory arrest for domestic violence and repeat offending: A meta-analysis. *Aggression and Violent Behavior* 53, 1359–1789.

Iyengar, R., 2009. Does the certainty of arrest reduce domestic violence? Evidence from mandatory and recommended arrest laws. *Journal of Public Economics* 93, 85–98.

Johnson, M.P., 1995. Patriarchal terrorism and common couple violence: Two forms of violence against women. *Journal of Marriage and Family* 57, 283–294.

Myhill, A., 2019. Renegotiating domestic violence: Police attitudes and decisions concerning arrest. *Policing and Society* 29, 52–68.

NHS, 2021. Overview – Cognitive behavioural therapy (CBT). nhs.uk. https://www.nhs.uk/mental-health/talking-therapies-medicine-treatments/talking-therapies-and-counselling/cognitive-behavioural-therapy-cbt/overview/ (accessed 11.29.21).

Oswald, M., Grace, J., Urwin, S., Barnes, G.C., 2018. Algorithmic risk assessment policing models: Lessons from the Durham HART model and 'Experimental' proportionality. *Information & Communications Technology Law* 27, 223–250.

Robertson, A., Featherstone, A., Phillips, J., McFadzien, K., Forthcoming. Family violence reported to Kent police: Classifying 371,000 cases by frequency and harm patterns 2003–2017.

Robinson, A.L., Clancy, A., 2020. Systematically identifying and prioritising domestic abuse perpetrators for targeted intervention. *Criminology & Criminal Justice* 687–704.

Sebire, J.A., 2013. Love and lethal violence: an analysis of intimate partner homicides committed in London 1998–2009 (Doctoral Thesis). University of Leicester.

Sherman, L.W., Berk, R.A., 1984. The specific deterrent effects of arrest for domestic assault. *American Sociological Review* 49(2), 261–272.

Sherman, L.W., Harris, H.M., 2015. Increased death rates of domestic violence victims from arresting vs. warning suspects in the Milwaukee Domestic Violence Experiment (MilDVE). *Journal of Experimental Criminology* 11, 1–20.

Sherman, L.W., Schmidt, J.D., Rogan, D.P., 1992. *Policing domestic violence: Experiments and dilemmas.* Free Press.

Spivey, E., Nodeland, B., 2020. The victim-offender overlap in intimate partner violence: Considering the role of self-control. *Deviant Behavior* 42(6), 735–746.

Strang, H., Sherman, L., Ariel, B., Chilton, S., Braddock, R., Rowlinson, T., Cornelius, N., Jarman, R., Weinborn, C., 2017. Reducing the harm of intimate partner violence: Randomized controlled trial of the Hampshire Constabulary CARA Experiment. *Cambridge Journal of Evidence-Based Policing* 1, 160–173.

Straus, M.A., Gelles, R.J., 1990. How violent are American families? Estimates from the National Family Violence Resurvey and other studies, in: *Physical Violence in American Families: Risk Factors and Adaptations to Violence in 8,145.* Transaction Publishers, pp. 95–112.

Westmarland, N., Thorlby, K., Wistow, J., Gadd, D., 2014. *Domestic violence: Evidence review.* N8 Policing Research Partnership.

Woolford, R., Wardhaugh, J., 2019. Help: A practitioners' perspective on programmes for domestic abuse perpetrators. A qualitative study. *British Journal of Community Justice* 15, 82–105.

Chapter 8

Coordinated solutions to domestic abuse

KEY POINTS

- Knowledge from research and practice signposts ways to respond to domestic abuse.
- Working together professionally and as a community protects victims and challenges perpetrators.
- The development of Multi-agency Risk Assessment Conferences and the role of the Independent Domestic Violence Advisors formalise the approach to risk assessment in cases of domestic abuse.
- Evidence-based solutions support practical policing.
- Domestic Violence Homicide Reviews enable lessons to be learnt – and acted upon – when things go wrong.

Introduction

This chapter reviews the significance of agencies working together in cases of domestic abuse. It reviews the strategic and tactical partnerships and highlights the importance of adopting a coordinated community response (CCR). This chapter offers an analysis of Multi-Agency Risk Assessment Conferences (MARACs), the role of the Independent Domestic Violence Adviser (IDVA), and, when these processes fail, the importance of recognising domestic femicide and learning from Domestic Violence Homicide Reviews (DVHRs).

Background

The model of working together has a long history but was often seen as an 'ideal' notion since it is complicated to put multi-agency strategies into practice. Successive governments have been keen to utilise partnerships to tackle crime and as such the concept of multi-agency working has been part of a ". . . political process towards a locally informed collaborative approach to developing policies and practice to improve citizenship and

DOI: 10.4324/9781003137412-8

local accountability" (Harvie and Manzi, 2011, p. 80). Whilst the focus was on good practice, there were other political and economic considerations within these governmental approaches including the possibilities of sharing costs and resources between agencies.

The foundations of the current multi-agency collaborations were laid down in the Thatcher era of the 1980s. Originally this was formulated under the Children Act 1989 following several child sex abuse scandals, the most significant of which resulted in the Cleveland Inquiry's (Department of Health and Social Security, 1988) recommendation that professionals must work together to better protect children. At a similar time, the Morgan Report's (Standing Conference on Crime Prevention, 1991) review of local crime realised that no one agency was ultimately responsible for prevention and recommended that the police should work in partnership with local authorities to enable a multi-agency approach to community safety. The Morgan Report recommendations were initially shelved by politicians and not implemented until 1998 through the Crime and Disorder Act, which established the principles in law. However, by this time many of the suggestions from the report had already been accepted and enacted by local authorities and police forces across England and Wales (Newburn, 2017).

What emerged, particularly with the Labour Government's 'third way' strategy in the early 2000s, was a move away from the past fluid collaborations between agencies towards coordination of partnerships with pre-set objectives, clear boundaries, and a whole systems approach of 'joined up' thinking (Ranade and Hudson, 2003).

Furthermore, the intention of these 'new' partnerships was to mitigate inequalities of power and status between NGOs and statutory organisations in order to exercise the 'principle of equal worth' of each individual member (Ranade and Hudson, 2003). This has not always worked out in practice which has sometimes risked the loss of local information and support from the grass roots membership. Local knowledge is important as it gives us a more in-depth narrative; it tells what is happening behind closed doors ". . . and as such (has) been key to furthering a more inclusive crime prevention and community safety strategy" (Davies, 2020, p. 285).

At the strategic level, amendments to the Crime and Disorder Act placed responsibility for reducing and preventing crime on Police Crime and Control Commissioners, local authorities, and clinical commissioning groups. Their remit was to form partnerships to set objectives using local knowledge. This way of working was perceived as the key to crime prevention and remains ". . .the touchstone for community safety and security" (Davies, 2020, p. 278).

During this period, multi-agency focus was towards public safety in public places and, as such, created problems for dealing with the typically private violence of domestic abuse. As we have already noted, most domestic abuse victims remain hidden within the domestic sphere and those who do come forward frequently have multiple needs such as housing, counselling, and child protection, which are beyond the scope of one agency. Partnerships could be seen as a success in areas such as anti-social behaviour but dealing with the private and complex nature of domestic abuse has not been so successful (Harvie and Manzi, 2011). Consequently, finding solutions to domestic violence has become a priority for police forces across the United Kingdom. Probably one of the key issues to emerge is that whilst the police may often be the 'first responders' to cases of domestic abuse, other organisations are involved with managing risk and protecting victims on several levels, including some statutory responsibilities. Thus, some domestic abuse cases may require an initial criminal justice approach, but ongoing support and safeguarding need a multi-agency response.

Part of the challenge has been to develop victim-led approaches to deal with domestic violence. There were two important global initiatives that led to a demand for change. First, the development of the Duluth programme in the United States, an innovative process to keep victims safe and hold perpetrators accountable that influenced responses to domestic abuse in the 1990s (Davies, 2020). Whilst there have been considerable criticisms of this programme, not least that the emphasis is on female victims and assumes male perpetrators, the model produced (see Box 8.1) has proved invaluable in professional training and is used as a basis for some perpetrator programmes. This is partly because it covers all aspects of domestic abuse and highlights the diversity of behaviours suffered by victims. Similarly, the Duluth model itself indicates an alternative way to deal with domestic abuse by moving any blame from the victim to the offender as well as offering a "...commitment to shift responsibility for victim safety from the victim to the community and state" (Domestic Abuse Intervention Programs, 2017).

BOX 8.1 THE DULUTH MODEL APPROACH

The Duluth Model approach is to keep victims of domestic violence safe and ensure any perpetrators are accountable for their actions. This is an 'evolving way of thinking about how a community works together to end domestic violence'. There are several key principles:

i A shift in blame from the victim to the perpetrator as well as the responsibility for safety and risk from the victim to the community and state.
ii A move to multi-agency and community shared processes and interventions for holding perpetrators accountable and keeping victims safe.

iii Agreed definitions between agencies of domestic violence, strategies and perceptions of danger, risk, and accountability.
iv Include the experiences of domestic violence victims in policy development and practice.

https://www.theduluthmodel.org/what-is-the-duluth-model/

The second global initiative was the Violence Against Women and Girls (VAWG) campaign led by the United Nations (UN); this has been on the UN agenda for over 20 years and is an ongoing concern for the UK government (Davies, 2020). As part of the UK government response (see Box 8.2) the action plans developed in 2014 and 2016 encourage the continuation of locally led partnerships to ensure early intervention, adequate service provision, and risk reduction and prevention. Both the Duluth Program and VAWG put victims at the centre of policy and practice.

BOX 8.2 VIOLENCE AGAINST WOMEN AND GIRLS: UK GOVERNMENT STATEMENT OF EXPECTATIONS

1. Put the victim at the centre of service delivery. Every victim, whether adult or child, is an individual with different experiences, reactions, and needs. Local areas should ensure that services are flexible and responsive to the victim's experience and voice.
2. Have a clear focus on perpetrators in order to keep victims safe. In order to keep victims safe, local areas should ensure that there are robust services in place which manage the risk posed by perpetrators and offer behavioural change opportunities for these willing and able to engage.
3. Take a strategic, system-wide approach to commissioning acknowledging the gendered nature of VAWG. Good commissioning always starts with understanding the issue and the problem you are trying to solve.
4. Services should be locally led and safeguard individuals at every point. Commissioned services should make use of local initiatives and services already in place to utilise resource, share best practice, and ensure that there are coordinated pathways of support.
5. Strategies need to be in place to raise local awareness of the issues and involve, engage, and empower communities to seek, design, and deliver solutions to prevent VAWG. Commissioners should work with local partners to provide a multiplicity of reporting mechanisms to better enable victims to come forward and access the support they need.

> The government recognises the disproportionate gender bias in many sexual and DA crimes, it is important to acknowledge that men and boys can be victims too. This statement of expectations should benefit all victims.
>
> (GOV.UK, 2016)

We know that domestic violence and abuse are complex issues that require sensitive handling by a range of police, health, social care, and NGO professionals. We also know that the cost in both human and economic terms is significant so any interventions that prove to be effective are worthwhile (NICE, 2014). The Home Office paper, *Call to End Violence Against Women and Girls* (2010), did not just stress the need to bring perpetrators to justice and reduce the risk of harm and support victims, but it also emphasised the need to challenge attitudes to domestic abuse and sexual violence within the national curriculum. Given this remit and the diverse nature of the crimes and abusive behaviour that are incorporated into the current understanding of domestic abuse, working in multi-agency partnerships must be the only effective way to approach the problem both at a strategic and operational level. This is particularly the case as we know that working together is effective in ". . . tackling complex problems that are perceived to be intractable and not amenable to resolution by any one agency working alone" (Percy-Smith, 2006, p. 313).

Types of domestic abuse prevention

Using knowledge from a practical and research basis is more likely to succeed as is understanding which approach is the most appropriate for any agreed goals. Domestic abuse prevention strategies can be divided into primary, secondary, and tertiary. Primary prevention focusses on measures to stop abuse from happening in the first place. Until recently this has been a neglected area, with more money invested in secondary and tertiary programmes. However, there has been a recent increase in the primary prevention strategies, particularly in public health (WHO, 2010) and education. An example is the move to make healthy intimate relationship education mandatory in schools in England and Wales (Page and Temple-Malt, 2018).

From September 2020, all schools in the United Kingdom have been obliged to teach relationship education to encourage positive and safe relationships at both primary and secondary school levels. This compulsory curriculum includes a wide range of topics including mental well-being, sexual consent, keeping safe online, sexual exploitation, grooming, coercion, harassment, rape, domestic abuse, forced marriage, honour-based violence, and female genital mutilation (Department for Education, 2019). Schools can provide the setting in which interventions aimed at preventing intimate partner violence and abuse are delivered to young people (Stanley et al., 2015). However, it is essential that such education is agile and kept up to date with the onset of new crime types such as cyber bullying, coercive control, and sexting which are becoming ever-increasing issues for young people.

Shifting social norms within a peer group is key to ensuring the success of any educational intervention (Stanley et al., 2015). Gains can be both short term, as young people embark on personal relationships that may involve domestic abuse, and long term as a preventative measure to influence adult relationships. What is clear from the limited research about the proliferation of adolescent domestic abuse is that it involves younger children than those covered by the government definition. It is therefore essential that educational interventions need to target children before they reach the age of 13 (Fox et al., 2014).

A systematic literature review of the impact of teaching about domestic abuse found that messages for boys should be positively framed to avoid a blaming approach that could provoke resistance (Stanley et al., 2015). Indeed, Fox et al. (2014) go further by explaining that, compared to cases of domestic abuse in the adult population, the situation amongst young people appears less overtly gendered. The data suggests there is much more gender equality in terms of both victims and perpetrators at this stage of a young person's life. As teenagers move from seeking advice from parent to peers, it is the lack of knowledge of how to prevent or deal with abuse which can lead to normalisation of behaviour and an absence of formal retribution or justice (Pensak, 2014).

A more recent development is the reducing age of victims and perpetrators, the normalisation of domestic abuse in teenage relationships, and the increasing and often unhealthy use of technology by young people. This combined with a lack of capability by police to respond to cyber stalking and other technology-assisted crimes is of significant concern (King-Ries, 2010). In order to ensure that policing has the capacity to deal with this moving forward, King–Ries (2010) suggests that more resources are required for the investigation of digital domestic violence, particularly that involving young victims and perpetrators, to prevent an epidemic moving forward. The recent all-party parliamentary response to tackling domestic abuse in a digital age noted that the age of those involved in domestic abuse is getting lower and online abuse and harassment plays a significant part in such violence against women and girls. Therefore, education at an early stage is key to primary prevention (Clark et al., 2017).

However, preventative education sits alongside community commitment. Children are often invisible to services, falling through the gap of child protection procedures and domestic abuse practices, and are further endangered by their reliance on technology to form and conduct relationships. The literature concerning teenage domestic abuse is limited, and there is little guidance or policy for practitioners and law enforcement personnel on how to deal with teenage victims and perpetrators of intimate violence. Forming a more coherent, coordinated response will break the "... generational cycle of violence" (Suarez, 1994, p. 471) that traps some children and young people (see Box 8.3).

BOX 8.3 CASE STUDY CHILD J

The murder of Child J in December 2013 sparked national concern and interest following her disappearance and the subsequent discovery of her body by police, buried in a grave in a churchyard in Didcot, Oxfordshire. The Joint Serious Case Review and Domestic Homicide Review that followed (Oxfordshire Safeguarding Children's Board, 2016) picked up on the seriousness of domestic abuse in teenage relationships, particularly in terms of the impact of coercive control, and the lack of domestic abuse support for young people. You can read the overview report on Child J here:

Child-J-OSCB-Overview-Report.pdf

The tipping point has been reached to suggest that teenage domestic abuse is a significant concern, and one which will only increase in the future unless we ensure our primary and secondary prevention programmes work.

Secondary prevention strategies are responses that focus shortly after the abuse has taken place or is recognised. Prevention activities include early intervention initiatives, such as screening for domestic abuse in National Health Service (NHS) settings. Such interventions have been trialled, implemented, and evaluated in several hospitals, with patients routinely asked whether they have experienced abuse when attending A&E or maternity services (Warren-Gash et al., 2016). Other secondary prevention strategies focus on preventing abuse amongst diverse sub-groups who are identified at being at increased risk of domestic abuse (NICE, 2013). The Early Intervention Foundation (EIF) estimates that the price of late intervention, the potentially preventable fiscal cost of short-term acute services, is £5.2 billion per year in England and Wales (EIF, 2018).

Tertiary prevention focusses on the ongoing support of those experiencing abuse and treatment and rehabilitation of those who are perpetrating the abuse. Much of the focus of criminal justice responses to domestic abuse is on tertiary prevention (WHO, 2010).

Complexities of trying to prevent domestic abuse

Trying to prevent domestic abuse is made difficult by the complex interplay of multiple risk factors that operate at different levels (WHO, 2012). The nuances of each individual case make it very difficult to apply a one size fits all approach to prevention. Figure 8.1 shows an ecological model of domestic abuse used by the World Health Organisation (WHO) to understand the different levels over which abuse operates. The model was initially developed in the late 1970s to understand child abuse, but it has since been expanded to look at youth violence, abuse of the elderly and intimate partner violence (Krug et al., 2002). The model identifies the characteristics at the individual, relationship, community, and societal level and the connection between each of the levels.

Table 8.1 details risk factors that have been identified at each level. Krug et al. (2002) identify that the key to prevention lies in promoting the development of cross-sectional programmes that make the links and interactions between the different factors and levels.

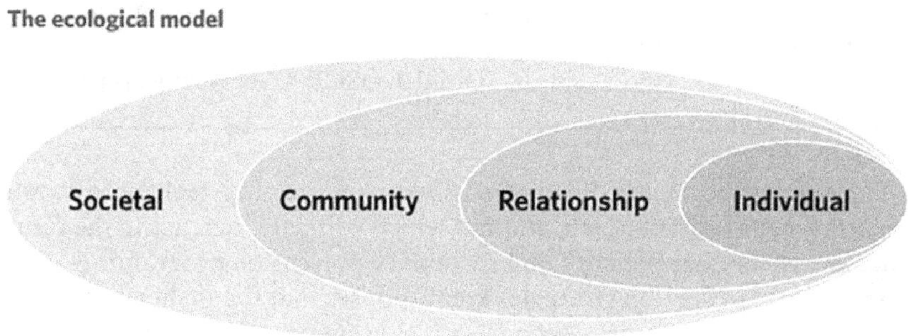

Figure 8.1 Ecological model of domestic abuse (Krug et al., 2002).

Table 8.1 Risk factors for domestic abuse by level

Individual	Individual attitudes Behaviour Health Social, personal, and biological history
Relationship	Family relationships/ Closest social circle Patriarchal culture Role of women Alcohol/drug use Poverty Employment

Community	Neighbourhood environment Culture of violence Access to services Quality of housing Drug use Social isolation Schools and workplaces Levels of anti-social behaviour Population density Deprivation
Societal	National, state, and local policy Education of women Gender inequality Religious and cultural belief systems Societal norms Public awareness Firearms policies Emergency systems

Beyer et al. (2015), Krug et al. (2002), Weir (2019), WHO (2012)

It is these multifarious risk factors that create a web of challenging dynamics for prevention and harm reduction in cases of domestic abuse. But highlighting them emphasises that the key element to managing domestic abuse lies within a partnership approach, which must be constructed on several levels to enable both strategic and operational responses.

Strategic partnerships

Partnerships are often various and complex but there are two defining strata. One level is strategic and the other relates to more operational activities. Partnerships at all levels are more than network groups. They are formal and organised in structure with agreed aims and objectives and plans to achieve these (Percy-Smith, 2006). To be successful, stakeholders need to develop a sense of trust, cooperation, and commitment. When this works, multi-agency partnerships can deliver a more consistent service to both victims and offenders and often develop innovative ideas to deal with difficult and complex situations (Percy-Smith, 2006). These groups offer an opportunity for cross-fertilisation of knowledge and experience not just as a one-off coming together but rather as a more integrated group. Burnett and Appleton (2004) highlighted this as the difference between a 'fruit salad' and a 'fruit cake', the fruit cake is solid and more consistent.

There are four clear requirements for successful strategic partnerships:

- Stakeholders at appropriate seniority to account for decision-making.
- Processes in place for budgeting, commissioning, and delivery of services.

- Regular review of service provision and evaluation of impact.
- Regular review of partnership stakeholders and renewal/change of membership to ensure effectiveness (Davies, 2020).

Partnerships stand outside of the bureaucracy and normal accountability methods of their agencies and so require robust mechanisms of both internal and external audits, action plans, and monitoring and reporting systems. These give the multi-agency partnerships credibility, encourage goals, and offer individuals a sense of purpose. The Home Office has a statutory framework published alongside the new Domestic Abuse Bill (Home Office, 2021), and these, alongside NICE guidelines (2016, 2014), offer clear directions for strategic partnerships and what is expected of them (Box 8.4). This statutory guidance increases credibility and supports cooperation between agencies.

BOX 8.4 MEMBERSHIP AND EXPECTATIONS OF STRATEGIC PARTNERSHIPS

NICE recommends that partnership should ensure the group is representative by including senior officers from the following organisations to participate in a local strategic partnership:

- Health services and local authority – to include the chairs of the adult and child safeguarding boards
- Police and crime commissioners
- Public health
- Sexual violence services
- Housing
- Education
- Community safety partnerships
- CJ agencies
- Specialist court representatives and advisers
- Specialist voluntary, community, and private sector organisations.

One partner should take the group lead to oversee service delivery, but all agencies work together in service provision. The role of strategic partnerships carries a number of expectations:

- To gauge the need for domestic abuse services by consulting victims – including women, men, and young people and victims from communities that are rarely heard – or rarely listened to.
- Map local domestic abuse service provision and adjust where necessary to provide a coordinated response to local need.

- Commission services using the consultations and mapping exercises.
- Consultation with regional and national strategic partnerships to ensure specialist services can be provided across local boundaries.
- Develop referral pathways to ensure victims can access services, especially for those with protected characteristics, for those with mental health issues, drug or alcohol dependency, and for young people and children caught up in violent households.
- Provide suitable pathways for managing perpetrators.
- Adopt protocols for information sharing such as the Caldicott guidelines (https://www.gov.uk/government/publications/the-caldicott-principles).
- Publish a directory of local and national services and how these can be accessed by service users.

It is important that any commissioned services are accessible and there are services addressing all levels of risk and severity of domestic violence.

(NICE, 2016)

Apart from the statutory expectations there are other elements that enable partnerships to be effective. Working with other agencies can put stakeholders outside of their comfort zone by challenging their normal agenda and working practices. People need time to build relationships and change their 'mental' maps in order to see themselves as part of a whole and stop shifting blame to other parts of the system (Percy-Smith, 2006). The more diverse the group, the greater the possibilities of new ideas emerging and increasing passion and energy to effect change. Facilitation by an experienced leader can develop a common focus and joint ownership of responsibility as well as the mutual trust required to ensure an active and proactive partnership. Even when problems arise, under ideal circumstances, these can be aired and resolved to ensure smooth working as well as success in achieving the agreed aims.

Of course, some problems are more difficult to resolve than others for instance,

- Budget constraints hold particular issues. Each organisation involved has fiscal and resource limitations, and these are exacerbated for many NGOs who are constantly developing bids for funding, often on a year-on-year basis. However, the new Domestic Abuse Commissioner is looking at new ways of procurement for core funding. This is alongside the Local Authority requirements to fulfil the responsibilities of the new Domestic Abuse Bill (2021) by developing a sustainable approach to the commissioning of appropriate services which is a step in the right direction.

- Different policies, procedures, and practices "... can act as barriers to effective partnership working" (Longden, 2014, p. 8). Awareness of the various roles and responsibilities of stakeholders as well as where possible multi-agency domestic abuse training, and updates, at all levels supports core aims and objectives and smooths day-to-day practice.
- As suggested above, power imbalances within partnerships can be detrimental to working together. But good leadership can resolve these. Noble and Jones (2006) have suggested one way to support trust and encourage 'joined-up' thinking is to use 'boundary spanners'. Boundary spanners are individual stakeholders with specific knowledge and skills who "... can play an important role in explaining and interpreting ... behaviour and resolving conflicts and misunderstanding" (Ranade and Hudson, 2003, p. 46).
- Another common and important difficulty presented in strategic partnerships concerning domestic abuse is the ongoing tension between protecting the victim and tackling the perpetrator. But as Davies (2020) suggests, such discussion is not always negative as, "(t)hese tensions serve as healthy reminders of the divergent paradigms, ideologies, politics and working cultures at stake in multi-agency partnerships" (p. 292).

Domestic abuse requires the combined efforts of agencies and NGOs working together – a whole systems approach – to protect victims and challenge perpetrators. There is plenty of discussion and agreement around the concept of a CCR. However, sometimes the practice is more complicated. Part of the problem certainly for England and Wales is the legacy dealing with domestic abuse as a crime – a police and judicial matter – and as such it places the focus of response on the criminal justice system, which as we know is only part of the answer.

Coordinated community response

A CCR goes one step further beyond partnership working arrangements by ensuring a community commitment to dealing with domestic abuse (see Box 8.5). There are some core requirements to ensure a successful and productive CCR mainly,

> ... mobilizing community leaders, connecting victims to resources, holding offenders accountable, maximising effectiveness and efficiency of responses, and avoiding duplication of services.
>
> (Johnson and Stylianou, 2020, p. 2)

BOX 8.5 WHAT IS A COORDINATED COMMUNITY RESPONSE (CCR)?

> The CCR is based on the principle that no single agency or professional has a complete picture of the life of a domestic abuse survivor and their children. Instead, agencies hold information that can be shared within an effective and systematic partnership, to increase the safety of survivors and their children. Central to the CCR is the aim of holding perpetrators account, underpinned by a full understanding of the perpetrators' pattern of coercive control, abusive behaviour and the impact this has on the survivor and any children.
>
> (Standing Together, 2021, p. 7)

The CCR is made up of 12 components behind which is a "set of core principles which agencies and partners need to share in order to make CCR work". These values, principles, and approaches include collaboration, an intersectional approach, holding perpetrators accountable, supporting the various responsibilities and approaches of other agencies, shared understanding, and shared leadership.

Three key and important issues required for CCR to be effective:

- Responsibility is spread across agencies not held with a single agency or person.
- A nominated lead is required to hold the group together alongside commitment from all partners.
- Responsibility for the safety of victims and their children rests with systems and the community not the victim.

(Standing Together 2021)

What is a CCR?

A CCR brings communities together to end domestic abuse. It is not just local agencies and statutory organisations but whole communities that are required to ensure the success of a response. Good coordination between agencies can work towards challenging the ways that organisations and individuals think about domestic abuse and as such is,

> . . . a collaborative multiagency effort to change the culture of tolerance of domestic abuse by embedding practices and procedures which integrates victim/survivor safety and holds the perpetrator to account for the abuse.
>
> (Standing Together, 2021)

Importantly, using this system ensures that the responsibility for safety shifts from the victim to the community and agencies involved and makes way for 'bystander' programmes "...that enable and equip residents to safely challenge unacceptable behaviour, ensuring awareness of unsafe interventions" (Haringey Borough Council, 2016). Successful CCRs ensure that leadership is shared, all stakeholders take ownership and shared responsibility of the goals and any problems in achieving these. Furthermore, a CCR that works well listens to the voices of victims to ensure the suitable frameworks are in place and uses IDVAs to supplement this data and enable a strategic approach to managing perpetrators (Standing Together, 2021). The behaviour of communities and individuals can be challenged, and victims better protected, through CCR and multi-agency partnerships. Community coordinated response is most significant through the role of the Multi-Agency Risk Assessment Conference (MARAC). Whilst not statutory, this bringing together of key partners is vital to reduce harm to victims.

The Multi-Agency Risk Assessment Conference

Part of the role of strategic partnerships is to research and assess service requirements and determine how these might be delivered in terms of commissioning. The delivery of these services is overseen by the operational multi-agency partnerships and local needs determine which agencies are involved, therefore this differs across England and Wales. However, all areas have a MARAC. Despite some difficulties and criticisms, MARACs have been held up as examples of successful multi-agency cooperation.

The MARAC brings together the criminal justice system as well as others such as health and social care, and appropriate third sector groups including domestic abuse charities. The aim is to provide a forum for information sharing and action planning to reduce harm to high-risk domestic abuse victims and their families. Central to the concept of a MARAC is the assumption that no single agency or individual can see the complete picture of the life of a victim, but all may have insights that are crucial to their safety (SafeLives, 2014). Domestic violence, and in particular risk of homicide or significant harm through such violence, is a multi-agency issue (Robbins et al., 2014) and working together to prevent such harm is imperative. Whilst the primary focus of the MARAC is to safeguard the adult victim, the MARAC will also make links with other fora to safeguard children and manage the behaviour of the perpetrator (SafeLives, 2014).

The first MARAC was held in Cardiff, Wales, in 2003 and came about following the introduction of the Multi-Agency Public Protection Arrangement (MAPPA) process under Section 67 of the Criminal Justice and Court Services Act 2000 (Robinson, 2006). The enormous benefits of such a process ensure a focus on the victim and a holistic look at the risk with a coordinated community response as the outcome. What one agency knows may be unknown to another, but discussing together means there can be constructive developments, and indeed challenge, on action and risk management. Limited time means the MARAC is unlikely to be able to delve into a case significantly and share in-depth knowledge but provides the opportunity to share information across agencies and ensure resources are allocated to address concerns raised.

Statistically there were 247 MARACs in England and Wales in the year ending March 2020 and 99,447 cases were discussed (ONS, 2020). Of these:

- 5% involved a male victim.
- 16% involved a black and ethnic minority victim.
- 7% of victims had a disability.
- 1% identified themselves as lesbian, gay, bisexual, or transgender (LGBT).

MARACs are most frequently chaired by the police. Just under two-thirds (65%) of MARAC cases were referred by the police in the year ending March 2020 (ONS, 2020) with the rest being referred by other front-line agencies who undertake risk assessments with a victim and determine whether their case meets the high-risk threshold. A victim cannot self-refer, nor does the victim attend the MARAC but is represented by an IDVA who speaks on their behalf. In the unusual case where a victim does not wish to be referred to MARAC, then agencies must assess on a case-by-case basis whether it is proportionate and legitimate to share information to protect the victim from harm.

Robinson (2006) remarks that MARACs are invaluable because agencies assist victims more efficiently due to enhanced information sharing, and this coordinated community response leads to 60% of victims discussed at MARAC not becoming re-victimised. However, research by Whinney (2015) suggested that whilst significant reductions in crime harm are associated with MARAC referral, reductions are also seen in cases where victims were not referred to MARAC and the process seems to be producing little reduction in subsequent domestic abuse that would not have happened anyway.

These dichotomies of opinion reflect the fact that there is a paucity of academic research on MARACs. Steel et al. (2011) found that MARACs have the potential to improve victim safety and reduce re-victimisation and therefore may be a cost-effective measure but the available evidence on MARAC outcomes is "relatively weak" and should be explored further. Berry et al. (2014) concluded that there is no robust evidence supporting the effectiveness of MARACs and concentrating on high-risk victims may be to the detriment of victims assessed at lower levels of risk who cannot access the services provided to those deemed of higher risk. As such, whilst MARACs no doubt add value in a complex landscape of risk assessment and management of domestic abuse, the question of whether they are fit for purpose is critical. Recent research by Adisa (2020) suggests there are still numerous barriers to effective outcomes such as a lack of accountability and no statutory obligation to attend for relevant partners, a lack of clarity of desired objectives and obligations, and a lack of monitoring and reflection, all of which can leave victims at future risk.

Despite these concerns, the MARAC is a place for partners to understand the voice and concerns of the victim through the medium of the IDVA, and for that reason the conferences are essential to ensuing these representations are heard.

The role of IDVAs

IDVAs are utilised throughout England and Wales to provide help and advocacy for victims of domestic abuse from the point of crisis through to any court case and sometimes beyond. They sit independently of any other service such as the police or courts but work closely with partners. Working often in the most high-risk cases, IDVAs are part of the multi-agency approach to protect and help victims of domestic abuse, ensuring the safety of the victim and their children is at the forefront of everything they do. The Children and Young People IDVA role (CYPIDVA) provides high-risk children and young people aged 13–17 with domestic abuse support. These are less well utilised nationally but are key to addressing some of the gaps that are quite significant when children are primary victims of domestic abuse.

The IDVA role was formally introduced in 2005 following the evaluation of Specialist Domestic Violence Courts in England and Wales. The IDVA role was defined by the Home Office (2005) as having seven key principles:

- Independence from any other agency with a focus on the victim.
- Professionalism through training.
- A good understanding of safety options including criminal and civil remedies.
- Crisis intervention.
- Ability to assess risk.
- Working in partnership with voluntary and statutory services.
- Measurable outcomes including reduced repeat victimisation and victim withdrawal.

Robinson and Howarth (2012) set out three reasons why IDVAs are considered specialist risk practitioners:

- They identify the level and type of risk that a victim faces.
- They work primarily with victims considered to be at "high risk" of further abuse.
- They aim to manage risk by developing and implementing safety plans for victims and coordinating access with other agencies that may help to keep victims safe.

There were 980 IDVAs working in England and Wales in 2020, of which 833 were IDVAs for victims at high risk from domestic abuse. This is an increase from 897 full-time equivalent IDVAs in 2017, of which 782 were for victims at high risk of domestic abuse. This small increase of 7% over the last two years is still a shortfall in the coverage of 26% against SafeLives recommended number of IDVAs to support high-risk abuse cases (ONS, 2020).

The IDVA role is inherently gendered, with the vast majority involving women assisting other women (Duggan, 2020). The number of IDVAs supporting male victims decreased from 71 in March 2018 to 64 in March 2020. However, there was an increase in the number of services offering refuge and outreach services to male victims (ONS, 2020).

Research by Howarth et al. (2009) exposed that the abuse experienced by victims accessing IDVA services was both multi-faceted and extremely serious. Three quarters of victims in this research had experienced severe abuse including violent behaviour causing injuries, strangulation, rape, other sexual abuse, stalking, and extreme controlling behaviour.

Kershaw et al. (2008) have suggested that domestic violence has more repeat victims than any other crime. Assertive outreach by IDVAs helps to address this with a professional focus to reduce repeat victimisation through a variety of means. Indeed, Howarth et al. (2009) research found there was a significant impact on the safety of a victim following intervention of an IDVA with over half seeing a cessation in domestic abuse, as well as large reductions in victims suffering more than one type of abuse, for example, physical abuse and stalking. This outcome was replicated in a study conducted by Howarth and Robinson (2016) which found that where IDVAs intervened with women at high risk of domestic abuse, the majority of women experienced measurable improvements in their safety despite the complexity and seriousness of the abuse they faced.

Further to safety improvements and reduced occurrences of domestic abuse, IDVAs are notably engaged much more widely in assisting victims as they transition out of the abusive situation. Support after the immediate referral and through the criminal justice process is paramount, but Taylor-Dunn (2016) also cites a number of other factors that IDVAs become intrinsically involved in when they work with a domestic abuse victim. These include emotional support, addressing the victim's wider needs, assisting with child contact arrangements, and balancing the involvement of children's social care, and often most importantly, unequivocal support even if the victim retracts from the criminal justice process and withdraws a complaint.

Over time the way the IDVA service is delivered has changed, making them more accessible and ensuring that interventions are more timely and appropriate. For example, IDVAs based in hospitals can identify survivors not visible to other services, encourage increased numbers of referrals from health professionals, and promote safety through intensive support and access to resources at an earlier stage (Halliwell et al., 2019). This is vital as Walby (2009) estimated that this includes health costs to the NHS of at least £1.73 billion annually. In the year ending March 2017, domestic abuse cost the state £66 billion (Home Office, 2019). Over the decade since Walby's research this will have undoubtedly increased substantially so any work to reduce domestic abuse and support victims is likely to have an impact in many arenas, but not least the NHS. More recent research by Dheensa et al. (2020) reviewed the impact of the co-location of IDVAs in Emergency Departments and Maternity Units at five hospitals in England between 2012 and 2015. The research identified two key themes in relation to hospital-based IDVAs. First, they fulfilled several crucial roles, enhancing the knowledge of healthcare professionals about domestic violence and abuse and providing immediate support and onward referrals for victims, who might otherwise have been lost or overlooked. Second, the research showed that the success of Hospital IDVAs hinges on a range of structural factors such as resources, space to work, and access to medical information.

Robinson and Howarth (2012) conducted a review of 2000 victims in the United Kingdom to assess how risk judgements were made by IDVAs. They found that IDVAs paid significant attention to victims' own perceptions of danger and, when they felt very frightened or afraid of further injury, IDVAs were more likely to label them as high risk. It is this in-depth appreciation of victims' knowledge and perceptions of risk that is important. These often challenge existing risk assessment tools and offer a more holistic, sometimes life-saving, approaches to risk management.

As well as managing risk, effective victim advocacy using IDVA can impact positively on the prosecution of domestic violence offences (Taylor-Dunn, 2016). This was always the initial ambition when IDVAs were introduced, attempting to reduce victim attrition through the criminal justice process.

Duggan's (2020) research into the emotional labour of IDVAs concentrates on the impact the burden of dealing with domestic abuse can have on those working in this complicated and often draining environment. Emotional self-protection for the IDVA is paramount, and Duggan reviews this in the context of Clare's Law disclosures where there is often a high risk of fatal harm. As with any role with critical risk management processes and serious consequences, the responsibility on IDVAs can be enormous and the well-being and welfare of those undertaking the role must be of paramount importance.

Police research and domestic abuse – 'what works'

There is a widespread understanding in policing that domestic abuse is one of the most prolific crimes dealt with by police officers. A shift does not go by without an emergency call to deal with a domestic incident of some sort.

But how do police officers know what the best way is to deal with such calls? Where is the evidence base around good practice, what works, strategic direction, victim safety, and harm reduction?

In many regards there is significant academic research around different areas of domestic abuse, but in an ever-evolving world this shifts regularly as new offending methods come to the fore and changes occur to the criminal justice system. As noted in Chapter 5, the introduction of new technology has led to an explosion of new capabilities for perpetrators to abuse victims, for example, through cyber stalking (Todd et al., 2021). With limited knowledge or evidence base in this domain, police, and academics alike, can have trouble keeping up with the nuances changes in technology can have. There are also many known gaps in academic research on domestic abuse. Within this book it has already been discussed that there would be significant value in more in-depth research on the value or otherwise of MARACs (Steel et al., 2011) or domestic abuse attrition rates through the criminal justice system (Barrow-Grint, 2016) for example. The wicked problem of domestic abuse requires more research and study, and academics and practitioners should work together to explore the evidence base as much as possible.

In 2017 the College of Policing completed a two-year programme of work called the Police Knowledge Fund (PKF) together with the Higher Education Funding Council and the Home Office, to increase the evidence base in several priority policing areas. Domestic abuse was one of these areas. The funding facilitated three key areas of development:

- A catalogue of research and policy-based articles useful for evidence-based policing.
- Development of skills to critique and use academic research in practice.
- Ongoing opportunities for knowledge sharing and collaboration across agencies (College of Policing, 2017).

More generally, the work of @WeCops provides a bi-monthly Twitter debate on a policing topic with the aim of sharing innovation and good practice (WeCops, 2021), and the College of Policing's publication 'Going Equipped' enables practitioners and academics alike to contribute to the evidence base at a much more general level (College of Policing, 2020). Both @WeCops and 'Going Equipped' have provided platforms for the policing of domestic abuse to be discussed over recent years, opening the debate to a much wider forum.

Training domestic abuse leaders

In policing, domestic abuse training and more widely public protection training for senior police leaders have been very limited until relatively recently with the introduction of the College of Policing Public Protection &

Safeguarding Leaders Programme (PPSLP) in 2019. At the Police Superintendent's conference in 2018, Chief Superintendent Gavin Thomas described how 87% of senior officers working in public protection had no specific training or development in the area. In response, Sajid Javid the then Home Secretary announced that this had to change (Javid, 2018). The introduction of the PPSLP has been significant in training law enforcement colleagues from many agencies in the legislation, evidence base, and practitioner perspectives of public protection including domestic abuse but is a timely reminder that there are still training gaps at every level from leadership teams to detectives, and learning must be a continuous exercise.

Practical policing solutions to improve service delivery and protect victims

Innovation in policing activity happens continually. In terms of policing domestic abuse, it is sometimes complicated especially where the level of risk to the victim is in doubt. However, there are many good examples of pioneering practice:

- In their progress report on the policing of domestic abuse, HMIC (2015) found that police and IDVA's co-locating resulted in quicker and better information sharing, risk assessing, and safety planning, all of which led to better outcomes for victims of domestic abuse.
- In terms of positive partnership working, in Northumbria, IDVAs accompany the police on patrol to ensure that they are on hand to attend domestic abuse incidents and can provide immediate support (Mayes et al., 2017).
- Digital technology has provided a paradigm shift for victim safety. Personal safety devices or mobile phone handsets such as TecSOS (2021) can be provided to victims as part of safety planning. Linked directly to the police or monitoring service, they can provide emergency services with GPS location and victim details and even a record of the call. As digital practices advance, so to do the capabilities available. There are now applications (apps) available for smartphones giving advice and links to victims when safe for them to access them, such as 'BrightSky' (Hestia, 2021).

In 2019 the' Make Yourself Heard' campaign commenced, backed by the charity Women's Aid, the Independent Office for Police Conduct, and the National Police Chiefs' Council. This campaign was instigated to raise awareness of the Silent Solution and how to safely dial 999 when it is too dangerous to speak by pressing '55' on the handset. The campaign followed the death of domestic abuse victim Kerry Power in 2013 who was strangled by an ex-partner. Kerry dialled 999 but was unable to speak and was unaware that dialling 55 when prompted by the automated Silent Solution mechanism would get her the help she desperately needed. With the police receiving over 12 million 999 calls every year and 20,000 silent 999 calls a day, it is vital that anyone who cannot speak to an operator has the opportunity to summon assistance and this is extremely important for domestic abuse victims (Women's Aid, 2019).

Policing innovations in domestic abuse were enhanced and developed at speed during the global COVID-19 pandemic, which started in 2020. In some respects, the relative drop in police demand experienced at the beginning of the pandemic when the first lockdown was introduced actually increased the capacity of the police to respond to domestic abuse and allowed improved opportunities for officers to spend more time with victims considering relevant safeguarding measures (Johnson and Hohl, 2021). Walklate et al. (2021) describe how the pandemic advanced the use of technology to increase the range of access to policing services available to victims of domestic abuse, such as online reporting tools. It also afforded different opportunities for physical engagement such as supermarket surgeries and encouraged improved partnership working with the use of online multi-agency risk assessment conferencing which sped up information sharing and decision-making.

Johnson and Kohl (2021) also found, amongst many improvements, improved strategic coordination of force responses to domestic abuse during the pandemic at a senior management level and increased engagement in evidence-based policing, with forces working closely with academics, as well as consulting academic research and international data on domestic abuse in other jurisdictions.

One such project involved researchers from the London School of Economics working with a police force to devise an outreach campaign targeted towards women at high risk of domestic abuse, to inform them how they could safely contact police. A randomised control trial was set up with the treatment group targeted for extra social media advertising with the campaign's message, whilst the control group was only exposed to the various national campaigns that were ongoing at the same time. The outcomes of this work showed a limited, statistically insignificant impact suggesting the extra campaign activity made little difference to the way victim's contacted police or variances in recidivism (Grogger et al., 2020). Importantly, this example shows the value in experimenting, even in times of national emergency, but reviewing and stopping when the evidence base shows no or limited positive impact.

There are many examples of qualitative and quantitative research, as well as practical examples based on testing in the field by practitioners, sometimes with, but often without academic support. Best practice is a tricky concept, because contexts will change, victims and perpetrators will be diverse, and what works for one individual might not work for another. If ethical considerations are deliberated appropriately, then there is certainly a space for innovation in policing domestic abuse, and indeed in reality, it is a necessity to ensure harm reduction is at the forefront of our thinking.

Domestic Homicide Reviews (DHR)

Despite many systems and processes put in place by police and partnership organisations for the effective management of domestic abuse, things can and do go wrong. Human error, failure to share information, lack of training and overwhelming caseloads, are common factors which contribute to circumstances where agencies have failed to adequately protect and support victims leading to serious injury and loss of life. Where incidents of this nature take place, they are often widely publicised in the media, and this can undermine public confidence. Therefore, it is essential that in all such cases the circumstances are fully reviewed and recommendations and actions for improvement are considered and acted upon in a timely manner. This section will collate the current research regarding system-failure leading to femicide and will detail the statutory process of Domestic Homicides Reviews (DHRs) which take place following a murder in domestic circumstances.

Regardless of the changes to legislation, prevention initiatives, and a renewed focus on domestic abuse within law enforcement and social care, the average figure of two female homicide victims per week has remained constant over the past decade. In many cases victims will have had some form of prior contact with voluntary or statutory services. Coroners' inquests, criminal proceedings, and internal agency reviews conducted into the circumstances of many of these deaths have continued to highlight areas of inconsistent practice, miscommunication between agencies, and poor recordkeeping that have led to missed opportunities to intervene.

In 2004 national concern over repeated 'failings' alongside the political focus on domestic abuse led to the introduction of new legislation – the Domestic Violence, Crime and Victims Act 2004. It was this act that mandated all local authorities in England and Wales completes a review of the circumstances and actions of involved agencies in cases of domestic abuse-related homicide.

The provisions of the 2004 Act direct that a review be conducted into:

> "the circumstances in which the death of a person aged 16 or over has, or appears to have, resulted from violence, abuse or neglect by—
>
> a a person to whom he was related or with whom he was or had been in an intimate personal relationship, or
>
> b a member of the same household as himself, held with a view to identifying the lessons to be learnt from the death".
>
> (Domestic Violence, Crime and Victims Act 2004, sec. 9:1)

The reviews are not intended to be punitive; any issues of negligence, poor performance, or misconduct are managed through the relevant agency's disciplinary procedures. Their key purpose is to identify both positive practice and areas requiring improvements both locally and nationally.

The authorities and agencies required by the Secretary of State to contribute to a DHR include police, probation, schools and education establishments, adult and children's social care, housing, and health services, including general practitioners and the local authority. Each agency will have a greater or lesser role to play in the victim's life depending on the circumstances, but all will be required to contribute to the review as well as implement any recommendations accepted and embed any identified changes to practice. Voluntary agencies and other service providers who may have had contact with victims or offenders may also be offered the opportunity to contribute to the review. Furthermore, as reviews are very focussed on understanding the life and experience of victims' family members, friends and associates are also encouraged to support and contribute.

There are other forms of statutory homicide and agency review processes such as safeguarding adult review (SAR), serious case review (SCR) or mental health investigation (MHI). Depending on the specific circumstances of the domestic homicide any one of these statutory reviews may also be commissioned. For instance, where another family member or child has been murdered in the same domestic homicide event. In these circumstances, whilst the respective parallel reviews will take place, they may be conducted jointly to avoid duplication.

Figure 8.2 illustrates the process set out in the Home Office Statutory Guidance (2016) for the completion of a DHR. Following a domestic homicide, it is the responsibility of the police force in the area to inform the Community Safety Partnership (CSP). The CSP is a multiagency body with representatives from the police, health, probation, fire and rescue, and the local authority. These agencies work together to protect the public against crime (see Chapter 6). Following a detailed report from the police, the CSP has 28 days to decide whether to commission a DHR and notify the Home Office of their decision. If a DHR is commissioned an independent chair and panel will be convened to oversee the review. This panel has representation from all agencies involved who review their own actions and conduct in relation to the circumstances. These internal agency reviews are known as Individual Management Reviews (IMRs). It may be that a particular agency had very limited contact with the victim. However, even then a review is needed to establish whether that limitation was due to an inability of the victim to access the service, or the appropriate service provision was simply not available. The completed IMRs are collated and form the basis of the final report which will outline a chronology of the victim's life and contact with agencies and identify any collective of individual agency failings, poor practice, positive interventions, and learning. Where appropriate, recommendations

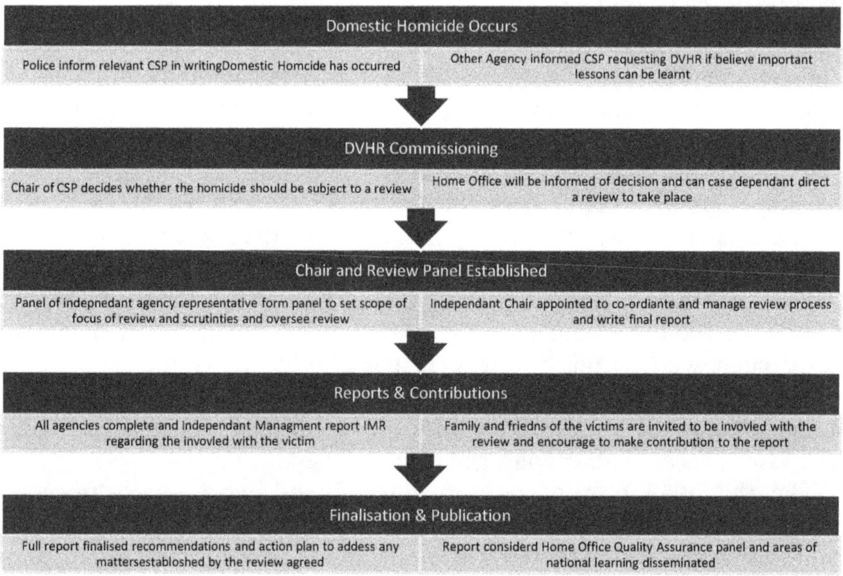

Figure 8.2 Home Office Statutory Guidance for completion of DHRs (2016).

and an action plan will be presented to the CSP for approval. Reports are submitted to the Home Office Quality Assurance Panel for the collation of national matters of learning. Once finalised, reports are then published on Local Authority websites.

The guidance advises that a DHR should be completed within six months; however, these time limits can be exceeded where cases are particularly complex or there are other parallel processes such as inquest, criminal trials, or family court proceedings which need to be finalised before the review can be completed.

Police services have a statutory role in both the review panel and providing an IMR of the material held and actions taken in association with the victims and perpetrators prior contact with law enforcement. All available material such as incident call recordings and logs, statements, DASH forms, crime reports, and notes will be required to be submitted for the report to be completed. It is important that all officers and staff are familiar with force standing operating procedures and policies when dealing with domestic incidents and follow them accordingly. Reviews will examine how staff from individual agencies complied with policies and procedures. Reviews may also assess the adequacy of training provision and resource allocation and appropriateness of supervision as well as individual actions and responses. It is essential that care and attention to detail are taken in all interactions with domestic abuse victims and perpetrators and material is recorded accurately and retained appropriately according to force policies. Where policies have found to be breached or misconduct identified the DHR chair will inform the relevant agency so those matters can be then be further investigated internally. As the examination of the circumstances of the review is so detailed there can be concerns those colleagues will be circumspect in providing detail of their involvement for fear of punitive consequences.

This is an inevitable way of working in a climate where, following a serious event such as a child death or domestic violence homicide, it is common to look for failure in practice and to hold individual practitioners publicly accountable (Robinson and Howarth, 2012, p. 1506).

Therefore, all reviews are framed with the objective of learning and embedding organisational learning. Whilst it is right that such reviews highlight missed opportunities as well as any organisational and individual failings they are also balanced and will share positive practice and commend individuals' actions as necessary.

BOX 8.6 DOMESTIC HOMICIDE REVIEW: REPORT INTO THE DEATH OF ANDREW

Andrew was a 54-year-old male who died at his home address from a single stab wound to his chest. His partner Olivia, 73, was charged with his murder and subsequently convicted of his manslaughter and was sentenced to a three-year prison sentence.

The Local Authority in which his death took place commissioned a DHR which is now published and provides an insight into the process of the completion of a DHR as well as providing specific information as Andrew's death and local partnership working arrangements. The report is clearly structured. It opens a summary of the circumstance of Andrew's death. It then continues with an identification of those agencies contributing to the panel, the terms of reference, scope of the enquiry, and the process the panel followed in completing the review. In this case 24 agencies were contacted; however, only four agencies including police provided IMRs. From these IMRs the report is able to compile a timeline of relevant events for both Andrew and Olivia and an analysis of the circumstances leading up to Andrew's death.

When considering Andrew, there was a reported incident where he was arrested and treated as a suspect for domestic abuse allegation against Olivia. However, his disclosures of being a victim himself were not considered. A DASH form was not completed detailing his allegations nor a crime report made of his allegations. The investigative focus remained solely on Olivia's safety. The tunnel vision therefore did not take into account the full relationship dynamics. The report identified that improved practice would have been for a more holistic review of their relationship considered at the time and Andrew's allegations have also been considered and responded too.

The review also identified there was positive practice in that police made referrals to adult social care; however, it highlighted concerns that case was closed when no contact could be made with Olivia. The family contribution to the review identified they held more information about Andrew and Olivia's relationship. Had these details been know it would have enhanced the risk assessment prior to the case being closed. The review identified three areas of concern: how male victims are dealt with by police, how domestic abuse within older couples is addressed, and finally provision of alcohol misuse services. The report concludes with a series of multi- and single-agency recommendations.

(Central Bedfordshire Community Safety Partnership, 2018)

The report of Andrew in Box 8.6 exemplifies how DHRs can explore in detail the actions of agencies and how they work together. For instance, the fact that Andrew's allegations were not recorded, nor any DASH completed, consequently meant this information did not then pass through to the social care team who were completing the risk assessment and would have been able to determine what support might be made available to him and Olivia. A prior hospital admission was not followed up through their GP, and a vital information was held by family members was not known to any agency. In isolation none of these incidents would potentially have changed the outcome but they would have allowed further engagement of agencies with the couple so a greater understanding of the relationship dynamics would have been available to make more balanced risk assessment decisions and safety plans. Through careful and clear understanding of the single- and multi-agency working environments the report was able to make recommendations that will inform the processes followed to improve current practice.

BOX 8.7 REVIEW OF THE DEATH OF CHILD J

The murder of Child J (aged 17) was committed by her ex-partner, Adult L. This would have given rise to a DHR; however, given her age and history with social care services the review remit combined both DHR and SCR to ensure all lessons regarding her care were considered. In December 2013 Child J was reported missing by the managers of her supported living placement. She had told them she believed she was pregnant and was going to inform her ex-partner, Adult L, with whom she had previously experienced domestic abuse. Despite her age and vulnerability and this previous history, the missing person's report was graded as MEDIUM risk. Adult L was arrested, interviewed, and bailed shortly after in relation to an allegation of possession of indent photographs. He was not questioned in relation to the missing person's matter. Furthermore, this information was not linked with the missing person's enquiries, or the existing history of domestic abuse held by police. Detailed interviews of the staff caring for Child J were only conducted some days following the missing person's report. It was only then officers were made aware that Child J had disclosed that Adult L threatened to kill her if she ever got pregnant. Following that information and given a fuller appreciation of her vulnerabilities and previous history with Adult L, her missing status was regraded to High risk. Fourteen days after she was reported missing, her body was found. Adult L was charged and subsequently convicted and sentenced to a minimum sentence of 20 years for her murder.

Oxfordshire Safeguarding Children Board (2016) Child J OSCB Overview Report Child-J-OSCB-Overview-Report.pdf

The review of the death of Child J offers a different example indicating the complexities of some domestic abuse situations (Oxfordshire Safeguarding Children's Board, 2016). This review was a combined process for the completion of a DHR and SCR (see Box 8.7). The conclusion of the report emphasises the significance of information exchange between and within agencies. It is vital to work with other agencies, seek out, and review all information and intelligence to assess victim vulnerability and the risk factors to appropriately understand and respond to risk presented; but there are sometimes difficulties in sharing information and knowledge.

Perennial issues

Analysis has been undertaken (Home Office, 2016; Robinson et al., 2018; Sharp-Jeffs and Kelly, 2016) which identifies several perennial issues commonly associated with how partners work together and within their own agencies when dealing with cases of domestic abuse. In many of the homicide reviews issues such as lack of communication and data sharing (particularly across geographical and professional boundaries, risk assessment), training and recordkeeping have been singled out as being potential failings and missed opportunities to prevent ongoing abuse and keep victims safe.

Silo working is often identified a blocker to information sharing. As was the case in the death of Andrew (Box 8.6), failure to record and refer allegations appropriately is a common occurrence when domestic homicides are reviews. The lessons learnt also highlight the importance of being open-minded and for professionals to make their assessment on all available information (Box 8.7).

DHRs provide an important function in supporting the development of best practice in managing services response to domestic abuse. However, despite the failings which have been identified it must be remembered it is the perpetrator who has the ultimate responsibility for their actions. Prevention and safety planning is, of course, essential and services and the police should always work toward ensuring the best quality of service, but their failures should not absolve the perpetrator or blame the victim of fatal actions.

Public confidence in the policing response to domestic abuse can be negatively influenced by a DHR. Officers and staff engaging with, or being subject to a DHR, can feel like they are being scapegoated for procedural issues and, in such circumstances, it can be helpful to take advice from the relevant staff association. However, the objective of DHRs is to support and facilitate learning with the cooperation of all concerned to improve outcomes for victims. At the time of writing, the HM government is in the process of creating a national digital registry of all DHRs to share identified themes and trends and highlight specific areas of good practice.

Conclusion

This chapter has considered a diverse selection of responses, innovations, and reviews that allow reflection on not only how domestic abuse can be policed, but also how the criminal justice system and partners can learn from both good and poor practices. The importance of good partnerships and highly capable IDVAs will ensure victims get the best possible service and risk management throughout their journey, whilst testing new technology and services will allow additional ideas and practices to be developed.

Despite the work of statutory agencies and NGOs, national statistics (CSEW – see Chapter 3) suggest that the incidence of domestic abuse remains at an unacceptably high level. However, challenging social attitudes to VAWG within organisations and more broadly, in society will support change. In the meantime, information sharing through multi-agency practice allows the development of appropriate interventions, one of the key processes for protecting victims and confronting the violent behaviour of perpetrators. However, even the best policies and practice can fall short and both good and bad practices must be reviewed to ensure balanced recommendations for change.

Reflective questions

- What do you feel the perennial issues in policing domestic abuse may be? What mechanisms can police and partners introduce so recommendations are effectively embedded?
- Discuss the purpose and effectiveness of DHRs.
- Why is the concept of working together considered so important when dealing with cases of domestic abuse?
- Critically review the role of data in the policing of domestic violence.
- Describe the best ways of sharing innovative practice and solutions in dealing with domestic abuse cases.

Useful websites

Authorised Professional Practice in Domestic Abuse: https://www.app.college.police.uk/app-content/major-investigation-and-public-protection/domestic-abuse/

College of Policing Domestic abuse|What Works Centre for Crime Reduction (college.police.uk)

CPS Guidance: https://www.cps.gov.uk/publication/domestic-abuse

MAPPA Guidance: https://www.gov.uk/government/publications/multi-agency-public-protection-arrangements-mappa-guidance

Nice Guidance: https://www.nice.org.uk/guidance/ph50

Respect: https://www.respect.uk.net

References

Adisa, O., 2020. Professionals' perceptions of MARACs and barriers to attendance: Headline findings from the 'Are MARACs still fit for purpose?' University of Suffolk Briefing Paper.

Barrow-Grint, K., 2016. Attrition rates in domestic abuse: time for a change? An application of temporal sequencing theory. *Policing: A Journal of Policy and Practice* 10, 250–263.

Berry, V.L., Stanley, N., Radford, L., McCarry, M., Larkins, C., 2014. Building effective responses: An independent review of violence against women, domestic abuse and sexual violence services in Wales. Welsh Government.

Beyer, K., Wallis, A.B., Hamberger, L.K., 2015. Neighborhood environment and intimate partner violence: A systematic review. *Trauma, Violence, & Abuse* 16, 16–47.

Burnett, R., Appleton, C., 2004. Joined-up services to tackle youth crime: A case-study in England. *British Journal of Criminology* 44, 34–54.

Central Bedfordshire Community Safety Partnership, 2018. Central Bedfordshire community safety partnership domestic homicide review executive summary. Report into the death of Andrew. Central Bedfordshire Community Safety Partnership.

Clark, H., Lumsden, E., Royal, P., West, H., Revel, E., Leech, G., Millington, M., Couchman, K., Gummer, A., Taylor, A., 2017. A report by the all-party parliamentary group on a fit and healthy childhood the impact of social and economic inequalities on children's health. All Party Parliamentary Group.

College of Policing, 2020. Going equipped. College of Policing. https://www.college.police.uk/tags/going-equipped (accessed 11.28.21).

College of Policing, 2017. PKF catalogue | What Works Centre for Crime Reduction. https://whatworks.college.police.uk/Partnerships/Knowledge-Fund/PKF_catalogue/Pages/default.aspx (accessed 11.28.21).

Davies, P., 2020. Partnerships and activism: Community safety, multi-agency partnerships and safeguarding victims, in: Tapley, J., Davies, P. (Eds.), *Victimology*. Palgrave Macmillan UK, pp. 277–299.

Department for Education, 2019. Relationships education, relationships and sex education (RSE) and health education statutory guidance for governing bodies, proprietors, head teachers, principals, senior leadership teams, teachers. https://assets.publishing.service.gov.uk/government/uploads/system/uploads/attachment_data/file/1019542/Relationships_Education__Relationships_and_Sex_Education__RSE__and_Health_Education.pdf (accessed 7.10.22).

Department of Health and Social Security, 1988. *Report of the enquiry into child abuse Cleveland 1987*. HMSO.

Dheensa, S., Halliwell, G., Daw, J., Jones, S.K., Feder, G., 2020. 'From taboo to routine': A qualitative evaluation of a hospital-based advocacy intervention for domestic violence and abuse. *BMC Health Services Research* 20, 1–13.

Domestic Abuse Intervention Programs, 2017. The Duluth model. Domestic Abuse Intervention Programs. https://www.theduluthmodel.org/ (accessed 11.27.21).

Domestic Violence, Crime and Victims Act, 2004. Statute law database. https://www.legislation.gov.uk/ukpga/2004/28/contents (accessed 7.10.22).

Duggan, M., 2020. Gendering emotional labour: Independent domestic violence advisors, in: Philips, J., Waters, J., Westaby, C., Fowler, A. (Eds.), *Emotional Labour in Criminal Justice and Criminology*. Routledge, pp. 138–149.

EIF, 2018. Early intervention in domestic violence and abuse. Early Intervention Foundation. https://www.eif.org.uk/report/early-intervention-in-domestic-violence-and-abuse (accessed 3.4.19).

Fox, C.L., Hale, R., Gadd, D., 2014. Domestic abuse prevention education: listening to the views of young people. *Sex Education* 14, 28–41.

GOV.UK, 2016. Strategy to end violence against women and girls: 2016 to 2020, https://www.gov.uk/government/publications/strategy-to-end-violence-against-women-and-girls-2016-to-2020 (accessed 7.10.22).

Grogger, J., Ivandic, R., Kirchmaier, T., 2020. Tackling domestic violence using machine learning. *CentrePiece* 25, 9–10.

Halliwell, G., Dheensa, S., Fenu, E., Jones, S.K., Asato, J., Jacob, S., Feder, G., 2019. Cry for health: A quantitative evaluation of a hospital-based advocacy intervention for domestic violence and abuse. *BMC Health Services Research* 19, 1–12.

Haringey Borough Council, 2016. Haringey VAWG strategy 2016–2026. https://www.haringey.gov.uk/social-care-and-health/health/public-health/domestic-violence-and-abuse-and-violence-against-women-and-girls/violence-against-women-and-girls/haringeys-approach-violence-against-women-and-girls (accessed 7.10.22).

Harvie, P., Manzi, T., 2011. Interpreting multi-agency partnerships: Ideology, discourse and domestic violence. *Social & Legal Studies* 20, 79–95.
Hestia, 2021. Bright Sky app. Hestia. https://www.hestia.org/brightsky (accessed 11.28.21).
HMIC, 2015. Increasingly everybody's business. Her Majesty's Inspectorate Constabulary.
Home Office, 2005, Domestic Violence: a national report. Home Office.
Home Office, 2010, *Call to End Violence against Women and Girls*, https://www.gov.uk/government/publications/call-to-end-violence-against-women-and-girls (accessed 7.10.22).
Home Office, 2016. Multi-agency Statutory Guidance for the Conduct of Domestic Homicide Reviews. Home Office.
Home Office, 2019. The economic and social costs of domestic abuse. https://www.gov.uk/government/publications/the-economic-and-social-costs-of-domestic-abuse (accessed 11.6.21).
Home Office, 2021. Domestic abuse act statutory guidance. GOV.UK. https://www.gov.uk/government/consultations/domestic-abuse-act-statutory-guidance (accessed 11.27.21).Howarth, E., Robinson, A., 2016. Responding effectively to women experiencing severe abuse: Identifying key components of a British advocacy intervention. *Violence Against Women* 22, 41–63.
Howarth, E., Stimpson, L., Barran, D., Robinson, A., 2009. *Safety in numbers: A multi site evaluation of independent domestic violence advisor services.* The Henry Smith Charity.
Javid, S., 2018. Home Secretary Police Superintendents' Conference speech 2018. GOV.UK. https://www.gov.uk/government/speeches/home-secretary-police-superintendents-conference-speech-2018 (accessed 7.10.22).
Johnson, K., Hohl, K., 2021. *Parliamentary Home Affairs Committee Home Office Preparedness for Covid-19 (Coronavirus) Consultation: Supplementary Call for Evidence Submission – The impact of Covid-19 on domestic abuse reported to the police, and policing responses.* Parliament, UK.
Johnson, L., Stylianou, A.M., 2020. Coordinated community responses to domestic violence: A systematic review of the literature. *Trauma, Violence, & Abuse* 23, 506–522.
Kershaw, C., Nicholas, S., Walker, A., 2008. Crime in England and Wales 2007/07, *Home office statistical bulletin.* Home Office.
King-Ries, A., 2010. Teens, technology, and cyberstalking: The domestic violence wave of the future. *Texas Journal of Women and the Law* 20, 131.
Krug, E.G., Mercy, J.A., Dahlberg, L.L., Zwi, A.B., 2002. The world report on violence and health. *The Lancet* 360, 1083–1088.
Longden, J., 2014. *A case study focussed around a police DV unit in the West Midlands examining how effective the unit is at working with other agencies to support victims of DV, Unpublished.* Newman University.
Mayes, A., Moroz, A., Thorsgaard Frolunde, T., 2017. *Survivor's Justice. How victims and survivors of domestic abuse experience the criminal justice system.* Victim Support.
Newburn, T., 2017. *Criminology*, 3rd ed. Routledge.
NICE, 2016. Overview|Domestic violence and abuse|Quality standards|NICE. https://www.nice.org.uk/guidance/qs116 (accessed 3.24.19).

NICE, 2014. Domestic violence and abuse: Multiagency working|Guidance and guidelines. https://www.nice.org.uk/Guidance/PH50 (accessed 2.11.19).

NICE, 2013. *Review of interventions to identify prevent reduce and respond to domestic violence.* National Institute for Clinical Excellence.

Noble, G., Jones, R., 2006. The role of boundary-spanning managers in the establishment of public-private partnerships. *Public Administration* 84, 891–917.

Office, H., 2016. *Multi-agency statutory guidance for the conduct of domestic homicide reviews.* Home Office.

ONS, 2020. Domestic abuse prevalence and trends, England and Wales – Office for National Statistics. https://www.ons.gov.uk/peoplepopulationandcommunity/crimeandjustice/articles/domesticabuseprevalenceandtrendsenglandandwales/yearendingmarch2020#crime-survey-for-england-and-wales (accessed 9.7.21).

Oxfordshire Safeguarding Children's Board, 2016. Child J OSCB Overview Report. http://www.oscb.org.uk/wp-content/uploads/Child-J-OSCB-Overview-Report.pdf (accessed 7.10.22).

Page, S., Temple-Malt, E., 2018. Healthy relationships education offers a real chance to reduce domestic violence. *The Conversation.*

Pensak, R., 2014. Must be 18 or older: How current domestic violence policies dismiss teen dating violence. *William and Mary Journal of Women and the Law* 21, 499.

Percy-Smith, J., 2006. What works in strategic partnerships for children: A research review. *Children & Society* 20, 313–323.

Ranade, W., Hudson, B., 2003. Conceptual issues in inter-agency collaboration. *Local Government Studies* 29, 32–50.

Robbins, R., McLaughlin, H., Banks, C., Bellamy, C., Thackray, D., 2014. Domestic violence and multi-agency risk assessment conferences (MARACs): A scoping review. *The Journal of Adult Protection* 16:6, 389–398.

Robinson, A., Rees, A., Dehaghani, R., 2018. *Findings from a thematic analysis of reviews into adult deaths in Wales: domestic homicide reviews, adult practice reviews and mental health homicide reviews.* Cardiff University.

Robinson, A.L., Howarth, E., 2012. Judging risk: Key determinants in British domestic violence cases. *Journal of Interpersonal Violence* 27, 1489–1518.

Robinson, A.L., 2006. Reducing repeat victimization among high-risk victims of domestic violence: The benefits of a coordinated community response in Cardiff, Wales. *Violence Against Women* 12, 761–788.

SafeLives, 2014. *Multiagency risk assessment conferences (MARACs).* SafeLives.

Sharp-Jeffs, N., Kelly, L., 2016. Domestic homicide review (DHR): Case analysis. https://www.standingtogether.org.uk/blog-3/domestic-homicide-review-dhr-case-analysis (accessed 7.10.22).

Standing Conference on Crime Prevention, 1991. Crime prevention, safer communities: The local delivery of crime prevention through the partnership approach. The Morgan Report. Presented at the Standing Conference on Crime Prevention, Home Office, London.

Standing Together, 2021. Domestic violence: In search of excellence. https://www.standingtogether.org.uk/blog-3/in-search-of-excellence (accessed 7.10.22).

Stanley, N., Ellis, J., Farrelly, N., Hollinghurst, S., Downe, S., 2015. Preventing domestic abuse for children and young people: A review of school-based interventions. *Children and Youth Services Review* 59, 120–131.

Steel, N., Blakeborough, L., Nicholas, S., 2011. *Supporting high-risk victims of domestic violence: a review of Multi-Agency Risk Assessment Conferences (MARACs). Research report 55 summary*. Home Office.

Suarez, K.E., 1994. Teenage dating violence: The need for expanded awareness and legislation. *California Law Review* 82, 423.

Taylor-Dunn, H., 2016. The impact of victim advocacy on the prosecution of domestic violence offences: Lessons from a realistic evaluation. *Criminology & Criminal Justice* 16, 21–39.

TecSOS, 2021. Home. http://www.tecsos.co.uk/index.html (accessed 11.28.21).

Todd, C., Bryce, J., Franqueira, V.N., 2021. Technology, cyberstalking and domestic homicide: Informing prevention and response strategies. *Policing and Society* 31, 82–99.

Walby, S., 2009. *The cost of domestic violence: Up-date 2009*. Lancaster University.

Walklate, S., Godfrey, B., Richardson, J., 2021. Changes and continuities in police responses to domestic abuse in England and Wales during the Covid-19 'lockdown.' *Policing and Society* 32:2, 221–233.

Warren-Gash, C., Bartley, A., Bayly, J., Dutey-Magni, P., Edwards, S., Madge, S., Miller, C., Nicholas, R., Radhakrishnan, S., Sathia, L., 2016. Outcomes of domestic violence screening at an acute London trust: Are there missed opportunities for intervention? *BMJ Open* 6, e009069.

WeCops, 2021. We Communities. http://www.wecops.org/ (accessed 11.28.21).

Weir, R., 2019. Using geographically weighted regression to explore neighborhood-level predictors of domestic abuse in the UK. *Transactions in GIS* 23, 1232–1250.

Whinney, A., 2015. *A descriptive analysis of Multi-Agency Risk Assessment Conferences (MARACs) for reducing the future harm of domestic abuse in Suffolk* (MA thesis), University of Cambridge Institute of Criminology.

WHO, 2012. *Understanding and addressing violence against women*. World Health Organization.

WHO, 2010. *Preventing intimate partner and sexual violence against women: Taking action and generating evidence*. World Health Organisation.

Women's Aid, 2019. Women's aid, the IOPC and the NPCC launch Make Yourself Heard campaign this National Stalking Awareness Week. *Women's Aid*. https://www.womensaid.org.uk/womens-aid-the-iopc-and-the-npcc-launch-make-yourself-heard-campaign-this-national-stalking-awareness-week/ (accessed 11.28.21).

Chapter 9

Policing domestic abuse within the organisation

KEY POINTS

- Many police officers and staff may have experienced domestic abuse in their private lives as either perpetrators or victims.
- Understanding the importance of Code of Ethics, Professional Standards, Performance, and Integrity in managing professional and private lives.
- Managing relationships within the workplace, abuse of power, and understanding when relationships should be declared.
- Recognising the impact of continued professional exposure associated with policing domestic abuse on well-being and mental health.
- Understanding the available tools and techniques for help and support.

Introduction

> "The police and the public are the public are the police".

Set out by Sir Robert Peel in 1829 (College of Policing, 2014) this phrase establishes the foundation for modern policing. There is therefore no reason to expect that the private lives of police officers will be any different to the experiences of members of the public. The Crime Survey of England and Wales indicated that 2.3 million adults within England and Wales had experienced domestic abuse within the last year ending March 2020 (ONS, 2020). Equating to 7.3% of women and 3.6% of men in the population, we can assume that some police officers, special constables, and police staff members will be amongst this cohort with some of those charged with policing domestic abuse professionally, also being victims or perpetrators in their private lives.

All criminal allegations of domestic abuse made against police officers and other members of police staff are dealt with through the various processes and criminal procedures referenced within this book, just as they would for any other member of the public. However, because of the

DOI: 10.4324/9781003137412-9

standards and ethical behaviours expected of police in their public as well as private lives, where allegations of domestic abuse are made against police personnel, additional procedures and safeguards may be required. This chapter will outline those procedures referencing the Code of Ethics, Police Conduct Regulations, and National Police Chief's Council policy.

This chapter will then move on to consider what additional steps may be required for those officers who are, or have been, victims of or witnesses to domestic abuse in the private lives. Again, support mechanisms provided to any other member of the public are available; however, additional consideration must be given to the potential re-traumatisation of staff in dealing with incidents that may strike a chord in their own lives and adversely impact their mental well-being.

Policing has a hierarchical rank structure which can lead to coercive relationships within the workplace. This chapter will consider best practice principles in relation to workplace relationships. An imbalance of power can also be evidenced where police officers or members of police staff form emotional or sexual relationships with vulnerable people with whom they have had a professional involvement. This chapter will also consider how such an abuse of power impacts on public confidence.

Finally, this chapter will explore the overall and sometimes enduring impact of policing domestic abuse. The demands of dealing with trauma and continued exposure to such events can affect mental well-being. The personal experience of intimate abuse as well as concepts of compassion fatigue and vicarious trauma suffered by some officers will be explored. Resources available to provide support for the mental health and well-being of staff who police domestic abuse will also be reviewed.

Expected standards of behaviour in public and private life

British policing is founded on the principle of consent. The public accept the legitimacy of the police in enforcing laws and keeping the peace to the overall benefit of society. Where the integrity of that legitimacy is brought into question through the actions of police forces or individual officers and staff that consent, which is essential for a stable nationhood, can be eroded. When police service employees appear to be corrupt, lacking integrity, biased, or enacting double standards, the confidence of the public can be negatively impacted.

However, police officers are human with the same frailties and challenges as everyone else. The Code of Ethics, the Police Conduct Regulations 2020, National Police Chief Council, and local forces are all mechanisms which set out expected standards of behaviour for police officers and staff in their professional and private lives which they should abide by in order that the public can have confidence in them to uphold the law with integrity.

The Code of Ethics was introduced in 2014 by the College of Policing and acts as code of practice for police forces within England and Wales. The Code of Ethics provides a guide for expected behaviours at all times, "whether at work or away from work, online or offline" (1.4.2; p. 2). In 2020, the Home Office published statutory guidance for all police officers in England and Wales entitled the Police Conduct Regulations. These outline the expected standards of behaviour and the legal process following any allegations that they have been breached. The standards again apply to both the public and private lives of officers. Conduct matters can directly relate to any behaviours "whether on or off duty, which brings discredit on the police service or undermines public confidence in policing" (The Police Conduct Regulations, 2020). Schedule 2 of the Police Conduct Regulations 2020 (Box 9.1) outlines the 10 standards of professional behaviour expected of all officers in England and Wales. There are equivalent expectations and standard operating procedures of Police Scotland and Police Service Northern Ireland.

BOX 9.1 SCHEDULE 2 OF THE POLICE CONDUCT REGULATIONS 2020

Code of Ethics – policing principles	*Conduct regulations – standards of professional behaviour*
Accountability	Honest & integrity
Fairness	Authority, respect & courtesy
Honest	Equality & diversity
Integrity	Use of force
Leadership	Orders and instructions
Objectivity	Duties & responsibilities
Openness	Confidentiality
Respect	Fitness for work
Selflessness	Conduct
	Challenging & reporting improper behaviour

Article 8 of the Human Rights Act 1998 affords the right to a private life. Yet this needs to be balanced with the duties and expectations held of police service employees both on and off duty. Officers and staff are therefore held to a very high bar both in their professional and public lives. Any allegations or complaints of domestic abuse made against officers and staff, even those which do not result in any criminal outcome, can have significant consequences for their professional careers. This is in order to maintain the highest standards of integrity and trust and is unlikely to be similar in other careers where allegations of domestic abuse which do not reach criminal trial or conviction would not lead to an impact on employment.

Police perpetrated domestic abuse

Reports collated from 32 forces indicate that there have been 829 criminal allegations of domestic abuse perpetrated by suspects employed as police officers reported over the last five years. It is suggested however that the real numbers may be higher than this (BBC News, 2021).

The investigation of any criminal allegations associated with domestic abuse will always take primacy over any internal misconduct investigations. Investigations of criminal behaviour by police force employees, whether an officer or staff member, will take place in the same way as they would for any member of the general public. The police must be held to accountable for their actions and should not be treated or seen to be treated in a favourable manner. However, because of their role as police officers or police staff members, there are certain technical challenges in investigating allegations which do not exist for members of the public.

For instance, because of their professional duties, police officers/staff members have access to sensitive intelligence systems which hold private information and personal data including home addresses, vehicle registrations, and previous contact with police services. If employees have a malign intent, they have the potential to unlawfully gain access through these systems to personal data regarding, for example, a victim or their new partner. Location, contacts, and other personal details can then be used by the perpetrator to control, stalk, or cause harassment. Police employee perpetrators may have networks of friends and associates within the police organisation who could be used to gain information about an ongoing investigation or be corrupted into influencing any investigation in the suspect's favour potentially by destroying or falsifying evidence. Due to the nature of their role some officers will also have access to weapons such as firearms and Conducted Energy Devices (CED common referred to as TASER), increasing their ability to threaten violence and exert control over a victim. Therefore, it is essential that safeguarding processes and risk assessments must be put in place. These measures are to ensure the integrity of the investigation and are in the interests of the suspected officer/staff member, victim, witnesses, and wider force reputation.

Given the potential likelihood of sanctions or potentially the loss of their career even if the criminal allegation is not proceeded with, the welfare impact on the accused individual must be recognised, and enhanced support provided where necessary. Each force will have its own specific policy as to how such matters are dealt with; however, best practice would include the following actions to be put in place:

- Arrangements for another force to carry out the criminal investigation.
- Where an arrest is made the suspect should be taken to a custody office where contact with colleagues or peers is less likely.

- Notification of the staff member's line manager and National Police Chief's Council senior officer for that relevant business area in force.
- Notification to the force's Professional Standards Department should be made as soon as is practically possible in order that a conduct investigation can be initiated.
- Crime reports detailing information regarding the case should be flagged as restricted and access to them limited.
- Arresting and Interviewing officers, where possible, should not be known to, or close colleagues of the suspect.
- The Investigating Officer should be one rank higher than that suspect. If the case involves a senior officer who is a member of the National Police Chief's Council, then the Office for the Police and Crime Commissioner should be informed and they will designate an appropriate officer to lead the investigation.
- Anonymity should be maintained; however, a short factual briefing may be provided to the suspect's immediate team, if necessary, to prevent rumours being spread and to allow appropriate peer support if required.
- A full risk assessment in relation to the suspect's mental health and well-being should be completed by custody healthcare if relevant or occupational health once outside of the custody environment. A 'welfare point of contact' should be provided. This would normally be a line manager who can assist with signposting to relevant support.
- Staff Associations such as the Police Federation or police staff union Unison may also be able to provide professional and welfare support.

Whilst any allegation of domestic abuse is being investigated, a severity assessment will be conducted by the force Professional Standards Department. Dependent on the level and severity of the allegation, consideration will be given to whether the officer or staff member ought to be suspended from duty or have restrictions placed on their current role. Should the allegation relate to an authorised firearms officer further consideration will be given to the suspension of their licence to carry a firearm whilst on duty. The decision to suspend or restrict will be made by a senior police officer. A police officer may be suspended from duty if the allegation is of misconduct or gross misconduct and:

- An effective investigation may be prejudiced unless the officer is suspended.
- The public interest requires the police officer should be suspended.
- A temporary move to a new location or role has been considered and is not appropriate.

There are different mechanisms should the employee be a member of police staff. In these circumstances the decision to suspend will be taken by a senior manager who has been designated to undertake the role. Their decision will take into consideration:

- Seriousness of the case.
- Risk to the force.
- Impact of continued attendance of the employee on the investigation.
- Precedent.

Restrictions to any police officer/staff member will be relevant to the individual circumstances of the case. General measures include the employee not being allowed to have any role that involves face-to-face contact with the public or any involvement in processing any evidential material. It can also include moving to another post or working from another location. Suspension and restriction decisions must be reviewed regularly, normally by the senior officer who heads up the Professional Standards Department.

Should the criminal case result in a charge and conviction of the police officer or police staff member, there will be a presumption of dismissal from the police service. Upholding the confidence of the public and that of domestic abuse victims to come forward and report allegations would be very difficult should the police service continue to employ someone who had been found to have committed such offences. It would be only under very exceptional circumstances that a police officer or police staff member convicted of a domestic abuse-related offence would not be dismissed.

Clearly once investigated not all criminal cases will result in any charge or criminal conviction. Under these circumstances the employee may be subject to a gross misconduct or misconduct investigation to assess whether there have been any breaches of the standards of professional behaviour. If there is evidence of such a breach, this may result in a misconduct hearing (officers) or meeting (staff members) where an employee may be found guilty of gross misconduct and be dismissed. If found guilty of misconduct, they may receive a written warning. For lower-level breaches reflective practice requiring improvement may be appropriate.

Furthermore, under the Police Reform Act 2002 where there is an allegation of significant injury being caused that is more serious than an assault occasioning actual bodily harm (Section 47 Offences Against the Person Act 1861), whether within a personal domestic incident or otherwise, this must be referred to the Independent Office of Police Conduct (IOPC). The IOPC, on consideration of the circumstances, can either conduct an independent investigation or remit it back to the home force, whilst potentially retaining oversight and direction of the investigation.

The processes of police employee conduct regulations (officers) or police staff disciplinary procedures are complex. Figure 9.1 provides a basic schematic outline of the key stages of the criminal and misconduct processes. Force Professional Standards Departments are subject matter experts and

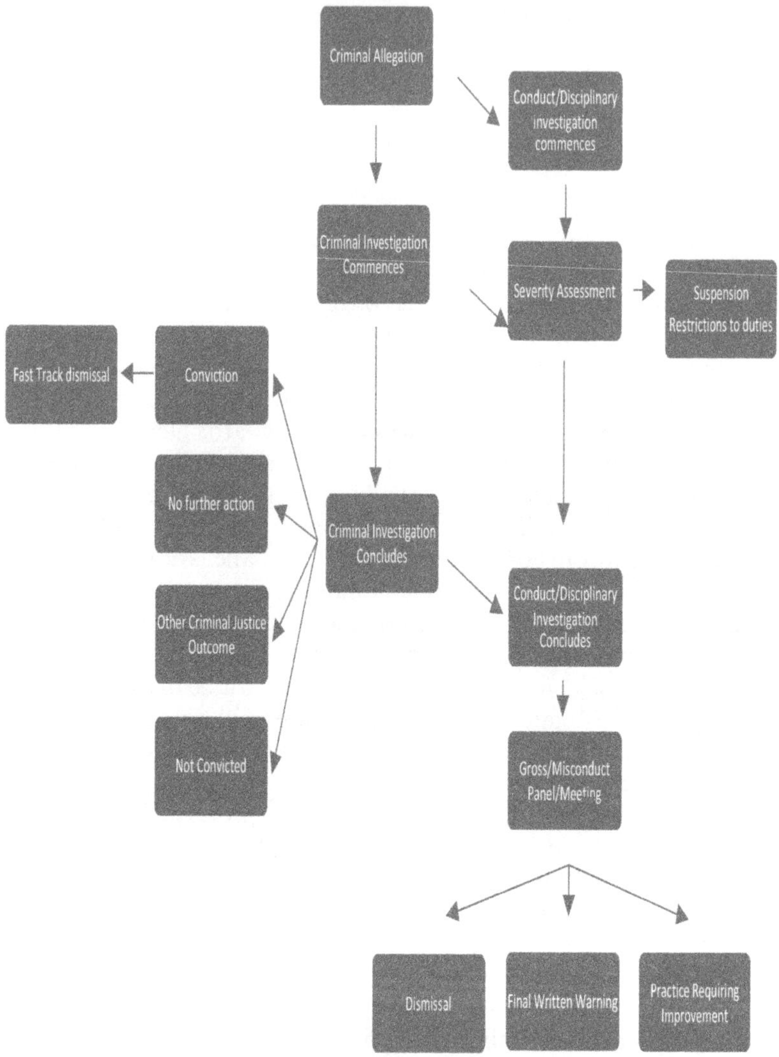

Figure 9.1 Key stages of the criminal and misconduct processes.

can provide help and support regarding how such processes should be managed.

Following any criminal or gross misconduct or misconduct finding where police service employees have been dismissed, those individuals will also be placed on the police barred list. Names will remain on the list indefinitely but can be subject to review after three and five years. This will flag in any vetting checks and is also publicly searchable, should the individual seek future employment re-joining another force or potentially undertaking careers with vulnerable people or within the security industry, for example. The seriousness with which police forces take any finding of domestic abuse against one of its employees is considerable.

The consequences of any finding are significant and long-lasting both personally and professionally for the perpetrator. This may be why some victims have reservations or are reluctant to come forward as the impact of any finding effects not only the perpetrator but also the wider family. Victims of police-perpetrated domestic abuse may also be reluctant to report allegations as they feel they will not be believed, or that their partner may be able to corrupt and influence any investigation because of their position. Concerns have been raised by the Centre for Women's Justice (2020) regarding the unique position of victims of police-perpetrated domestic abuse in the form of a super complaint. From a review of 25 cases a number of common themes have been identified. Primarily these relate to a lack of trust in the integrity of the investigative process and fear that they will not be protected by a policing system that the perpetrators themselves work within. Whilst the super complaint awaits resolution, the collective concerns reported by the victims should be recognised and any allegation of police-perpetrated domestic abuse treated compassionately, professionally, and according to Code of Ethics and Standards of Professional Behaviour.

Police employees experiencing domestic abuse

All victims or complainants of domestic abuse who are police officers or staff members will be entitled to the same level of support as any other member of the public. However, additional measures can also be put into place. Investigation reports should have restricted access only. Line managers and investigating officers must maintain confidentiality and provide support and understanding to staff experiencing domestic abuse. Additional support can be accessed through force occupational health units or other support services and staff associations; however, any referrals should be discussed with the employee.

Challenges also arise if the allegations have taken place within a workplace relationship. Whilst there are many happy and appropriately conducted workplace relationships between police employees as in other workplaces, due to the rank structure or potential conflicts of interests, all workplace relationships should be declared and conducted with complete professionalism in order not to undermine service confidence internally and externally. Where there are allegations of domestic abuse between workplace partners and family members, temporary relocation, roles, or changes to shift patterns can be made available to support the victim in the workplace. The National Police Chief's Council and the College of Policing (2019) have produced guidance regarding appropriate relationships and behaviours in the workplace, and officers and staff should make themselves aware of the requirements when forming any intimate attachments or working with family members.

It can be incredibly challenging for police officers who are in abusive relationships to speak out. There can be a cultural issue within police forces that staff are somehow immune from the crimes that take place in wider society. There may be an expectation that officers should know how to deal with violence and abuse within their own personal lives and if they admit otherwise this may be seen as impacting on their ability to do their job. In several cases this has led to police employees remaining silent or denying what was happening to them. In recent years, a number of high-profile self-disclosures made by senior ranking female officers has ensured these officers have acted as role models for others. They have courageously shared their experiences to support other colleagues in reporting abuse (Boxes 9.2 and 9.3).

BOX 9.2 CASE 1: OFFICER WHO SPOKE OUT ABOUT DOMESTIC ABUSE RECOGNISED WITH AWARD – CHIEF INSPECTOR SHARON BAKER (JUN 9, 2021)

An Avon and Somerset Constabulary officer who spoke out about her experiences of domestic abuse – and encouraged colleagues to do the same – has won the Annual Outstanding Contribution to Women in Policing award from the Police Federation of England and Wales (PFEW).

Chief Constable Andy Marsh, Chief Inspector Sharon Baker and Avon and Somerset Police Federation Chair Iain Prideaux.

Thompson T (June 9th, 2021) Police Professional

https://www.policeprofessional.com/news/officer-who-spoke-out-about-domestic-abuse-recognised-with-award/

BOX 9.3 CASE 2: FORMER CHIEF SUPERINTENDENT SALLY BENATAR

Former Chief Superintendent Sally Benatar

Sally Benatar is a former Chief Superintendent and Borough Commander with the Metropolitan Police. She retired in 2020 after a 31-year career. During this time, Sally was in a controlling and abusive marriage for 17 years.

> "It can happen to anyone; I know this because it happened to me" she said.

Livadeas C November 5th, 2020, Police Oracle, https://www.policeoracle.com/news/Former-chief-superintendent-speaks-out-on-domestic-abuse-_106123.html

Abuse of power

This chapter opened by outlining how the police only remain legitimate where they have the trust and confidence of the public. As we have already considered, police employees are expected to display the highest standards of behaviour in their public and private lives. There are, however, rare incidents where staff do not uphold these standards and use their role and power to take advantage of vulnerable people whom they encounter as part of their professional duties. Where power is abused in this way it can have a detrimental impact on the victim concerned, as well as wider public trust and confidence in policing.

In relation to the policing of domestic abuse, the abuse of power can operate in various circumstances such as employees using the power associated with their position to form emotional or sexual relationships with victims of domestic abuse or through being pursued by a victim who wishes to form a relationship with them. Where an employee forms a relationship with a victim of domestic abuse, it can be exploitative from the outset. The imbalance of power between the officer or staff member and victim is already out of kilter and potentially coercive. So, whilst it does not necessarily fall into the Home Office definition of domestic abuse which has been referred to through this book, it is abusive. Where officers or staff members feel an emotional or sexual attraction to any victim but especially one who has experienced domestic abuse, they should refrain from acting on these feelings and always maintain professional boundaries. Once all professional contact has ceased between both parties, it is potentially possible for relationships to form. However, in these circumstances the relationship should still be declared to a line manager and advice and guidance sought from the force Professional Standards Department.

Many professions which are associated with power and positions of authority over others can be an attractive career choice for those individuals who are predatory in nature and who seek to exploit others more vulnerable, deliberately, and repeatedly for their own advantage (Stinson et al., 2015). There have been rare occasions where members of the police service, primarily male, have used their role in order to gain access to vulnerable victims for their own sexual gain. This behaviour is not tolerated within the service and causes outrage both internally and externally by the discredit it brings to policing. All forces are inspected regarding their policies and procedures of identifying and dealing with members of the police service who abuse their position for sexual or emotional gain, on or off duty, by the HMICFRS as part of the assessment of force legitimacy. Any peer or colleague who has intelligence or concerns about the actions of a colleague must report these concerns, or they may potentially be in breach of committing a conduct offence themselves.

Where officers have been found guilty of misconduct/gross misconduct their actions will be subject to press reporting given the breach of public trust they have committed. Below (Box 9.4) are two such examples. In the first, a male officer approached female domestic abuse victims making sexual advances towards them and asking them for nude photographs. In the second, a male officer pursued a female for a relationship knowing she was vulnerable and a victim of domestic abuse.

On occasions domestic abuse victims may seek to pursue a sexual relationship with a police officer or staff member with whom they have had contact. This can be out of a sense of attraction or a need for further protection and safety that potentially comes from an attachment to someone in a position of authority. Should this happen, they should be treated respectfully

BOX 9.4 CASE 1: POLICE OFFICER SACKED FOR 'TRYING IT ON' WITH VULNERABLE DOMESTIC ABUSE VICTIMS

An employment tribunal heard how the West Midlands Police officer asked one of the victims for nudes and suggested she unbutton her shirt during a visit to her home (Hainey F, April 20th, 2021, Manchester Evening News).

Case 2: West Midlands Police officer dismissed after forming inappropriate relationship with vulnerable woman

A West Midlands Police officer has been dismissed – after a disciplinary hearing was told he had formed an inappropriate relationship with a vulnerable woman he met on duty.

(Farrington D, January 15th, 2021, Express & Star). https://www.expressandstar.com/news/crime/2021/01/15/west-midlands-police-officer-dismissed-after-forming-inappropriate-relationship-with-vulnerable-woman/

but all requests for a relationship declined, and professional boundaries maintained. Should the requests continue the officer or staff member, and their line manager should seek a route for the employee to disengage from the individual. Any direct policing services can be provided by a colleague as necessary.

Whilst they do sometimes happen, officers and police staff members abusing their power for sexual gain or forming relationships with domestic abuse victims are relatively rare occurrences. The majority of police officers and staff members who respond to a domestic abuse incident are highly professional and compassionate. It has, however, been recognised that this is a stressful area of policing and continuous exposure to such trauma can negatively impact on a police service employee's mental health and well-being.

The impact of dealing with domestic abuse

Law enforcement is an occupational group that is "at risk" of physical and psychological harm, as its members are called on to be first responders to traumatic events (Drew & Martin, 2020). Police officers suffer from mental health problems at a rate greater than the general population (Hartley et al., 2011), and policing is one of the most mentally taxing occupations (Stogner et al., 2020). The changing nature of police work towards more complexity, increasing demand, and significant victim focus naturally leads to increased stress and trauma on those dealing with the aftermath of serious crime.

The police recorded a total of 1,288,018 domestic abuse-related incidents and crimes in England and Wales (excluding Greater Manchester Police) in the year ending March 2020 (ONS, 2020). There were 129,110 full-time equivalent police officers during the same period (Home Office, 2021), and whilst many will not be dealing with those cases, a large proportion will be dealing with them repetitively. Indeed, Rudofossi (2009) suggests that police officers will attend between 10 and 900 incidents that could be classed as traumatic or severe stress-related during their career and, considering the figures above, many of these will be domestic-related. Research by Robinson et al. (2016) suggests that the vast majority of incidents are dealt with in a professional and empathetic manner, but negative and uninformed attitudes towards domestic abuse do still prevail, particularly when officers see the same couples repetitively, and become vexed at lack of engagement of the victim or the minor nature of the incidents. These frustrations can contribute to a general weariness felt by officers attending domestic abuse incidents and in certain cases compassion fatigue. However, the stress of trying to ensure you get everything correct when dealing with domestic abuse work is not lost on officers who cite the concern that "if you're going to lose your job [in policing], it will be over a domestic abuse case" (Robinson et al., 2016, p. 21). Invariably, not only this is related to the very real risk domestic abuse victims face if not appropriately dealt with and safeguarded by the police, but also the significant scrutiny domestic abuse investigators now face, both internally in force and externally through HMICFRS.

Domestic abuse is one of the most prevalent issues policing deals with, and the ever-increasing numbers of incidents and crimes means that daily police officers and staff are dealing with perpetrators, safeguarding vulnerable victims, and protecting innocent children. The impact this can have on individuals working in law enforcement should not be underestimated, whether they are working in control rooms answering 999 calls, providing an immediate response, and dealing with often horrific scenes of violence, or investigating the long-term suffering and coercive control that comes with years of abuse. As a service the effect this has on the mental health and well-being of those in the force must be considered and alleviated as much as possible.

Workplace Occupational Health reviews in policing are generally associated with physical surveillance checks to ensure officers, and sometimes police staff in relevant positions, are physically fit to perform the role. It is less common to find screening for psychological conditions such as anxiety, depression, and post-traumatic stress (Tehrani, 2018). Where such screening has taken place for certain roles, such as child abuse investigators, there is clear evidence that working in such departments poses a risk to mental health (Tehrani, 2018) and therefore a significant duty of care is placed on the police service to ensure staff are appropriately screened, monitored, and cared for.

There are numerous terms which can be used to describe the experiences of professionals who work with those who have suffered trauma in their lives. These include compassion fatigue and vicarious trauma.

Compassion fatigue

Charles Figley (1995, p. 1) introduced the term "compassion fatigue" to describe the "cost of caring" for those who suffer. Also sometimes referred to as secondary traumatic stress (Figley, 1985), compassion fatigue can have a negative effect on well-being and occupational performance. It can have impact on external behaviours, concentration, and feelings of helplessness, and can ultimately lead to burn out, which is associated with serious mental health conditions such as post-traumatic stress disorder (PTSD) and depression (Andersen & Papazoglou, 2015).

Tehrani (2010) discusses how in certain professions, and policing is likely to be such an occupation, there is a high level of exposure to negative emotions from members of the public who expect help and support, and this can lead to unintended consequences such as compassion fatigue. Compassion fatigue is described by Tehrani as leading to the professional experiencing symptoms similar to those they are engaging with, such as distress and trauma, and can lead to a change "underlying beliefs, values or assumptions at a pre or unconscious level" (Tehrani, 2010, p. 133). The outcomes of Tehrani's research suggest that the provision of professional or peer supervision may be helpful in increasing reflection and 'sense making' when individuals are exposed regularly to negativity and distress, in order to allow time and space to process and reduce anxiety and depression.

Despite Tehrani's research, it is clear that compassion fatigue in police officers is underresearched (Andersen & Papazoglou, 2015), and even more specifically, there is very limited discussion on the explicit impact of dealing with domestic abuse cases in terms of compassion fatigue.

Vicarious trauma

Ben-Porat and Itzhaky (2009) explain that vicarious trauma focusses on internal experiences and how the reaction an individual has when having to deal with something traumatic can change how they view the world from an internal perspective. It is rarely considered in the domestic abuse practitioner context, but the mental health issues associated with vicarious trauma have been recognised in Canada since 2017 amongst jurors having to listen to serious and traumatic criminal, civil, and coronial cases. So serious is the impact on jurors being taken, they are being offered psychological counselling and therapy to minimise the consequences of hearing about significant crimes (Bradford and de Amorim Levin, 2020).

Radu (2013) conducted qualitative research with domestic abuse therapists and found that being exposed daily to the trauma of their clients made the participants ruminate about their own intimate partners and relationships and changed how they saw aspects of both their work and family life. This led to many blurred lines and themes such as reliving their own trauma, using abusive practices in their private lives, and showing compassion for abusers as very unexpected results.

A lack of research into the vicarious trauma affecting police officers dealing with domestic abuse is a concern, and one which should be considered carefully in policing moving forward.

Protecting the well-being of police officers and staff

The National Police Wellbeing Service Oscar Kilo was launched in 2017 with the aim to provide evidence-based research to help shape well-being provision across the service and beyond into all emergency services. Oscar Kilo (2021) provides forces with practical support in eight key areas around the well-being and welfare agenda:

- Leadership
- Individual Resilience
- Peer Support
- Psychological Risk Management
- Trauma and Post-Incident Management
- Wellbeing at Work
- Wellbeing Outreach Service
- Physical Fitness.

Full of excellent resources, guidance, toolkits, and more, Oscar Kilo is a fundamental source of information and contacts to help both individuals and forces deal with issues related to trauma. In 2021, Oscar Kilo introduced the National Investigator Wellbeing toolkit to provide bespoke advice to investigators of serious crime following a review which suggested that investigators have the lowest levels of well-being across policing, which is having an impact on force's abilities to recruit and retain detectives and police staff investigators (Oscar Kilo, 2021).

Another useful mechanism for in service mental health support is Mind, the mental health charity, who set up blue light champions to provide those working in the emergency service – police, ambulance, fire, and search and rescue, the ability to set up formal networks in service of blue light champions to support those with mental health issues (Mind, 2021). Wide ranging in nature and made up of practitioners wanting to help colleagues rather than mental health professionals, the champions raise awareness about mental health issues and the impact working in the emergency services can have on an individual's health and well-being.

Whilst these resources are not only for officers and staff dealing with the domestic abuse and other crime types may also have similar personal impacts, it is important to recognise that individuals may be affected in many different ways, some many years after dealing with a traumatic event. Therefore, having a range of complementary resources to help facilitate recovery and mental health improvements will allow the policing community to continue to deal to the best of its abilities with the stress and pressure of dealing with domestic abuse, and many other shocking and distressing issues in society.

Conclusion

This chapter has considered domestic abuse within policing from a number of different angles. First, there was a discussion around police officers and police staff members committing offences of domestic abuse within their own private relationships and the impact this had, not only on the victim of such crimes but also on police legitimacy more generally. A detailed overview of the potential ramifications of such crimes, particularly in terms of the employment outcomes, was discussed, together with the courageous accounts of female police officers who had been the victim of domestic abuse and yet had been too traumatised and embarrassed to disclose to their employer the situation they were in. This chapter then moved on to consider those who utilise a focussed abuse of power for sexual gain or to form relationships with domestic abuse victims and the consequences of such relationships. Finally, the impact dealing with domestic abuse can have on police officers and staff was examined. An area lacking in vital academic research, it is clear that the trauma and stress of continuous exposure to such crime can have a long-term, detrimental impact on individuals in the policing profession. A number of key resources were considered to assist in this vital arena.

Reflective questions

- How do police draw a line between their public and private lives?
- How would you approach a police colleague who discloses to you they are experiencing domestic abuse but does not wish to make a formal allegation?
- How would you spot compassion fatigue in yourself and in a colleague?
- What are the signs that you may be suffering from stress?
- Can you write a self-care plan and where would you access the resources you may need for dealing with stress?

Useful websites

Code of Ethics (2014): https://paas-s3-broker-prod-lon-6453d964-1d1a-432a-9260-5e0ba7d2fc51.s3.eu-west-2.amazonaws.com/s3fs-public/2021-02/code_of_ethics.pdf

College of Policing, NPCC – Appropriate personal relationships and behaviours in the workplace: https://paas-s3-broker-prod-lon-6453d964-1d1a-432a-9260-5e0ba7d2fc51.s3.eu-west-2.amazonaws.com/s3fs-public/2021-02/appropriate_personal_relationships_and_behaviours_guidance.pdf

Maintaining a professional boundary between police and members of the public: https://paas-s3-broker-prod-lon-6453d964-1d1a-432a-9260-5e0ba7d2fc51.s3.eu-west-2.amazonaws.com/s3fs-public/2021-02/college_of_policing_guidance_on_professional_boundaries.pdf (accessed 15.05.21).

Mind Blue Light staff and volunteers – Blue Light staff and volunteers | Mind, the mental health charity – help for mental health problems: National Investigators Wellbeing Toolkit – Wellbeing of Investigators Toolkit – Oscar Kilo

Oscar Kilo – Oscar Kilo – Evidence Base & Best Practice for Emergency Services Wellbeing

Professional Standards, Performance and Integrity in Policing (2020) Home Office Statutory Guidance – England and Wales: https://assets.publishing.service.gov.uk/government/uploads/system/uploads/attachment_data/file/863820/Home_Office_Statutory_Guidance_0502.pdf (accessed 15.05.21).

Police Code of Conduct – Police Service of Northern Ireland: https://www.psni.police.uk/globalassets/inside-the-psni/our-policies-and-procedures/corporate-policy/professional-standards-111016.pdf

Police Code of Conduct – Police Scotland: https://www.scotland.police.uk/spa-media/uvyogah0/disciplinary-sop.pdf

References

Andersen, J.P., Papazoglou, K., 2015. Compassion fatigue and compassion satisfaction among police officers: An understudied topic. *International Journal of Emergency Mental Health and Human Resilience* 17, 3, 661–663.

BBC News, 2021. Victims of police domestic abuse "feel silenced." BBC News.

Ben-Porat, A., Itzhaky, H., 2009. Implications of treating family violence for the therapist: Secondary traumatization, vicarious traumatization, and growth. *Journal of Family Violence* 24, 507–515.

Bradford, J.M., de Amorim Levin, G.V., 2020. Vicarious trauma and PTSD in forensic mental health professionals. *The Journal of the American Academy of Psychiatry and the Law* 48, 315–318.

Centre for Women's Justice, 2020. *Failure to address police perpetrated domestic abuse.* Centre for Women's Justice.

College of Policing, 2014. Code of ethics. College of Policing. https://www.college.police.uk/ethics/code-of-ethics (accessed 11.28.21).

Drew, J.M., Martin, S., 2020. Mental health and well-being of police in a health pandemic: Critical issues for police leaders in a post-COVID-19 environment. *Journal of Community Safety and Well-Being* 5, 31–36.

Farrington, D., 2021. West Midlands Police officer dismissed after forming inappropriate relationship with vulnerable woman. https://www.expressandstar.com/news/crime/2021/01/15/west-midlands-police-officer-dismissed-after-forming-inappropriate-relationship-with-vulnerable-woman/ (accessed 11.28.21).

Figley, C. R. (1985). From victim to survivor: Social responsibility in the wake of a catastrophe, in: C. R. Figley (Ed.), *Trauma and Its Wake: The Study and Treatment of Post-Traumatic Stress Disorder* (pp. 398–415). New York, Brunner/Mazel.

Figley, C.R., 1995. *Compassion fatigue: Coping with secondary traumatic stress disorder in those who treat the traumatized.* Brunner/Mazel.

Hainey, F., 2021. Police officer sacked for "trying it on" with vulnerable domestic abuse victims. *Manchester Evening News.* https://www.manchestereveningnews.co.uk/news/uk-news/police-officer-sacked-trying-on-20418874 (accessed 11.28.21).

Hartley, T.A., Burchfiel, C.M., Fekedulegn, D., Andrew, M.E., Violanti, J.M., 2011. Health disparities in police officers: comparisons to the US general population. *International Journal of Emergency Mental Health* 13, 211.

Home Office, 2021. Police workforce, England and Wales: 31 March 2020 third edition. GOV.UK. https://www.gov.uk/government/statistics/police-workforce-england-and-wales-31-march-2020 (accessed 11.28.21).

Home Office, 2020. Professional standards, performance and integrity in policing. HM Government. Gov.uk.

Mind, 2021. Blue light – your mental health in the pandemic. https://www.mind.org.uk/news-campaigns/campaigns/blue-light-programme/blue-light-information/emergency-responders-your-mental-health-in-the-pandemic/ (accessed 11.28.21).

ONS, 2020. Domestic abuse prevalence and trends, England and Wales. Office for National Statistics. https://www.ons.gov.uk/peoplepopulationandcommunity/crimeandjustice/articles/domesticabuseprevalenceandtrendsenglandandwales/yearendingmarch2020#crime-survey-for-england-and-wales (accessed 9.7.21).

Oscar Kilo, 2021. Oscar kilo Evidence base & best practice for emergency services wellbeing. Oscar Kilo. https://oscarkilo.org.uk/ (accessed 8.5.21).

Police Conduct Regulations, 2020. The police (conduct) regulations 2020. https://www.legislation.gov.uk/uksi/2020/4/schedule/2/made (accessed 11.28.21).

Police Oracle, 2020. Former-chief superintendent speaks out on domestic abuse | UK Police News – Police Oracle. https://www.policeoracle.com/news/Former-chief-superintendent-speaks-out-on-domestic-abuse-_106123.html (accessed 11.28.21).

Police Professional, 2021. Police Professional | Officer who spoke out about domestic abuse recognised with award. https://www.policeprofessional.com/news/officer-who-spoke-out-about-domestic-abuse-recognised-with-award/ (accessed 11.28.21).

Radu, A., 2013. *'The work chips away parts of yourself' – Exploring therapists' experiences of working with survivors of domestic violence.* City University of London.

Robinson, A.L., Myhill, A., Wire, J., Roberts, J., Tilley, N., 2016. *Risk-led policing of domestic abuse and the DASH risk model. What works: Crime reduction research.* Cardiff University, College of Policing and UCL Department of Security and Crime Science.

Rudofossi, D., 2009. *Death, value and meaning series. A cop doc's guide to public safety complex trauma syndrome: Using five police personality styles.* Baywood Publishing Co.

Stinson Sr, P.M., Brewer Jr, S.L., Mathna, B.E., Liederbach, J., Englebrecht, C.M., 2015. Police sexual misconduct: Arrested officers and their victims. *Victims & Offenders* 10, 117–151.

Stogner, J., Miller, B.L., McLean, K., 2020. Police stress, mental health, and resiliency during the COVID-19 pandemic. *American Journal of Criminal Justice* 45, 718–730.

Tehrani, N., 2018. Psychological well-being and workability in child abuse investigators. *Occupational Medicine* 68, 165–170.

Tehrani, N., 2010. Compassion fatigue: Experiences in occupational health, human resources, counselling and police. *Occupational Medicine* 60, 133–138.

Chapter 10

Policing domestic abuse

Reflections and new directions

Introduction

This book has illustrated throughout the dynamic nature of domestic abuse. It is a social and legal construct and our understanding and acceptance of it has changed rapidly over the last three decades. From being an accepted form of chastisement, to being tolerated if it took place behind closed doors, it has historically been seen as a private matter, therefore not a role for police. Finally, domestic abuse is now being seen as a serious criminal offence and strategies to reduce it are key role for policing. Our understanding of the circumstances in which domestic abuse takes place is constantly evolving, and policing must continue to be at the forefront of responding to change and understanding what works, when, and why. However, as resources dwindle and other agencies better equipped to manage perpetrators and support victims become more stretched, policing is falling in to breach the gaps. This chapter will consider some of the key current and future challenges facing the policing of domestic abuse.

Policing domestic abuse within a pandemic – impact of COVID-19

The COVID-19 pandemic has had a particularly devastating impact on victims of domestic abuse across the world, with the UN describing a 'shadow pandemic' where survivors have been forced to lockdown with their abusers and have faced increased barriers to support and reporting (Johnson and Hohl, 2021; UN Women, 2020).

Lockdowns exacerbated the hidden element of abuse and changed the nature of help seeking and reporting. In the United Kingdom, the first lockdown in 2020 saw a tenfold increase in the amount of traffic on domestic abuse support pages and a 700% increase in calls to the national helpline run by Refuge (Refuge, 2020). However, reporting to the police initially declined, with victims unable to seek help whilst locked down with their perpetrator. Where incidents were reported there was a shift in who

DOI: 10.4324/9781003137412-10

was disclosing the incidents, with third party reporting from neighbours substantially increased, particularly in densely populated areas (Ivandic et al., 2021).

When lockdown measures were eased there was a pronounced increase in reporting to the police, with a significant rise in first time disclosures. Whilst overall levels of abuse have remained similar to pre-pandemic levels, the nature of abuse was found to change under lockdown and reinforced the need to undertake detailed statistical analysis. For example, research found a change in reporting by relationship type with increases in abuse amongst current partners and family members, but a decline in abuse from ex-partners (Ivandic et al., 2021).

The COVID-19 pandemic has led to changes in the way that the police respond to domestic abuse, with new channels opened to enable victims to seek support from the police online and improvements in the way in which technology is used. There have, however, been concerns that one of the reasons that the police response during lockdown has been effective is because it has been prioritised whilst demand for resources to police other crimes such as burglary and night-time economy disorder has been reduced (HMICFRS, 2021a). Research conducted during the pandemic not only identified the devastating impact of domestic abuse during COVID-19 but has also found that there was a pre-existing domestic abuse crisis prior to the pandemic, with analysis finding that levels of abuse had been increasing in the two years before the onset of COVID-19 (Johnson and Hohl, 2021). The challenge therefore is ensuring that domestic abuse remains a priority for policing as life returns to normality.

Another further issue caused by the pandemic has been the delays in the criminal justice system. The backlog in court cases and postponements in cases coming to trial increases the likelihood of victims disengaging with the process. The delays in timely justice for perpetrators also increase the chances of reoffending and the likelihood of further harm being caused to families (HMICFRS, 2021a). At a time when Her Majesty's Inspectorate of Constabulary and Fire and Rescue Services (HMICRFS) have also identified that three-quarters of domestic abuse cases are closed early without the suspect being charged (HMICFRS, 2021b), this further emphasises the need for the police and the criminal justice system to prioritise tackling domestic abuse. One of the ways in which this could be addressed is through a range of legislation that is currently being advanced.

Governmental and legislative change

The plethora of legislation, strategies, and guidance being developed presently covering the Violence against Women and Girls agenda and more specifically domestic abuse provide many opportunities to work strategically and tactically, in partnerships, and with victims to improve their safety and security. However, there is a balance to be had in order to ensure success rather than confusion, and for those involved in policing, particularly, to prioritise resources accordingly in response to domestic abuse.

The introduction of an overarching Tackling Violence Against Women and Girls Strategy (HM Government, 2021) is an unambiguous communication of intent to take this issue seriously, cross cutting government departments and statutory partners to ensure this is a priority for all. It makes it clear that legislation such as the Domestic Abuse Act, and a new domestic abuse strategy that will follow, will be complementary to the Tackling Violence Against Women and Girls Strategy, with harm reduction integral to both.

The publication of the HMICFRS (2021b) report into the Police Response to Violence against Women and Girls finds the police alone cannot 'solve' violence against women and girls. It is a societal problem, but the police do have unique powers and responsibilities to protect victims from further harm, pursue perpetrators, and prevent crime. This report was commissioned following the horrific murder of Sarah Everard and considers Violence Against Women and Girls both in domestic abuse situations and more widely in society. It draws on several themes and concerns at individual victim, force, local partnership, and national levels which all need addressing to improve the response. In essence, violence against women and girls must be funded and resourced similarly to other thematic areas such as counterterrorism and county lines for there to be a marked improvement to the whole system approach.

At the same time, the launch of the Police, Crime, Sentencing and Courts Act 2021 anticipates changes to Section 6 of the Crime and Disorder Act 1998, requiring Community Safety Partnerships to formulate and implement a strategy to prevent and reduce serious violence – a 'serious violence prevention duty' (Home Office, 2021). The duty does not explicitly include domestic homicide, domestic abuse, or sexual violence in the definition. Whilst it does place a duty on local partnerships to work together to reduce violence across society, there are calls by the Domestic Abuse Commissioner (2021) for amendments to be made to the bill to ensure partnerships include domestic abuse in their prevention strategies.

Finally, the introduction of the Domestic Abuse Act (UK Parliament, 2021) marks a significant milestone in the legislative support provision to victims and management of perpetrators in England and Wales. The often-lacklustre interventions in the decades that preceded meant that domestic violence was dealt with as a private issue, and in the margins, laws were passed to allow abuse and control of women by their husbands with no blame attached as discussed in Chapter 5. As we move into the 21st century, the landscape has significantly changed for the better, with both criminal and civil laws available to assist criminal justice agencies and victims in ensuring their safety and security as well as bringing perpetrators to justice.

The multitude of powers can be confusing however and can take time to be understood and utilised appropriately by law enforcement. A good example of this is the use of Domestic Violence Protection Notices and Orders, introduced in 2010 and soon to be repealed and replaced with Domestic Abuse Protection Notices and Orders, with many Forces using them sporadically, and with limited understanding of the impact and indeed the preventative possibilities of such orders (Blackburn and Graca, 2021; Ewin et al., 2020).

Even with the multitude of pieces of criminal and civil legislation, court processes are too slow, particularly in the criminal court, leading to significant attrition rates (Barrow-Grint, 2016; Hester, 2006). The impact of austerity, and then the COVID pandemic, on the criminal justice system cannot be under-estimated. With court listings running with a significant backlog in most areas throughout the country, focussed attention on prioritising the most vulnerable victims must take precedence.

Of concern too is recent research by the Domestic Abuse Commissioner and Safelives (2021) who found that once cases do reach court, many victims are traumatised by the criminal justice or family court processes, mainly due to a lack of understanding from judges and other court officials, which often allows the perpetrator to use the system for coercive control, questioning the value of the processes currently available.

What is clear, however, is that domestic abuse is now a central tenet in several areas of very new guidance and legislation, brought in to empower victims and bring perpetrators to justice. This is positive, there is no doubt, but clarity of use, prioritisation of problems, and comprehensive local partnerships are key to successful delivery. Legislation alone is not enough to help deal with the complex public health issue that is domestic abuse. Without a whole systems approach that incorporates the wide-ranging legal framework to deal with domestic abuse from both a criminal and civil perspective, together with appropriate education, and sufficient funding to support victims, there will be limited impact. It is the responsibility of society to resolve this problem, not simply the law alone.

Demand, digital technology, and data

Reported levels of domestic abuse both crimes and incidents have continually increased over recent years (ONS, 2020). As reflected in Chapter 3 interpretation of any official crime figures should be caveated with concerns about the robustness of recording practices. The official figures, of course, do not account for the whole picture. The Crime Survey of England and Wales (CSEW) reveals only 21% of domestic abuse is reported to police; thus, there are the hidden harms and demands by those who are victims and communities which do not have sufficient trust and confidence in the police or partners to report. Surveys do provide additional data on levels of abuse. However, as noted, they also are not full proof measures. The British Crime

Survey does not cover juvenile domestic abuse, and this only represents a small population size from which results of overall trends are extrapolated. However, despite all the increased focus and partnership prevention initiatives, the levels of domestic abuse and intimate partner homicide are not falling.

This presents a real dichotomy and challenge for policing. On the one hand, police actively encourage reporting and thus numbers increase as a consequence; however, there is also an expectation that the levels of investment and focussed activity on prevention would result in a sustained reduction of victimisation. In short, even with the acknowledgement that there are hidden victims and underreporting still the levels of demand are outstripping police and their partners ability to manage it particularly given the austerity measures public services have experienced (National Audit Office, 2018).

The consequences of this inability to manage demand are twofold. Victims may receive inconsistent and potentially inadequate responses. Perpetrators are not brought to justice, and this toxic situation impacts on the mental health and future life chances of children growing up in such environments. In short, domestic abuse within society is and remains a public health issue that needs to be addressed for social well-being, growth, and stability of individuals and communities. However, it also creates an internal critical crisis for policing where increasing requirements are being placed on officers and staff from managing increased call volumes, prioritisation of front-line response activities to the investigators who are holding rapidly increasing caseloads, and leadership decisions making complex resourcing decisions based on competing priorities impacting on public safety. These cumulative pressures may impact on individual's welfare and resilience as detailed in Chapter 8. Officers and staff want to provide a professional service but are often constrained in doing so by issues outside their control such as levels of demand, partnership capability, and delays in the criminal justice system. This can lead to frustration and stress over the levels of risk staff are responsible for managing and impact on their effective decision-making. These internal and external factors present an incredible challenge to policing and there are no simple answers. Current strategies for demand management are founded on risk assessment, digital technology, and data.

Chapter 4 outlined in detail how risk assessment is a tool employed by policing to manage demand by effectively triaging or screening cases. Resources can be more effectively deployed to those cases where is there the greatest risk of serious harm. A position Connor-Smith et al. opine "(a) ccurate assessment of risk for future violence is crucial to determining the optimal use of limited resources" (2011, p. 323). However, the challenge for policing is that if risk assessment is being used as a demand management tool its success is dependent on the tool itself being accurate as well as its application being professionally deployed. Questions have been raised by HMIC (2014) and academics (Medina et al., 2016; Sebire and Barling, 2016) as to the ongoing accuracy of DASH, the most common form of risk assessment, in terms of its sensitivity and validity as tool as well as its training, application, and usage. Recognising these concerns, new risk assessment tools such as DARA are being developed and rolled out across police services in England and Wales. However, there are positive impacts associated with DASH including the joint levels of partnership working, understating of a common language. The processes of risk management must be maintained to ensure the system continues to work collaboratively to support victims and manage perpetrators. However, addressing the concerns regarding training, supervision, and application in the completion of risk identification, assessment, and management should be recognised and taken forward and applied whichever tool being used.

Where applied effectively risk assessment conducted by police in domestic abuse cases can ensure that the right resources are deployed appropriately, and victims are protected. Police must continue to ensure whatever tool is employed, it is continually evaluated to ensure it remains fit for purpose and based on the most accurate and complete data set available. It must be accompanied with appropriate ongoing training and supervision in its effective use. Whilst this is an important approach, risk assessment is only a tool, not a remedy. As commented by Baldry and Sebire "risk assessment is useful but not enough" (2016, p. 324).

Another explanation as to why domestic abuse has increased is related to the emergence of new technologies and platforms which have been exploited by perpetrators to offend against, control, and harass victims. Mobile devices, social media, and digital technology have also brought an increased access to support networks and knowledge for victims. Technology despite its shortcomings also provides innovation opportunities for prevention and protection (PenzeyMoog and Slakoff, 2021). Electronic tagging and silent and recordable alarms within devices allow victims increased safety and confidence (Natarajan, 2016). Apps and digital platforms can encourage online and third-party reporting and victims to be able to access help and information. This was increasingly the case during the pandemic. There are also several apps such as Domestic Abuse Reference Tool (DART) available for police and partners to ensure they have information and legislation available to assist the work at the touch of a button to support their knowledge and practice.

The challenge for policing remains how to keep ahead of the technology curve, anticipating what new features can be exploited by abusers and how then they can be used to gather evidence. From encryption in commonly used apps such as WhatsApp through to dark web platforms, perpetrators (both domestic and non-domestic) can hide their activities in plain sight. Front-line responders and investigators should consider all technological opportunities in both evidence gathering and innovation in their pursuit of effectively dealing with domestic abuse.

The increase in reported crime has led to police holding increased amounts of data regarding victims, suspects, locations, and circumstances in which domestic abuse and violence take place. The advantages of this, where data has been accurately recorded and appropriate ethical considerations regarding the use data are made, allow for deeper research in the social science fields of criminology and sociology psychology to assist in our understanding of it and inform our response to it. Problem profiles of domestic abuse within local forces and neighbourhood areas can be produced by police intelligence analysts to target bespoke communication and prevention activities. The possession of big data allows forces to conduct more detailed research and supports the testing of previously held theories such as the 'myth' that a victim will be assaulted 35 times before calling police (Strang et al., 2014), the creation of offender typologies (Robertson et al., Forthcoming), and new information regarding perpetrators and precursor suicide ideation (Sherman et al., 2017). The more policing and partners have evidence-based research within the field of domestic abuse, the better able policing is to develop appropriate strategies to respond and prevent it.

The opportunity to mine data in such a manner has also led to the creation of algorithms and computer-generated decision-making within policing. It has been shown that such systems can make accurate assessments; however, their use presents ethical dilemmas (Bland, 2020). The challenge for policing is how it embraces new technologies and capabilities to increase its effectiveness through the benefits of AI (such as freeing up staff posts and supporting more effective decision-making) with the ethical tensions of holding and processing personal data especially where there are no human decisions-makers to imbue the processes with professional expertise and compassion. The risks of becoming too reliant on technology become evident where there are limited contingency plans to deal with systems failures, security issues regarding holding sensitive data. Ethically there are challenges over the morality of machine learning replacing people and their capacity and capability to manage such significant personal information.

Trust and confidence in the police

According to the Femicide Census two women a week are killed by a partner, ex-partner, or family member (femicidecensus.org). One woman a week reports a serving police officer for domestic abuse or sexual violence. Overall rape convictions are at their lowest level since records began in 2009, as outlined by the Victims Commissioner, Dame Vera Baird (2021). These statistics are stark and can impact negatively on womens' trust and confidence in policing to support them when they report domestic abuse.

However, the murder of Sarah Everard by Wayne Couzens, a serving Metropolitan Police Officer in 2021, has brought UK policing to a crisis point over how to build and maintain the trust and confidence of women in the policing and criminal justice system. Given that over 70% of domestic abuse victims are female, rebuilding trust and confidence in policing will be a substantial task. The challenges of regaining and restoring public trust and confidence are many. Processes and systems require drastic change and need to be appropriately resourced. However, whilst systematic change is needed individual trust and confidence can be built on an individual level. Each individual interaction will make a difference in how overall policing response to domestic abuse is perceived by communities. How individual officers and staff respond to and deal with victims and perpetrators of domestic abuse can make a difference. Professionalism, compassion, and an adherence to the policing principles outlined throughout this book can make a positive difference to the victim's experience and increase their trust and confidence in the system that is established to keep them safe.

Conclusion

The objective of this book has been to provide a practical and theoretical guide to the policing of domestic abuse. It outlines the theories advanced to explain why and how domestic abuse takes place within intimate relationships and families. It details the evolution of the law and police responses to abuse as society grows to accept that this is a serious crime which impacts on both individuals and society (emotionally, culturally, and economically). It suggests best practice in the management of both victims and offenders and highlights that this is not a binary division and there will be circumstances police officers and staff come across overlapping and complex incidents where it is not always obvious who has done what to whom and why. Each case must be carefully examined, and the risk identified, assessed, and managed. It also considers the hidden victims of abuse, where police must be additionally curious and sensitive to their needs to make an accurate assessment of the circumstances and support required.

Policing cannot be responsible as a lone entity for preventing and responding to domestic abuse. The effective mechanisms of partnership working through CCR and MARAC are outlined. It is only through working together with each agency, understanding their role and communicating clearly with one another, and implementing evidenced-based best practices, will victims be supported appropriately and perpetrator behaviour best managed. It is essential that all agencies learn from circumstances when partnership working does not meet its obligations and the importance of continuous reviews and training cannot be understated.

What does all of this mean for you, the police professional, partner agency, or researcher having now read this book for your own practice? It is suggested that you consider the material through a reflective learning cycle (Boot and Boxer, 1980).

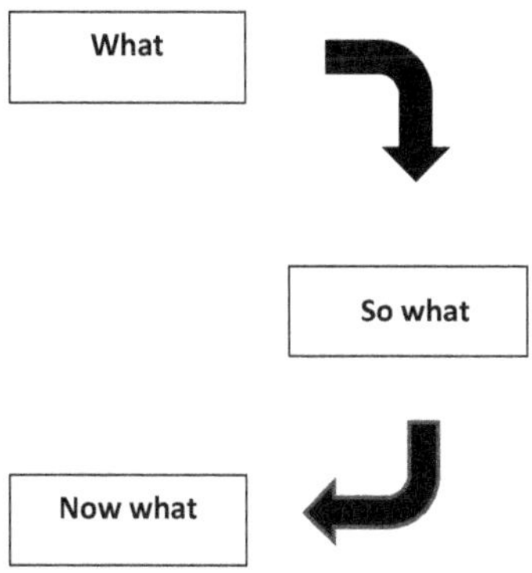

What have you learnt, **so what** does this mean for you and your practice, and **now what** will you do to change your approach and behaviours as a result? Understanding best practice in the policing of domestic abuse is an ongoing and iterative process. It is essential the police and partners continue to understand what works and prioritise this most serious of crimes to build and maintain trust and confidence within the communities we serve.

Reflective questions

- How can police and partners better understand and future-proof the use of technology to manage and prevent domestic abuse?
- What are the ethical issues in using big data to identify and track vulnerable victims and recidivist perpetrators and how would you mitigate these concerns?
- What steps can the police take to regain the confidence of untrusting communities and victims of domestic abuse to report allegations and support prosecutions?

Useful weblinks

https://janemsblog.wordpress.com/dart/

This Forensic Criminology website contains a range of information and training materials regarding intimate partner homicide. It also hosts access to the Domestic Abuse Reference Tool app which is a mobile app and resource for information regarding coercive control, homicide stalking evidence gather and risk assessment https://www.improdova.eu

Improdova is a EU funded innovate and research project. The site host research and training materials from agencies across Europe focussing on improving front line response to domestic abuse. It has online training facilities available as well as often hosts research seminars and conferences details of which are contained in the news section.

https://www.college.police.uk

This site hosts all Approved Professional Practice authorised by the College of Policing for use of police officers and staff primarily in England and Wales. It contains detailed guidance and instruction on a range of policing areas including public protection, major investigations, domestic abuse, child protection and risk assessment. It also hosts a 'what works' centre where evidence-based research on prevention is published.

References

Baldry, A.C., Sebire, J., 2016. Policing and domestic abuse: challenges and ways to go. *Policing: A Journal of Policy and Practice* 10, 323–327.

Barrow-Grint, K., 2016. Attrition rates in domestic abuse: Time for a change? An application of temporal sequencing theory. *Policing: A Journal of Policy and Practice* 10, 250–263.

Blackburn, K., Graca, S., 2021. A critical reflection on the use and effectiveness of DVPNs and DVPOs. *Police Practice and Research* 22, 23–39.

Bland, M., 2020. Algorithms can predict domestic abuse, but should we let them? in: Jahankhani, H, Akhgar, B., Cochrane, P., Dastbaz, M (Eds.), *Policing in the Era of AI and Smart Societies*. Springer, pp. 139–155.

Boot, R.L., Boxer, P.J., 1980. Reflective learning, in: Beck, J., Cox, C. (Eds.), *Advances in Management Education*. Wiley. 387–404.

Connor-Smith, J.K., Henning, K., Moore, S., Holdford, R., 2011. Risk assessments by female victims of intimate partner violence: Predictors of risk perceptions and comparison to an actuarial measure. *Journal of Interpersonal Violence* 26, 2517–2550.

Domestic Abuse Commissioner, 2021. Letter to the Home Secretary on the need to amend the Policing Bill. Domestic Abuse Commissioner. https://domesticabuse-commissioner.uk/letters/letter-to-the-home-secretary-on-the-need-to-amend-the-policing-bill/ (accessed 12.1.21).

Domestic Abuse Commissioner, Safelives, 2021. Understanding court support for victims of domestic abuse. https://domesticabusecommissioner.uk/wp-content/uploads/2021/06/Court-Support-Mapping-Report-DAC-Office-and-SafeLives.pdf (accessed 7.10.22).

Ewin, R., Bates, E.A., Taylor, J.C., 2020. Domestic abuse orders: Risk, vulnerability and training. *Journal of Criminological Research, Policy and Practice* 6(2), 151–167.

Hester, M., 2006. Making it through the criminal justice system: Attrition and domestic violence. *Social Policy and Society* 5, 79–90.

HM Government, 2021. Tackling violence against women and girls strategy. HM Government.

HMIC, 2014. Everyone's business: Improving the police response to domestic abuse. London: Her Majesty's Inspectorate of Constabulary.

HMICFRS, 2021a. Review of policing domestic abuse during the pandemic – 2021. HMICFRS. https://www.justiceinspectorates.gov.uk/hmicfrs/publication-html/review-of-policing-domestic-abuse-during-pandemic/ (accessed 10.21.21).

HMICFRS, 2021b. Police response to violence against women and girls: Final Inspection Report. https://www.justiceinspectorates.gov.uk/hmicfrs/publications/police-response-to-violence-against-women-and-girls/ (accessed 7/10/22).

Home Office, 2021. Police, crime, sentencing and courts bill 2021: draft guidance. GOV.UK. https://www.gov.uk/government/publications/police-crime-sentencing-and-courts-bill-2021-draft-guidance (accessed 12.1.21).

Ivandic, R., Kirchmaier, T., Linton, B., 2021. The Role of Exposure in Domestic Abuse Victimization: Evidence from the COVID-19 Lockdown (May 27, 2021). https://ssrn.com/abstract=3686873 or http://dx.doi.org/10.2139/ssrn.3686873.

Johnson, K., Hohl, K., 2021. The impact of Covid-19 on domestic abuse reported to the police, and policing responses, in: *Parliamentary Home Affairs Committee Home Office Preparedness for Covid-19 (Coronavirus) Consultation: Supplementary Call for Evidence Submission*. Parliament, UK. https://committees.parliament.uk/writtenevidence/22280/pdf/ (accessed 7.10.22).

Medina, J., Robinson, A., Myhill, A., 2016. Cheaper, faster, better: Expectations and achievements in police risk assessment of domestic abuse. *Policing: A Journal of Policy and Practice* 10, 341–350.

Natarajan, M., 2016. Police response to domestic violence: A case study of TecSOS mobile phone use in the London Metropolitan Police Service. *Policing: A Journal of Policy and Practice* 10, 378–390.

National Audit Office, 2018. *Financial stability of police forces in England and Wales 2018*. National Audit Office.

ONS, 2020. *Domestic abuse in England and Wales overview*. Office for National Statistics. https://www.ons.gov.uk/peoplepopulationandcommunity/crimeandjustice/bulletins/domesticabuseinenglandandwalesoverview/november2020 (accessed 11.28.21).

PenzeyMoog, E., Slakoff, D.C., 2021. As technology evolves, so does domestic violence: Modern-Day tech abuse and possible solutions, in: Bailey, J., Flynn, A., Henry, N. (Eds.), *The Emerald International Handbook of Technology Facilitated Violence and Abuse*. Emerald Publishing Limited.

Refuge, 2020. Refuge sees online traffic to its National Domestic Abuse Helpline website rise by 700%. Refuge Charity – Domestic Violence Help. https://www.refuge.org.uk/refuge-sees-700-increase-in-website-visits/ (accessed 10.21.21).

Robertson, A., Featherstone, A., Phillips, J., McFadzien, K., Forthcoming. Family violence reported to Kent Police: Classifying 371,000 cases by frequency and harm patterns 2003–2017.

Sebire, J., Barling, H., 2016. Assessing the assessors: An analysis of the consistency of risk grading by police when conducting domestic abuse investigations. *Policing: A Journal of Policy and Practice* 10, 351–360.

Sherman, L., Strang, H., O'Connor, D., 2017. *Introduction—Key facts about domestic abuse: Lessons from eight studies*. Springer.

Strang, H., Neyroud, P., Sherman, L., 2014. Tracking the evidence for a 'mythical number': Do UK domestic abuse victims suffer an average of 35 assaults before someone calls the police? *Policing: A Journal of Policy and Practice* 8, 222–228.

UK Parliament, 2021. *Domestic abuse act 2021 – Parliamentary bills.* UK Parliament. https://bills.parliament.uk/bills/2709 (accessed 12.1.21).

UN Women, 2020. The shadow pandemic: Violence against women during COVID-19. UN Women. https://www.unwomen.org/en/news/in-focus/in-focus-gender-equality-in-covid-19-response/violence-against-women-during-covid-19 (accessed 12.1.21).

Victims Commissioner, 2021. Victims' Commissioner responds to Home Office figures showing just 1.5% of rape cases result in a prosecution. Victims Commissioner. https://victimscommissioner.org.uk/news/home-office-rape-figures/ (accessed 12.1.21).

Index

For Product Safety Concerns and Information please contact our EU representative GPSR@taylorandfrancis.com
Taylor & Francis Verlag GmbH, Kaufingerstraße 24, 80331 München, Germany

www.ingramcontent.com/pod-product-compliance
Lightning Source LLC
Chambersburg PA
CBHW071250180926
51613CB00002B/187
9780367684143